4-11

This book is provided by funds donated by
The Friends of the Nipomo Library. Gifts to
the Friends are tax deductible. All proceeds
go to purchase library materials and support
library programs. Won't you join us?

P.O. Box 1330
Nipomo, CA 93444

The FRIENDS of the

Nipomo
Library

Italian, My Way

Jonathan Waxman

Foreword by
TOM COLICCHIO

Photographs by
CHRISTOPHER HIRSHEIMER

Simon & Schuster
NEW YORK   LONDON   TORONTO   SYDNEY

Simon & Schuster
1230 Avenue of the Americas
New York, NY 10020

First Simon & Schuster hardcover edition April 2011

SIMON & SCHUSTER and colophon are registered trademarks of
Simon & Schuster, Inc.

For information about special discounts for bulk purchases,
please contact Simon & Schuster Special Sales at
1-866-506-1949 or business@simonandschuster.com.

The Simon & Schuster Speakers Bureau can bring authors to
your live event. For more information or to book an event contact
the Simon & Schuster Speakers Bureau at 1-866-248-3049 or
visit our website at www.simonspeakers.com.

Designed by Kyoko Watanabe

Manufactured in the United States of America

10 9 8 7 6 5 4 3 2 1

Library of Congress Control Number: 2010039637

ISBN 978-1-4165-9431-4
ISBN 978-1-4516-1108-3 (ebook)

To my brother Richard Waxman, who tirelessly watches over me

With great love and affection

CONTENTS

FOREWORD

Tom Colicchio

The definition of Italian food has come a long way in this country in the past half century. When I was a kid growing up in New Jersey in the sixties, "Italian" meant macaroni and Sunday gravy, sausage and peppers, and *baccalà*. By way of Italian culinary icons we had the big-bellied pizzeria owner, the Sicilian *nonna* making meatballs in her kitchen, and oh yeah, Chef Boyardee.

By the 1970s, the seeds of change were already being sown out West. Chefs like Alice Waters, Jeremiah Tower and Jonathan Waxman were experimenting with a new style of cooking, one that shined a spotlight on ingredients. Thanks to a large Italian immigrant population and a climate conducive to growing things like tomatoes, olives, figs and basil almost year round, spectacular raw materials were in ready supply. Nobody called the food they were making "Italian," of course—dishes like heirloom tomato salad, wild nettle frittata and salmon in fig leaves were "New American." But their DNA was pure *Italia*: ingredient-driven food cooked simply and served without fanfare.

Jonathan was born and raised in the Bay Area, so it comes as no surprise that he was drawn to cooking with the ingredients that he grew up on. First as the cook at Chez Panisse and then as a chef/owner at Michael's in Santa Monica, Jonathan made a reputation early on as a chef who really understood how to make his ingredients stand out. In this way Jonathan has always been, without talking about it and maybe without realizing it himself, an Italian chef.

Already an innovator in California, Jonathan was the first person to bring this new style of cooking and eating to the Big Apple. When he opened Jams in 1984, it changed the way that people dined in New York City. Up until that point good food had been formal, and formal dining was always French. Then came Jonathan, like a cool California breeze washing over Manhattan. For the first time New Yorkers ate serious food in a casual environment. Jams had that Italian sex appeal too: celebrities and socialites dining on flattened chicken and frites, a chef who drove fast cars and was one of the first to own restaurants scattered around the globe.

I was a young chef, just on the cusp of getting my first New York City cooking job, when Jonathan opened Jams. It wasn't long after meeting him that I discovered another aspect about Jonathan that has always struck me as very Italian: his warmth and generosity of spirit. Jonathan was very supportive of me at an early point in my career, and that meant a lot to a kid from the 'burbs trying to make a name for himself in the big city. He was always someone that I looked up to; one of the good guys, with a trademark big grin and an easy way with people.

It was only when Jonathan opened Barbuto in 2003 that his food—food that was so very Italian in its soul—finally began to be called Italian by name. Barbuto is located a block away from my apartment, and I go there more than any other restaurant in New York. I'm always surprised to see how much Jonathan is there. His constant presence and his limitless caring shows in the food; he's cooking the best food of his life these days. It also shows in the familiar faces that I see there night after night—Jonathan treats first-time guests like regulars, and regulars like family.

In this book, Jonathan sets down the dishes that we have all come to love at Barbuto. It is well worth the wait. Gnocchi with spring vegetables and basil; stewed chicken with Meyer lemon, garlic, and white wine; asparagus and poached eggs; this is food that is *meant* to be made in your home. Cook it according to the seasons, with the utmost attention to your raw materials. Cook it with love and for your family and friends. That's Italian, Jonathan's way.

INTRODUCTION

Barbuto is located in the corner of an old garage in Manhattan's West Village, built to sell Rolls-Royce automobiles in 1939. We have about two thousand square feet, which makes for a smallish restaurant. The old garage doors were replaced a few years back, and the three new doors roll up anytime the weather allows. This gives us the air of a vacation spot, despite the grittiness of the city. We are close to the Hudson River and the breezes off the water are magnificent. The kitchen, with its huge pizza oven and grill, is wide open to the dining room. It also has a big kitchen table that is the setting for many a festive occasion.

The chairs are mismatched, the wine list mainly Italian, the tables unadorned mahogany, the napkins are kitchen towels. The waiters' shirts are etched with a caricature of our Barbuto dog. The clientele encompasses a wide demographic: locals, models (from my partner's fashion studio upstairs), tourists from all over the world, business types, families with raucous children, single diners, young, old and in between.

The mix lends itself to a rather casual atmosphere, albeit loud—definitely not intimate—just the way I like it. The food is a bit brash and is served on simple white or off-white Barbuto plates. The coffee is Italian; the bread is breadsticks or *ciabatta*; and good olives and olive oil garnish the table. The bar can get pretty hectic, especially in summer, but everyone loves eating and drinking at the bar.

The kitchen table is my favorite spot. It was built with two-hundred-year-old oak planks from a Pennsylvania barn and was tailor-made for the kitchen, and seats up to fourteen. Here is where Barbuto really exudes its charm. I cook whatever is seasonally available and good. The food is presented either on long platters or on big hunks of rough-hewn butcher block, and the guests serve themselves. This kitchen table is a perfect example of my cooking style at Barbuto: huge mounds of *fritto misto,* simply adorned *insalata mista,* steaming heaps of pasta *carbonara,* whole fish baked in sea salt. You could very well be eating in my house!

Barbuto has become a New York restaurant icon, an Italian brasserie that serves food that is fun, gutsy, and seasonally spontaneous.

The seeds of Barbuto were sown when an Italian couple moved into the penthouse directly above my family's apartment. He was a bearlike, cuddly character and his wife, in contrast, was petite and elegant, almost waiflike. Her name was Alessandra Ferri. She is a principal dancer at the American Ballet Theatre—perhaps the greatest emotive ballet dancer of her generation. Her husband, Fabrizio Ferri, is one of the greatest fashion photographers in Italy.

I often encountered Fabrizio exhausted from traveling. I asked once if he wanted a bite to eat, and he was soon at our little kitchen table devouring two portions of my home-cooked beef stew. He was charming, effusive and very enthusiastic about the food. We did this little dinner thing a few more times, until one evening he asked if I might be interested in a restaurant he owned downtown.

Busy with my restaurant, Washington Park, I refused, but Fabrizio prodded me for a few weeks until I ventured down to his studio, Industria, which occupies the upper floors of an old garage on the northeast corner of Washington Street in the West Village. The restaurant on the ground floor had large garage doors on two sides. It was a funky place, haphazardly put together as if the proprietors weren't interested in doing business. When I went back one Sunday evening with my chef pal Jimmy Bradley, he looked at me and said, "No way!"

Fabrizio did not give up. He explained that my sensibilities and cooking style were very Italian even though I wasn't. He said I cooked like his Roman grandmother. He thought that I could create a special Italian place that would make us both proud. Recognizing a kindred creative spirit, he set me free to rebuild and design the space. For the name, I chose Barbuto, the Italian noun meaning "beard," which described our trio—two scruffy bearded fellows plus Fabrizio's Irish wolfhound, Gideon. He serves as Barbuto's mascot on the restaurant's sign hanging over West 12th Street.

As Washington Park dissolved, I wanted something different. In Barbuto, I wanted the menu to be spontaneous, earthy, rustic and authentic. I wanted it to be creatively Italian but deeply rooted in tradition and Italian products. This meant that we would cook all pasta to order, grill and roast meats using a wood fire, and create old-fashioned pizzas, hearty soups and seasonal salads. The most important component was a philosophical one: I longed for the food to be affordable and comfortable. To achieve this I needed to free myself from any set menu. I envisioned a daily, ever-changing, seasonal menu, punctuated by dishes such as our shaved raw salad of Brussels sprouts with toasted walnuts, pecorino cheese and good olive oil. The dish was a defining moment, a cornerstone of Barbuto's style. Inspired, I decided to use as few as two or three ingredients per dish. This simplicity, fully intended to make a culinary as well as philosophical point, has served Barbuto well.

I love simplicity. Yet I was weaned on three-star food in France. It took a long time to realize that it really wasn't much fun to dine for six hours and eat dishes that had two bites, paired with an equal amount of wine, and achieve what my wife, Sally, calls a food hangover. No, the real food memories of my youth came flooding back when I spent time in Italy.

Simply braised rabbit on a bed of buttered noodles, grilled branzino with olive oil and lemon, a baked dish of creamy polenta with grilled porcini on top. The notion that Jonathan Waxman, a Berkeley boy educated in French haute cuisine with a Californian's penchant for idiosyncratic cooking philosophy, could embrace Italian sensibilities—well, it began to make sense.

This is my personal take on Italian food; it adheres to the "keep it simple" philosophy. I embrace Americans' passion for all things Italian, from Ferraris to Prada, from Pisa to the Amalfi coast, from Michelangelo to Giotto. The most widespread of these Italian passions is the essence of *cucina Italiana.*

I was lucky to have been raised in the San Francisco Bay area. Italians immigrated there in good numbers from the time of the Gold Rush, but the 1880s saw a steep increase. They brought samplings of grapes, olive trees and tomatoes, and found lush and verdant valleys of native olive-producing trees, acres of grapes and vast valleys of vegetables, fruits and grain. They quickly planted their particular varieties. The ingredients their cuisine demanded were sometimes very easy to find, like our wonderful crabs, wild boar and grass-fed cows, goats and lambs. And what they couldn't find, they quickly adapted using our native ingredients. We are the beneficiaries of cioppino, ravioli *malfatti,* San Francisco pizza, and so much more.

Pesto was easy here; basil grew well in the foggy climate. Rosemary, tarragon and fennel grew wild in the hills, as they do in Sicily. The majority of the Italian immigrants to California came from Genoa and Piedmont. Restaurants and wineries with Italian varietals began to flourish.

Mario Fontana and his fellow Ligurian Antonio Cerruti established a chain of canneries under the Del Monte label. Domenico Ghirardelli, who traveled through the gold mines in the 1850s selling chocolates and hard candies, settled in San Francisco and founded the Ghirardelli chocolate empire. He used Italian immigrant labor, right at the site of the present-day Ghirardelli Square.

Grapes and winemakers from Italy have long been a part of our American history. Filippo Mazzei planted vineyards with Thomas Jefferson. The founding of the Italian Swiss Colony wine cooperative at Asti, California (named for the Asti in Piedmont, famous for sparkling wine and Nebbiolo), in 1881 was a milestone in California-Italian wine making. Other immigrants from wine-growing regions led to the widespread participation and success of the Italians in the California wine industry and the vineyards of the Napa and Sonoma valleys.

What made California so enticing to these immigrants? The most obvious element is the weather. The temperate climate, cool, rainy winters and heat in the south is much like Italy. California also has an extensive seacoast like Italy, massive mountains, and vast acreage attached to vineyards, olive trees, etc. Beyond the geography are the people. Californians, too, love the outdoors and live to eat.

My passion for Italian food is rooted in San Francisco's Little Italy. Vanessi's, sadly long gone, was a masterpiece of Italian-Californian cooking. A cook (usually Chinese!) would prepare pasta, grill meats on a Montague grill (made by Italian immigrants in Hayward, California—the best grill in the world) in front of you, and they would serve a good rustic Zinfandel or Barbera. All was good. Or in Occidental, the Union Hotel had a set menu, with olives, celery and breadsticks followed by a minestrone, then salad, pasta and finally roasted and grilled meats. You would waddle out, happy as a wild boar in a field of acorns. Other San Francisco restaurants included the Joe's restaurants. These casual, open-kitchen joints were small: six guests at a counter and five tables. However, Original Joe's on Chestnut Street was huge, with decoration dating to the 1930s, and wonderful food. The piers were the center for the Italian fishermen and their restaurants: Labruzzi and Genoa, Castagnola, Tarantino and Alioto, all producing steaming Dungeness crabs and gallons of cioppino. Our most famous San Franciscan, the amazing Joe DiMaggio is still represented by an eponymous restaurant there. As is Alioto's (Alioto was a well-loved mayor during my youth). The restaurants are still thriving and so are the fishermen. The boats have not changed at all since the 1930s.

And then there were the cafés of North Beach, where I had my first espressos—Vesuvio, Caffè Trieste, Tosca Café and Enrico's Sidewalk Café. The rich culture that I grew up with subtly influenced my cooking: the desire to cook in an open kitchen, the use of a Montague grill and a *piastra* (or griddle), the liberal use of garlic and olive oil.

Throughout all the time I spent in France absorbing the great culinary wealth there, I harbored a secret desire to go to Vanessi's and have sand dabs in brown butter, baked lasagne and a grilled New York steak with rosemary potatoes, or simply a bowl of cioppino.

My passion for all things Italian was further ignited when I passed through Liguria, Piedmont and Valle d'Aosta in 1976. I was attending cooking school in Paris and I had decided to give Italian cooking a look-see. It was but a short trip that resulted in many more. Perhaps my seminal voyage was a week in Milan attending the annual decoration and furniture show. I felt a strong affinity to the Milanese style of cooking—it just felt "right."

In France, all things food-related can be rather formal and serious. I find the Italians livelier; they actually have a sense of humor. Their attitude toward cooking is strikingly different from that of the French. They enjoy food with a deep passion, while their French neighbors seem to imbue French cuisine with a certain formality.

Restaurants in the 1970s in Italy were a strange lot. The serious Michelin-starred joints all wanted to emulate the French. The small mom-and-pop places were slightly dotty and lacking in culinary strength. There were, of course, the standouts: Harry's Bar in Venice was at its apogee, packed with fantastic people eating great food. There were also the new upstarts who were impassioned to build on Italian traditions and use the momentum provided by French stars such as Paul Bocuse and Michel Guérard. I was lucky to see this evolution and to witness its beginnings in America and England as well.

The best Italian food was (and continues to be) in the homes of good cooks. And Italy abounds in good home cooks. They are the backbone of the tradition and the continuation of Italian food. The other stars are the winemakers, farmers, cheese makers and ranchers. Their passion is unflagging and now their products are better than ever.

Italy is enjoying a great renaissance in food, and, unlike in America, big stars do not dominate it. Gualterio Marchesi, Gianfranco Vissani and Fulvio Pierangelini qualify as bona fide "stars," but enthusiastic younger chefs and their spouses, all eager to cook their version of Italian regional cuisine, have buoyed the simple country places. It is a good time for Italian food.

In America, our Italian restaurants have changed as well. The traditional model was either the Brooklyn/Little Italy red-sauce-and-meatball joints or the sophisticated quasi-French places. I like both styles, but their ubiquity was crowding out any chance for regional Italian cookery. The American Italian revolution really started in Los Angeles in the 1980s with the onset of Rex il Ristorante (owned by the late, lamented Mauro Vincenti), Johnny Paoletti's eponymous Brentwood establishment and Valentino (Piero Selvaggio's sleek outpost) in Santa Monica. In New York, there were Trattoria da Alfredo,

Parioli Romanissimo, San Domenico and Lydia Bastianich's Felidia. In Philadelphia, De Lullo had a huge impact, and many of the new wave had their start there. These restaurateurs elevated the cause of Italian food awareness in America.

The problem for modern Italian restaurants in the United States was the unavailability of good raw products. Fava beans, true prosciutto, wonderful olive oils and great wines were not grocery staples. Even now, radicchio, good *balsamico* and other items are sometimes hard to come by. When I first arrived in New York in the early 1980s, I discovered the joys of fantastic arugula from Brooklyn, the handmade *salumi* from Salumeria and the amazing breads of Policastro in SoHo. But if you weren't centered near an Italian stronghold in one of our major cities, you were out of luck. Now, you can walk into any good supermarket in any city in America and see ten kinds of olive oil, five *balsamico,* six types of Arborio rice and a plethora of other Italian specialties.

The Italian culinary wave is here, spearheaded by the chefs who exploded from these beautiful restaurants. Cesare Casella, Mario Batali, Franceso Antonucci, Marc Vetri and many others have helped to set the bar at a very high level; they have seen the future and they love it.

Another great influence has been the River Café in London. The proprietors, Rose Gray and Ruthie Rodgers, developed a version of Italian food that is so simple and basic, it's truly amazing. They took out all the nonessential bits and operate on a very pure level. I love their style and perhaps I owe more to them than I realize.

So where do I fit in? I am happily ensconced in the middle, neither innovator nor strictly traditional. I love it all and I steal from everyone. I learned much from Mauro Vincenti and Piero Selvaggio, but most of all I owe Colman Andrews, who rather cagily allowed me to accompany him on many trips to Italy (and other places as well). His generosity is astounding.

Italian, My Way

I f the core of Italian cookery is seasonality, then nothing defines seasonality more than fresh greens. Lettuce can be a basic term for all greens; in Italy they grow an amazing variety. In America we tend to stick to the same old standbys; in Italy they have fifty varieties of *treviso*! I am constantly awed at what I find in the Italian markets when I wander around the countryside. Italians like their greens crisp, bitter and colorful, and this style appeals to me. A classic example is arugula. In Italy, some varieties of arugula are large and soft; others, small, crisp and spicy. I happen to like the wild variety, the small, bitter, almost blue-tinged *sylvetta*.

With the greening of the American food industry, arugula no longer rests in the hands of the Mediterranean farmers. We produce amazing arugula here. Nothing, absolutely nothing, compares to a freshly made salad of arugula and real Parmigiano-Reggiano cheese tossed with great olive oil and sea salt.

Early on in my career I became impassioned by the world of warm salads, which the Italians have enjoyed for centuries. I am particularly enamored with the classic *bagna cauda,* which I have adapted to my taste. I often wonder why eggs taste better in the hills of Piedmont than in downtown New York. I think pedigree might have something to do with it. In any case, a perfectly poached egg atop a curly endive salad, mixed with freshly picked herbs, pancetta, crispy torn bread croutons, true balsamic vinegar (more on that later) and, of course, that fantastic walnut oil from Abruzzi, is heaven!

I quite like the idea of a colorful, composed salad. Roasted apples, toasted walnuts and freshly made goat cheese, delicately but firmly tossed with lemon juice, good olive oil and black pepper, is an autumnal treat.

Then there is my absolute favorite: the raw vegetable salad. I was a picky and not at all adventuresome eater as a child. I came late to the game of delicious, freshly picked vegetables. Raw beets, asparagus, summer squash and even Brussels sprouts have all entered my daily menus. The only "trick" with raw vegetables is to choose farm fresh. A Brussels sprout gone past its prime is no one's friend. My first raw salad came in the guise of a shaved black truffle and mâche (lamb's tongue lettuce) salad—very decadent, and truly delicious. I have tried to enhance my repertoire along this theme. A trick I employ with raw vegetables is to use a lovely and sharp Japanese mandoline. This amazingly simple and precise tool makes quick work of a raw artichoke, cauliflower or turnip, making delicate, tender shavings. Again, tossed with great olive oil and salt, they are transcendent.

Raw shaved asparagus with lemon dressing

This is the quintessential late-spring offering. This idea originally came via the café at Chez Panisse in Berkeley. Technically chefs don't really "steal" a recipe; we euphemistically "adapt" it. It's a subtle but interesting difference. The use of raw asparagus had tantalized me, but I was too timid. Alice Waters is never timid.

Here's my advice about asparagus: First, please don't serve asparagus from five thousand miles away; it is neither sensible nor tasty. Second, freshness is paramount; the stalks need to be crisp, not limp or tired. Last, not all asparagus are created equal. Look for tips that have not bolted. The leaves should lie flat against the stalk. The spears should taste sweet and almost grassy, and they should need some cleaning (dirt left by the farmer is a good sign of freshness, usually). Shopping for them is the lengthiest portion of the process; the recipe will take about ten minutes. Try and shave the asparagus at the very last second. If you shave them ahead of time, keep them undressed in the refrigerator until ready to serve.

¼ cup hazelnuts
1 pound farm-stand asparagus
Juice of 1 lemon
¼ cup soft extra-virgin Spanish or
    Provençal olive oil

Sea salt and freshly ground black
    pepper to taste
1 tablespoon grated Parmesan

1. Toast the hazelnuts on a baking sheet for 5–8 minutes in a preheated 350° oven; cool and then crush in a towel using a rolling pin.
2. Wash and snap the asparagus spears at their base (the white, bitter part can be used for a delicious soup, see page 69). Upend a small bowl, place a spear on the flat bottom and, using a vegetable peeler, gently shave long thin slices.
3. Mix the lemon juice with the olive oil and add sea salt and black pepper.
4. At the very last second toss the dressing with the hazelnuts and asparagus. Serve on a platter decorated with the Parmesan.

Serves 3–4, depending on the size of the asparagus spears

Asparagus and poached eggs

Asparagus is a delightful vegetable. It is extremely nutritious, crisp and, best of all, easy to cook because it is good raw, grilled, poached, sautéed or stir-fried. I love the little ones we get from the North Fork of Long Island. In Italy as a first course they poach asparagus and serve it with a poached egg and grated Parmesan. Here I twist the recipe, cooking the egg in brown butter, then adding a sprinkle of red wine vinegar and olive oil and topping the egg with shaved Parmesan. The asparagus can be grilled or sautéed.

12 spears asparagus

4 eggs

4 tablespoons extra-virgin olive oil (preferably a fruity Tuscan variety)

Sea salt and freshly ground black pepper to taste

1 tablespoon red wine vinegar

4 tablespoons (½ stick) unsalted butter

12 thin slices Parmesan, shaved with a vegetable peeler

1. Break off the asparagus ends and wash the spears in cold water.
2. Break the eggs into 4 nonstick poaching cups that have been well buttered.
3. Heat a heavy cast-iron skillet and add 1 tablespoon of the olive oil. When hot, sear the asparagus until crispy and season with sea salt and black pepper. Transfer to 4 plates. Add the remaining olive oil and the vinegar to the skillet and taste for seasoning. Set aside.
4. Fill a wide, shallow saucepan with 4 inches of water and bring to a simmer. Place the egg cups in the water and cook until the egg whites are set, approximately 3 minutes.
5. Add the butter to a pan large enough to hold the eggs. When melted and lightly browned, slide the eggs into the pan. Heat until golden, then spoon an egg on top of each asparagus plate.
6. Spoon a bit of the butter over each egg, drizzle the oil and vinegar over the asparagus and top each egg with 3 shavings of Parmesan.

Serves 4

Poached artichoke hearts with fried egg and anchovy sauce

I love artichokes and treasure their arrival in the spring. I believe that artichokes have magical powers. It is said that when Catherine de' Medici first arrived at the Luxembourg Palace in Paris, she demanded that artichokes be sown in the garden. It takes two to three years before a fresh crop can be harvested, but the beds yield for up to fifteen years. Spain (which is the leader) and Italy account for about 50 percent of the world's artichoke production. Artichokes are not as popular in America as in Italy, where it is quite normal to see them everywhere when they're in season. I am very picky about my artichokes: I like them with a deep purple–green color, no signs of damage, and they need to be very rigid and crisp (not limp). I look for large ones that are as fat as your father's fist.

The eggs of Italy are works of art. They tend to have orange yolks, are usually impeccably fresh, and when poached, they are firm with an amazing, creamy white.

The dressing here is quite tangy: freshly smashed garlic with chopped anchovy and olive oil. The anchovies in the sauce are not particularly fishy, and the sauce does not overpower the eggs. This is a perfect luncheon main course and a great starter on those cool spring evenings by the fire.

4 large artichokes

5 tablespoons extra-virgin olive oil

Juice of 2 lemons

½ teaspoon sea salt, plus more to taste

1 tablespoon unsalted butter

Freshly ground black pepper to taste

8 anchovy filets, rinsed and chopped

2 cloves garlic, minced

2 shallots, minced

1 teaspoon mustard powder

4 very fresh eggs

1. To clean the artichokes: Pull off the outer leaves until you see the white, softer base; then cut 1½ inches off the top and scoop out the fuzzy core. Using a vegetable peeler, trim the tough skin from the base. Cut the hearts in half and place in a bowl. Toss with 1 tablespoon of the olive oil. Put the hearts in a saucepan with half of the lemon juice and ½ teaspoon sea salt and add enough water to cover them. Bring the artichokes to a simmer, place a clean kitchen towel directly on top of them to keep them

submerged and cook for about 15 minutes, or until tender. Let them cool in their liquid, then drain.

2. In a sauté pan, heat the butter and cook the hearts until they are golden. Season and keep hot.

3. Make the dressing: In a bowl, combine the anchovy filets, garlic, shallots and mustard powder. Dribble in the remaining lemon juice and then whisk in 2 tablespoons of the olive oil. Season with black pepper but no salt.

4. Fry the eggs: In a nonstick frying pan, heat the remaining 2 tablespoons of olive oil over medium-high heat. Slide the eggs into the pan and cook until just set.

5. Place 2 artichoke halves on each plate. Top with an egg and 2 tablespoons of the anchovy sauce. Serve hot.

Serves 4

Baby spinach, Maine sardines and pine nuts

I love the combination of grilled sardines and lettuce, particularly a hearty lettuce like spinach, which makes a perfect foil for any fish. Maine produces much more than just lobsters and moose. It has a fantastic array of fish; its stocks of sardines are perhaps the least known. In winter, fishermen there send me scallops, oysters, gorgeous pink shrimp and fat, juicy sardines. I grew up fishing in San Francisco Bay with sardines as bait. My brother, who loves eating at my restaurants, once remarked on how pathetic it was that I only served bait! Well, if bait can catch a beautiful bass in San Francisco Bay, then it must be a great delicacy. Sicily is an influence for this salad, but it could be from anywhere that sardines are caught.

8 whole sardines, cleaned
6 tablespoons extra-virgin olive oil
Juice of 2 lemons
Sea salt and freshly ground black
    pepper to taste

½ cup pine nuts
2 bunches baby spinach, washed and
    stemmed

1. Preheat the broiler and oil a baking sheet. Rinse and dry the sardines.
2. Place the sardines on the sheet, dribble 2 tablespoons of the olive oil and half of the lemon juice over them and season with sea salt and black pepper.
3. Place the pine nuts in a sauté pan with 2 tablespoons of the olive oil. Cook the pine nuts over low heat, stirring frequently, for 3 to 4 minutes, until lightly browned.
4. While the pine nuts are cooking, cook the sardines under the broiler, 2 minutes per side. Remove them from the oven and set aside.
5. Place the spinach on a platter and add the remaining 2 tablespoons of olive oil, the remaining lemon juice, the pine nuts and some sea salt and toss well. Place the sardines on top (the spinach will wilt ever so slightly; this is good). Serve.

Serves 4

Wild arugula salad with shaved Parmesan and extra-virgin olive oil

"Wild" is a somewhat loose term in the culinary world. We buy "wild" salmon, knowing full well that its trips to the ocean were minimal, save for a glimpse through a large net. The same philosophy applies to salads; arugula started as a field green, but today is cultivated. So I mean cultivated wild, a little like Bob Dylan in a Brioni tuxedo.

Sylvetta is most commonly referred to as wild arugula, but feel free to use any decent local variety.

This salad is an elegant, simple *contorni* that is a good foil for grilled steak or poultry. It is equally scrumptious atop any pizza.

½ pound arugula, washed and dried
¼ cup extra-virgin olive oil

Sea salt to taste
¼ pound chunk Parmesan

1. Place the arugula in a chilled stainless-steel bowl (this helps to keep it crisp).
2. Toss the arugula with the olive oil. Add sea salt.
3. Using a vegetable peeler, shave long, thin strips of cheese and place them on top of the salad. Toss gently (to keep the shavings intact). Place on 4 plates and serve.

Serves 4

Tomato, *burrata* and lavender blossom salad

Here are two of the finest ingredients from the Italian larder. *Burrata* is the Lamborghini of mozzarella. It has a pure, creamy texture and its almost milky, ricotta taste is divine. It does not travel well, and it does not last. A good cheese shop will supply you with it, but the natural substitute is buffalo mozzarella.

Tomatoes are not indigenous to Italy. I find that mind-boggling because they are in almost all of the dishes you see there. Please take heed: All tomatoes are not equal. Lately, we have seen a tremendous surge in heirloom tomatoes, those ugly guys that every Ag Department in America tried to stomp out like smallpox fifty years ago. They almost succeeded, but thanks to brave seed companies and hardy old-fashioned farms, they live again. Yet please remember, tomatoes need good parents, weather and some luck. I find hothouse varieties better than soggy, overripe, rotten tomatoes or tomatoes that qualify as baseballs. The only true way to know is to taste them, or buy some slightly unripe Jersey tomatoes and let them ripen on your windowsill.

4 nice, ripe tomatoes (I like to mix and match different colors. If large ones aren't available, by all means use cherry tomatoes.)

1 pound *burrata*, at room temperature

¼ cup extra-virgin olive oil

¼ teaspoon sea salt

½ teaspoon fresh lavender petals (available in pots at better groceries and nurseries, or substitute ¼ teaspoon dried lavender)

Freshly ground black pepper to taste

1. Remove the stem portion of the tomatoes using a paring knife and trim off any ugly or damaged parts. Carefully slice off the bottoms. Slice larger tomatoes into ⅛-inch-thick rounds and place them on a cold platter. Cut the other tomatoes into any shape you like. Lay them on top.
2. Gently slice the *burrata* and decorate the tomatoes with the cheese.
3. Mix together the olive oil, sea salt, lavender and some black pepper, sprinkle onto the tomatoes and *burrata* and serve.

Serves 4

Raw shaved Brussels sprouts with pecorino and toasted walnuts

This has become one of my most famous dishes, and it has enhanced the reputation of a vegetable that haunted many a childhood, Brussels sprouts. I'm always up for a challenge and one afternoon I thought, if asparagus is good raw, why not Brussels sprouts? Shaving the vegetable transforms its flavor, and tossed in a bowl with salty pecorino cheese, a rich Ligurian or Napa Valley extra-virgin olive oil, crunchy toasted walnuts and a squeeze of lemon, this salad is crunchy, delicious and healthy. It will make a Brussels sprouts believer out of even the most finicky eater.

½ cup shelled walnut halves
2 pints very fresh whole Brussels
  sprouts
Juice of 1 lemon
¼ cup extra-virgin olive oil (preferably
  Ligurian or Napa Valley)

Sea salt and freshly cracked black
  pepper to taste
4 tablespoons grated pecorino
  cheese

1. Spread the walnuts on a baking sheet and toast in a preheated 350° oven for 8–10 minutes, remove, let cool and lightly crush using a rolling pin or wine bottle.
2. Wash the Brussels sprouts and trim off the hard stem portion. Using a very sharp knife or mandoline or a Japanese vegetable mandoline, shave the sprouts into a large bowl.
3. Add the lemon juice, olive oil and walnuts to the sprouts and toss well. Season with a small pinch of sea salt, freshly cracked pepper and 2 tablespoons of the pecorino cheese.
4. Toss the salad well and place on a rustic platter, sprinkle the remaining cheese over the salad and serve at room temperature.

Note: The standard mandoline is made for high volume rather than precise slicing. The Japanese versions, with numerous blades, are far more sharp and exacting.

Serves 4

Baby beets, farmer's cheese, beet top greens and walnut oil

Beets have become a gourmet's staple. In Europe, one can buy precooked beets, which takes away the effort and also the pleasure of cooking them yourself. I love the new varieties available: Chioggia, rainbow golden, purple, yellow, white and many others. The tried and true method of cooking beets is poaching them in simmering water, but I believe it zaps their flavor and intensity. Here we roast them with salt, which intensifies the flavors. You'll be transformed into a beet lover if you aren't one already.

Walnut oil is a gorgeous agent for all salads, especially for strong-flavored ingredients like beets. The walnut oils we produce in America sadly pale next to those of the Alps. Spend some money to buy the best, but buy in small quantities (250 milliliters is perfect) so the oil won't go rancid. A viable substitute for walnut oil is hazelnut oil.

¼ cup walnuts

2 pounds small fresh beets with the leaves and stems intact

1 pound kosher salt

¼ cup extra-virgin olive oil

2 tablespoons walnut oil

1 tablespoon good-quality red wine vinegar

½ pound fresh farmer's cheese

Sea salt and freshly ground black pepper to taste

1. Spread the walnuts on a baking sheet and toast in a preheated 350° oven for 8–10 minutes, remove, cool and crush slightly with a rolling pin or wine bottle.
2. Cut off the beet leaves and stems. Wash and dry them and place in the refrigerator.
3. Pour half of the kosher salt on a rimmed baking sheet, place the beets on top and cover them with the remaining kosher salt. Bake for 1½ hours.
4. Remove the beets from the oven and let them cool on the salt. When the beets are cool, discard the salt and peel the beets. Cut them into quarters and chill.
5. To make the vinaigrette: Whisk together the olive oil, walnut oil and vinegar.
6. In a bowl, toss the greens, beets and walnuts with the vinaigrette. Place on a platter, sprinkle with the cheese and season with sea salt and black pepper.

Serves 4

Long Island chicory, white anchovy and garlic toast

Chicory is a mainstay of the Veneto, the region surrounding Venice, which is the center for radicchio, *treviso* and other members of the chicory family. Some find it a bit strident, but chicory has a slight bitterness that I love. (For this salad, I use curly endive, which is yet another variety of chicory.) Both to temper and enhance this bitterness, I like this combination of vinegar-and-olive-oil-marinated white anchovy, shaved Parmesan and the crunchy wholesomeness of garlic toast. Anchovies are ubiquitous throughout Italy as a *condimento* or an appetizer, meant to be eaten on toast or in salads. I like using them whole, and tossed gently with chicory, they create a mellifluous salad.

2 heads curly endive (it looks like
Tallulah Bankhead's hair-do)

1 baguette

1 clove garlic, halved

2 tablespoons extra-virgin olive oil

One 6-ounce package marinated
white anchovies

2 large shallots, peeled and minced

2 ounces *speck*, diced

4 eggs

Sea salt and freshly ground black
pepper to taste

Juice of 1 lemon

1. Wash, dry and separate the curly endive. Save the green tops for another use and cut the white inner cores into bite-size pieces.
2. Cut the baguette in half lengthwise. Toast in a preheated 350° oven until golden brown, then rub the cut sides with the garlic and drizzle with up to 1 tablespoon of the olive oil. Cut the baguette into bite-size pieces.
3. Drain the anchovies and reserve the oil.
4. In a small saucepan, heat 1 tablespoon of the reserved anchovy oil to medium. Add the minced shallots and cook for 2 minutes. Add the *speck* and cook for 3 minutes. Break the eggs into the pan, season with sea salt and pepper and cook sunny-side up.
5. In a large bowl, toss the curly endive, croutons, lemon juice and 1 tablespoon olive oil. Gently toss in the anchovies and season with sea salt and freshly ground black pepper. Place the eggs and *speck* carefully on top of the salad and serve.

Serves 4

Blood orange and shaved raw fennel with black olives

Ah, blood oranges, the fantastic fruit of Sicily. I grew up on delicious oranges in California, but the majestic blood oranges of Sicily are transcendent. The flesh is heavier, a resplendent purple-red, and the flavor divine. The season is only a month long, from about December to January, but the oranges are now produced in America, where we have a later season. The season for these beautiful beasts coincides brilliantly with artichokes, Meyer lemons, scallops, shrimp and hard-shell lobsters. I use every bit of these oranges, from the multicolored rind to their fantastic juice. It feels exotic to wake up in Venice to the bells of St. Mark's, stroll across the piazza and sit down to a perfect breakfast of crisp, freshly baked rolls, extremely thin prosciutto from San Daniele and a glass of fresh-squeezed blood orange juice—nothing starts the day off better.

4 blood oranges
3 tablespoons extra-virgin olive oil
Juice of 1 lemon
Freshly ground black pepper to taste

1 pound small fennel bulbs
½ cup salted Moroccan black olives,
  pitted

1. Zest 1 orange into a small bowl.
2. Section all the oranges: Cut off the top and bottom of each orange, then cut away the peel and pith. Using a paring knife, carefully slice each segment away from the membrane and add them to the zest. Toss with the olive oil, lemon juice and some black pepper.
3. Wash, trim and core the fennel. Shave the fennel on a Japanese mandoline or slice paper thin with a very sharp knife. Wash in cold water and then dry.
4. Add the olives and fennel to the oranges, toss well and serve.

Serves 4

Shaved carrot, turnip and radish salad with garlic dressing and green olives

We are in a carrot renaissance: white, burgundy, pale orange, black and even multicolored carrots are showing up in markets. Sadly, when they are cooked, the carotene tends to lose its color and in turn muddle the dish, but raw, you get everything: the majestic color, the impeccable crispness of these heirloom varieties, the perfume of a real carrot and the juice that blends so well with lemon, saffron, orange and olive oil. The garlic is really a tease here; the radishes add a bit of heat; and the olives, the meaty component. All together they spell a salad that would please any carnivore. It is gorgeous to behold.

1 pound carrots, peeled

4 baby turnips, trimmed and peeled

½ cup radishes, trimmed and washed

2 cloves garlic, minced

3 tablespoons chopped green olives

¼ cup extra-virgin olive oil

2 tablespoons lemon juice

Sea salt to taste

1. Using a vegetable peeler or Japanese mandoline, carefully shave all the carrots, turnips and radishes into a bowl.
2. Make the dressing: Combine the garlic, olives, olive oil and lemon juice and season with sea salt.
3. Toss the shaved vegetables with the dressing and serve cold.

Serves 4

Warm dandelion greens with scrambled eggs and chives

In Italian dandelion is called *tarassaco* and in Latin *Taraxacum officiale.* As a kid I loved dandelion flowers, but little did I realize their culinary potential. We considered them weeds, but to pull weeds and then enjoy them on the dinner table is a double lagniappe. This dish works on many levels: It has an unusual taste and a breath-taking texture. The quality of the ingredients matters most. Fresh eggs, preferably a day old, small dandelion leaves, not overgrown stalks, pancetta cut into tiny pieces—all add up to a wonderful whole.

3 cups dandelion leaves, washed, dried and cut into 1-inch lengths
1 tablespoon extra-virgin olive oil
½ cup diced pancetta
4 eggs
2 tablespoons heavy cream

Sea salt and freshly ground black pepper to taste
6 tablespoons (¾ stick) unsalted butter
1 tablespoon *balsamico*
1 tablespoon fresh minced chives

1. Place the dandelion leaves on a platter.
2. Heat the olive oil in a heavy pan over medium heat and add the pancetta; cook until crispy, about 5 minutes. Remove and drain on paper towels.
3. Break the eggs in a bowl and whisk in the cream. Season with sea salt and black pepper. Melt 3 tablespoons of the butter in the pan over medium-low heat and add the eggs. Cook, stirring with a wooden spoon for 5–8 minutes, until the eggs are cooked but still soft. When the eggs are nicely scrambled, transfer them to the dandelion platter.
4. Immediately add the remaining butter to the pan and turn up the heat. When the butter is brown, add the *balsamico*, whisk for a second and pour over the eggs. Sprinkle the chives and pancetta on top and serve.

Serves 4

The term *antipasti* literally means "before the *paste* (pasta) course." In Italy, the progression of courses in a meal is not to be taken lightly. At our rustic kitchen table at Barbuto, we serve a myriad of appetizers or *antipasti*. Some of these are the essence of simplicity, like thinly sliced prosciutto on a platter with freshly baked focaccia and breadsticks. Other dishes might be *baccalà* (salt cod cakes) on grilled toast with aioli, or smoked trout crostini. *Bruschette* are great starters: crusty rustic bread, grilled and rubbed with olive oil and garlic, then spread with a flavorful pumpkin purée. Another antipasto could be a warm salad of grilled octopus and calamari tossed with bread crumbs and a lemony aioli.

My kids love making little hors d'oeuvres. (I think they like eating them more, but who's telling?) A fun group effort can start with breadsticks. The dough is easy (just some leftover pizza dough), the rolling out simple and the execution fun. Or bruschetta, which is fun to grill, then rub with garlic and olive oil and top with any number of things. Kids love beans, cheese, tomatoes, prosciutto (my son Alexander thinks prosciutto is the food of the gods and he's correct) or any other ingredient you can think of. Kids can also help with polenta; they don't mind stirring for long periods and actually enjoy it.

Cold dishes are a wonderful addition to anyone's repertoire. I learned many years ago that an essential element of customer satisfaction is getting the food to the table in an expeditious fashion. The easiest way to ensure this is with cold *antipasti,* and they are slowly coming back into fashion. The pace of our lifestyles and the need to cook at odd times, both favor cold dishes. I really love them all, and the advantages are many. Pulling a perfectly seasoned tart or *crudo* from the fridge and serving it with a chilled glass of Prosecco or Erbaluce makes quite an impression.

In Italy, meals might consume the better part of a day, and if it's a holiday, the entire day. A typical meal at someone's house in Italy starts formally, with drinks in the living room if it's cool and on the terrace if it's hot.

The small bites served at this sitting come under the heading of *antipasti*, but this is only the first stage. The hour or so of getting reacquainted or perhaps gossiping is then followed by the true *antipasti* course, served *a tavola* (at the table). This is where the real meal begins. Many cold dishes such as terrines, *bagna cauda* or other *antipasti* can be served here, but hot appetizers almost always distinguish a serious meal.

So, before the soup, before the pasta, before the *secondi* (main course) and the dessert, you've already spent two hours eating and drinking! In most Italian households it's about ten p.m., and the main course probably won't hit the table until eleven thirty.

Pesce crudo

I've always been drawn to the food of Japan. The freshness of the seafood, the meticulousness of the preparations, the presentation all speak to me. When I first ate sashimi in the early 1970s it was a revelation. To discover that the Italians were enamored of this style of cookery thrilled me no end. Gualtiero Marchesi, the three-star Michelin master chef from Milan, spent time in Japan and brought back recipes that he quickly manipulated into his own lexicon. Here in New York we have David Pasternak of the wonderful Italian fish house Esca. David is passionate about fish and his *crudi* are world class.

12 ounces pompano or red snapper filet (skinless)
Sea salt to taste

Extra-virgin olive oil
Pink peppercorns to taste

1. Using a very sharp knife, slice the fish as thinly as possible and place on a long chilled platter.
2. Sprinkle with sea salt, then olive oil and finally freshly ground peppercorns.

Serves 4–6

Prosciutto *con burrata*

Prosciutto is truly an Italian national treasure. The pigs that go to slaughter to make these gorgeous hams are extremely rare. Of the thousands raised, only a small percentage makes the premier grade. The exact weight and proportion of the legs are regulated. According to the law, they must be slaughtered and butchered precisely. Any imperfection will result in their being downgraded. The legs are cured in pure sea salt for a minimum of eight months. They are tested constantly, graded again, and only the best are selected. These are then packed for export (Italian prosciutto is relatively new in the United States; it has only been imported since 1998). Some are packed deboned, but I only use the bone-in variety. At Barbuto we spend about $100,000 a year on prosciutto. We never use domestic because, sadly, our industry doesn't match the peerless quality of Italy.

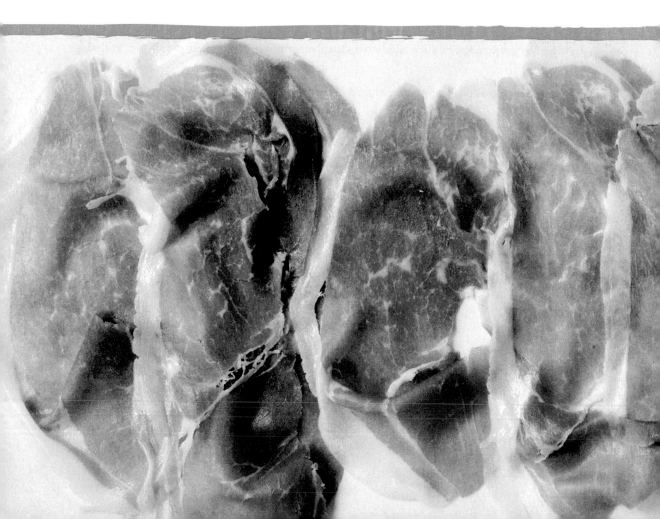

16 slices good prosciutto
(experiment with your butcher to
see which type you like the most)
3 whole *burrata*, at room
temperature

¼ cup extra-virgin olive oil
1 teaspoon *balsamico*
Sea salt and freshly ground black
pepper to taste

1. Place the slices of prosciutto on a platter.
2. Slice the *burratas* crosswise like a fig (see page 58), or to resemble a paper cootie-catcher, and decorate the prosciutto with the slices.
3. Drizzle with olive oil and then a few drops of *balsamico*. Sprinkle with sea salt and black pepper.

Serves 4–6

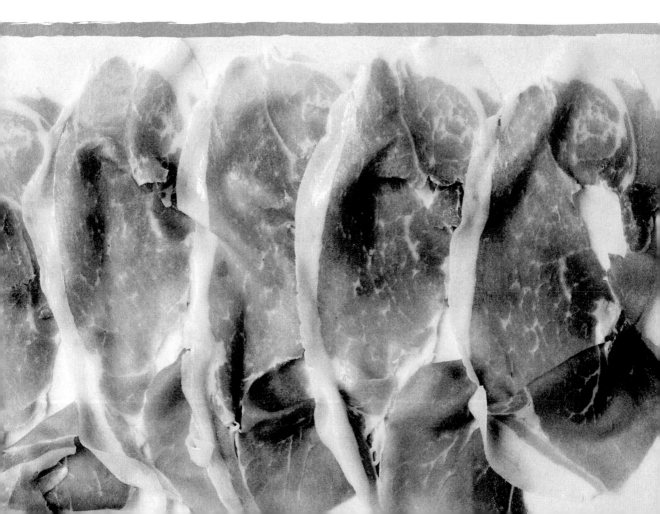

Lardo on toast

My pal Cesare Casella, head of the Italian Culinary Institute, is one of the better-known Italian chefs in America. With his distinctive cowboy boots, his Florentine proboscis and the permanent bouquet of herbs in his chef coat pocket, he is an amazing expert on all foods Italian. His family once had the best restaurant in Lucca.

One dish that is near and dear to him is *lardo.* On paper, *lardo* sounds rather indigestible, yet if you ate it blindfolded, you would think it perhaps the greatest thing that has ever sat in your mouth. It is the pure fat of the gorgeous pigs from Tuscany, cured in salt for six months, then sliced as thinly as possible and laid on some charred Tuscan toast. Remember, Tuscan bread is saltless. The salty fat that melts into the warm bread has all the salt necessary to provoke our senses.

8 slices country bread
Extra-virgin olive oil

8 slices *lardo* (have your Italian deli
slice them very thin)

1. Toast the bread.
2. While it is warm, drizzle with olive oil and then top with *lardo.* Serve immediately.

Serves 4

Ippoglosso tartare

I love the Italian name for halibut; it comes from the Latin for water horse: *hippoglossus!* These water horses are great fish. Halibut is endangered, so I suggest you buy with care. The best size is about five to ten pounds; bigger, and the fish is meatier but less tasty.

The trick to this delicately flavored tartare is to find the freshest fish possible. Trim the filets of all skin, sinew, fat and any unsavory material. Try to keep the fish, the container, even the cutting board as cold as possible. I know this sounds extreme, but it's worth it. You can make the tartare with a food processor, but you'll be far happier with the results if you hand-cut the fish. I love the herbs here—dill, chives, tarragon and parsley—plus the zest of lemon and a tiny dice of red pepper. The addition of shallot adds complexity, and the dribble of pure, fantastic green Tuscan olive oil is mandatory. I like serving this with a cold Sauvignon Blanc from Voglar, but cold beer is a good substitute.

½ pound very fresh halibut filet
1 lemon
1 jalapeño
1 red bell pepper
1 shallot, peeled and minced
2 cloves garlic, 1 minced, 1 halved

1 teaspoon each chopped fresh dill,
    chives, tarragon and parsley
3 tablespoons extra-virgin Tuscan
    olive oil
1 baguette
Sea salt to taste

1. Trim the halibut and finely dice. Return the fish to the fridge.
2. Zest the lemon into a small bowl and add the juice.
3. Remove the seeds from and finely mince the jalapeño and the bell pepper and add to the bowl.
4. Combine the shallot, minced garlic, the herbs and 2 tablespoons of the olive oil. Mix all the ingredients with the halibut and refrigerate until very cold.
5. Split the baguette in half lengthwise, toast, rub with the garlic halves and dribble with the remaining tablespoon of olive oil.
6. Season the tartare with sea salt and spoon into cold cups. Serve with the toasted baguette.

Serves 4–6

Crostini with smoked trout and mascarpone

The mountainous regions of Abruzzi and Liguria have very good trout, with a long tradition of smoking the fish. The delicate smoked flesh is placed on freshly toasted bread, rubbed with garlic and olive oil, and dabbed with mascarpone. It's a lovely match for a glass of Erbaluce.

2 whole smoked trout
1 baguette
2 cloves garlic, halved
Extra-virgin olive oil to taste

One 500-gram tub imported
mascarpone
Lemon wedges (optional)

1. Preheat the oven to 400°.
2. Skin and remove the bones from the trout. Gently flake the flesh, but don't overdo it!
3. Slice the baguette slightly on the bias to create angled rounds.
4. Toast the bread in the oven. When it is lightly golden brown, rub each piece with the cut garlic cloves, then dribble olive oil on top.
5. Add a dab of mascarpone and a few pieces of trout. Serve at room temperature, with lemon if desired.

Serves 4–6

Swordfish carpaccio

This dish was devised at Harry's Bar in Venice and named for the famous Venetian Renaissance painter Vittore Carpaccio. He was a student of the better-known Bellini (whose name the Ciprianis gave to their peach and Prosecco cocktail), and his fifteenth-century paintings are a visual delight.

The dish is quite straightforward. Swordfish makes the best carpaccio, but any sturdy-bodied fish like mahi, striped bass or salmon may be used. The trick here is to cut each three-ounce portion as thinly and with as large a surface area as possible. Then using a meat tenderizer, gently pound the steaks into very thin, almost translucent, plate-size carpaccio. The sauce is very easy, just some shallots, mustard, a good white vinegar (rice wine vinegar is excellent), some fresh herbs, ideally straight from your garden, and a great olive oil—fresh, spicy and green.

12 ounces fresh swordfish	1 teaspoon Dijon mustard
2 tablespoons plus 4 teaspoons extra-virgin olive oil	1 tablespoon rice wine vinegar
	1 teaspoon lemon juice
1 tablespoon each fresh chives, tarragon and basil	Sea salt and freshly ground black pepper to taste
2 shallots, peeled and minced	

1. Cut the swordfish into 4 steaks; slice off any bloodline and skin.
2. Rub each steak with 1 teaspoon of the olive oil, then place in a large resealable plastic bag. Gently pound each steak as thinly as possible using a rolling pin or a heavy-bottomed saucepan.
3. Place the steaks on 4 chilled plates. Cover and refrigerate while you make the sauce.
4. To make the sauce: Tear the herbs into tiny pieces. Combine the shallots, mustard, vinegar and remaining 2 tablespoons of olive oil and then add the torn herbs. Mix well and add the lemon juice. Season with sea salt and black pepper.
5. Drizzle each serving of carpaccio with a bit of sauce and serve cold.

Serves 4

Terrine of artichoke and ham

Terrines are deemed a bit old-fashioned these days by the powers that be, but I still crave them. Italian terrines are a bit smaller and more finely chopped than their French cousins; they seem denser and may be aged longer. This delightful terrine featuring spring peas, onions, carrots and artichokes is easy to make. The ham helps create a fluffy, delicate texture.

1 cup each peas, baby carrots and pearl onions

4 large artichokes (see directions for cleaning on page 7)

1 pound ham, diced

1 cup crème fraîche

4 egg yolks

1 tablespoon chopped fresh tarragon

Sea salt and freshly ground black pepper to taste

Extra-virgin olive oil

Ciabatta, to serve

1. In boiling water, cook the peas, then the carrots and finally the baby onions until just tender. Drain and let cool.
2. Cook the artichokes for 35 minutes in a steamer. Let cool and cut into quarters.
3. Place the ham, the crème fraîche and the egg yolks in the bowl of a food processor fitted with a metal blade. Add the tarragon, sea salt and black pepper. Pulse until just combined.
4. Preheat the oven to 300°.
5. Line a terrine with parchment paper that has been coated with olive oil.
6. Spread an inch-thick layer of the ham mousse, and then a layer of vegetables in the terrine. Repeat 3 times, finishing with the ham mousse. Cover with a piece of parchment paper, then aluminum foil. In a roasting pan, make a *bain-marie*: Pour in 2 cups water and place the terrine in the water. Bake for 1 hour 15 minutes. Remove from the oven.
7. Place a heavy weight on top and let cool. When cool, place in the fridge overnight.
8. When ready to serve, remove the terrine from the fridge, take off the weight, aluminum foil and parchment paper and cut into 1-inch slices. Serve with grilled *ciabatta*.

Serves 6–8

Bruschetta of wild mushrooms and goat curd

I love to make hors d'oeuvres. I use these delightful open-faced sandwiches as often as possible for small and big parties. They are easy and fast, and a great crowd-pleaser. The basic recipe can be augmented. For instance, you can use morels when in season, grilled *cèpes* instead of sautéed mushrooms, ricotta instead of goat cheese. I do like the sweetness of heirloom cherry tomatoes and they make a colorful presentation.

1 pound chanterelles

7 tablespoons extra-virgin olive oil

Sea salt and freshly ground black pepper to taste

1 whole-wheat country *boule*

2 cloves garlic, 1 halved, 1 minced

½ pound fresh goat curd (substitute fresh chèvre if you can't find curd)

1 pint cherry tomatoes, halved along the equator

1 tablespoon chopped fresh chives

1. Wash the chanterelles and then dry them in front of a fan. Slice into small pieces.
2. In a sauté pan, heat 2 tablespoons of the olive oil and sauté the mushrooms until golden, then season with sea salt and black pepper. Let cool in the pan.
3. Slice the bread and toast; rub with the garlic halves and drizzle with 1 tablespoon of the olive oil.
4. Mix the curd with the cherry tomatoes and 3 tablespoons of the olive oil, the minced garlic and the chives.
5. Coat each slice of bread with goat curd, then top with chanterelles, drizzle each piece with the remaining olive oil and serve.

Serves 4–6

Three crostini
Fava bean purée
Goat cheese and prosciutto
Tomato with fresh herbs

Crostini—pieces of either baguette or *ciabatta,* toasted or grilled, rubbed with olive oil and fresh garlic and topped with a savory topping—are ubiquitous in Italy. They are served at every trattoria, wedding, wine bar, etc. Here are three easy and fun variations; you can experiment with your own. The tomatoes and herbs are gorgeous and tasty and the fava bean is my favorite. You can use dried beans cooked with garlic and laurel (bay) leaves.

1 baguette

1 clove garlic, halved

2 tablespoons extra-virgin olive oil

1. Preheat the oven to 350°.
2. Split the baguette in half lengthwise, toast in the oven for 6 minutes, rub with garlic and dribble with the olive oil. Cut into 2-inch slices.

FAVA BEAN PURÉE

2 cups shelled fresh fava beans

2 tablespoons extra-virgin olive oil

2 cloves garlic, minced

½ cup cold water

1 teaspoon fresh oregano leaves

Sea salt and freshly ground black
    pepper to taste

1. In a 4-quart pot of boiling salted water, cook the favas for 3 minutes, drain and let cool. Remove the husks.
2. In a sauté pan, heat the olive oil, garlic and beans and sauté for 3 minutes; add the cold water and the oregano.
3. In a blender, purée the fava beans and season with sea salt and black pepper; they will remain bright green. Spoon the purée onto the toasted bread.

GOAT CHEESE AND PROSCIUTTO

4 slices prosciutto

1 cup fresh goat cheese

2 tablespoons unsalted butter, at
room temperature

1 tablespoon minced fresh chives

Sea salt and freshly ground black
pepper to taste

1. Roll the prosciutto up and slice into ¼-inch-wide ribbons.
2. Mix the prosciutto with the goat cheese, butter and chives and season with sea salt and black pepper.
3. Spread generously on the toasted bread.

TOMATO WITH FRESH HERBS

1 pint mixed tomatoes

2 tablespoons extra-virgin olive oil

3 tablespoons roughly chopped
mixed fresh herbs (basil, oregano,
chives, parsley, etc.)

1 clove garlic, minced

Sea salt and freshly ground black
pepper to taste

1. Wash and stem the tomatoes. Slice into quarters, put in a bowl with the olive oil, herbs and garlic and season with sea salt and black pepper.
2. Spoon onto the toasted bread.

Serves 4–6

Asparagus wrapped with prosciutto

This perfect party appetizer is easy to make and its effect is beautiful. The asparagus should be fairly large and very fresh. The prosciutto must be very thinly sliced for the dish to come together.

6 asparagus spears
12 thin slices prosciutto
Extra-virgin olive oil

Sea salt and freshly ground black
pepper to taste

1. Preheat the broiler. Blanch the asparagus spears in boiling water for 1 minute. Cool. Remove the tough ends from the asparagus and cut each spear in half lengthwise.
2. Wrap each prosciutto slice around an asparagus half like a maypole.
3. Place the wrapped asparagus on an oiled sheet pan, brush them with olive oil, season with sea salt and black pepper and broil for 1 minute. Turn them over and broil for another minute. Serve warm with a drizzle of olive oil and sea salt.

Serves 4

Ciabatta, chunked Parmesan and twelve-year-old *balsamico*

At an Alicia Keys concert a few years back, we struggled to feed 450 hipsters in a room suited for 200 maximum. The crowning moment was when Prince was carried over the heads of the crowd by his massive bodyguards so he could grab a bite of food! It was a waiter's nightmare, and once the thirty-minute concert started, I realized that there was no way any food would be served during it. After Keys finished, we resumed the food festivities. One dish that stood out was perhaps the simplest: a fifty-pound wheel of Parmesan hacked off in chunks and served with twelve-year-old *balsamico* and rounds of freshly baked *ciabatta*—sheer bliss.

CIABATTA

6 cups strong organic bread flour

1 package active dry yeast

2 tablespoons whole milk

1 tablespoon honey

2 tablespoons extra-virgin olive oil

2¼ cups warm water

1 tablespoon sea salt

————

A chunk of the best Parmesan, weighing about 2 pounds

1 bottle superior twelve-year-old *balsamico*

1 bottle extra-virgin olive oil

1. In a ceramic bowl, combine 2 cups of the flour, the yeast, milk, honey and olive oil. Add 2¼ cups of warm water. Stir together with a wooden spoon, then beat until fully incorporated. Cover and let sit at room temperature for several hours, then refrigerate overnight.
2. Add the remaining flour and the sea salt and mix well. The dough should be moist and slightly sticky. Dump the dough onto a work surface, dust with flour and knead for 10 minutes. Clean the bowl and coat with olive oil. Return the dough to the bowl and let rise for 2 hours.
3. Preheat the oven to 425°.
4. Cut the dough in half and form a slipper 12 inches long, 5 inches wide and about

3 inches high. Roll the *ciabatta* in flour and place on a baking sheet. Repeat with the second half of the dough. Let the loaves rise for 30 minutes.

5. Put the *ciabatta* in the oven and bake for 30 minutes. If they brown too much, lower the temperature and continue baking.

6. To serve: Let the *ciabatta* cool and cut them into rounds. Serve each with a chunk of Parmesan. Dribble a tiny amount of *balsamico* on top, then a bit of olive oil.

Serves 6–8 as a starter

Fried whitebait with aioli

The quintessential fried starter. Whitebait is ubiquitous on menus along the Italian coast. Fresh sprats, net-caught in the morning, are tossed with low-gluten, fine white flour and fried. They are served with fried lemon and maybe parsley, but always sea salt. Nothing else is needed; it's a perfect way to begin a meal.

3 cups peanut oil

2 cups very fine organic pastry flour

1 teaspoon sea salt

2 pounds small fry fish (see Note)

Aioli (page 219)

Lemon wedges

1. Heat the oil to 325° in a deep, heavy pan.
2. In a paper bag, combine the flour and sea salt, add the fish and shake vigorously.
3. Deep-fry the fish in batches until golden, 2–3 minutes, and drain on paper towels. Serve with aioli and a wedge or two of lemon. (I dislike the lemon but most people are addicted to it.)

Note: The fish can be from the sea or fresh water. Baby trout, tiny herring and baby perch all work well.

Serves 4–6

Grilled porcini

Ah, the fabulous porcini. We chefs call fresh ones *cèpes* in America (the French translation) and generally refer to only the dried variety as porcini. Many years ago I was surprised to hear that porcini exist in forests around the world. On a bachelor weekend with my pals in the mountains of Aspen, Colorado, we foraged for mushrooms and discovered porcini at thirteen thousand feet. At first they looked like stones, but when harvested, they were perfect: no blemishes, no trace of worms, the best porcini I've ever had. Cooked like steaks, coated lightly in olive oil with a hint of garlic and fresh-chopped herbs, they were magnificent. I've had porcini many ways, in fancy preparations with foie gras, short ribs and masses of black truffle, but truly, grilled or sautéed in olive oil is the way to go.

1 pound fresh *cèpes*	¼ cup extra-virgin olive oil
4 cloves garlic	Sea salt and freshly ground black
½ cup fresh parsley leaves	pepper to taste

1. Preheat a grill or broiler.
2. Gently clean the *cèpes*. Wash the stems and cut off any dirt or other material and slice into ¼-inch "steaks."
3. To make the dressing: Put the garlic and parsley in a mortar and mash together well with a pestle. Dribble in the olive oil and season with sea salt and black pepper to taste.
4. Grill the *cèpes* 2–3 minutes per side, or until golden, place in a bowl, toss with the dressing and serve warm.

Serves 4–6

Griddled razor clams with spicy dressing

In Venice many years ago, I heard of a new restaurant that was off the beaten track, where a woman was cooking arguably the best seafood in Italy. Getting reservations was virtually impossible, but I succeeded in snatching one for lunch. It is called Da Fiore and is a traditionally decorated restaurant with few seats. As I passed the host stand I was greeted by a treasure trove of cooked seafood. When the menu arrived I was speechless. The variety of seafood was endless. I wisely gave up and asked the husband of the chef to choose some dishes and wine.

After a remarkable prosciutto, we were presented with tiny razor clams cooked in olive oil and garlic, with a touch of red pepper and sea salt. I had never had such delicious clams. The rest of the meal was equally wonderful—tiny fried soft-shell crabs (*moleche*), whole branzino, pasta with baby shrimps and those weird prehistoric crustaceans that looked like langoustines from hell. But those clams!

The tiny, fragile razor clams from that luncheon are the inspiration for this dish. In Venice, the chef split them open raw, then seared them briefly in the shell on a very hot griddle with olive oil and some chives.

2 shallots, peeled and minced

1½ tablespoons lemon juice

¼ teaspoon red pepper flakes

4 tablespoons extra-virgin olive oil (preferably Ligurian)

Sea salt to taste

2 slices fresh sourdough bread, crusts removed

1 clove garlic, halved

12 razor clams

1 tablespoon unsalted butter

1 small bunch very thin chives, finely chopped

1. To make the dressing: Combine the shallots, lemon juice, red pepper flakes and 2 tablespoons of the olive oil. Season with sea salt and set aside.
2. Toast the bread, rub with the split clove of garlic, dribble with 1 tablespoon of the olive oil and finely chop into bread crumbs. Set aside.

3. Wash the clams to rid them of any sand, drain them and toss with the remaining tablespoon of olive oil.

4. Heat a pancake griddle over medium-high heat. Lightly coat the surface with olive oil and place the clams on top.

5. Cook until the shells pop open. Add the butter and let it sizzle. Turn the clams onto the meat side and cook about 2 minutes, until golden.

6. Place the hot clams on 4 plates, spoon the dressing on top and sprinkle with bread crumbs and chives.

Serves 4 as an appetizer

Oven-roasted mussels with cilantro and red chilies

Mussels are everywhere and almost always overlooked. They are cheap, delicious and nutritious—the pristine, beardless ebony-colored tiny mussels from Maine, Puget Sound and Nova Scotia are all luxuriously rich and briny. They need to be fresh and have only a faint odor of the ocean. When cooked they should open completely. Closed mussels should be discarded (though sometimes a little whack with a spoon can hurry up the opening process).

Chilies are a grand foil for mussels; they really perk up the flavor and add incredible bounce.

2 quarts fresh mussels, scrubbed and the beards removed	2 shallots, peeled
	¼ cup fresh cilantro leaves
2 tablespoons extra-virgin olive oil	1 lime
2 red Fresno chilies	

1. Preheat the oven to 450°. Place an empty cast-iron skillet inside and let it heat for 30 minutes.
2. Pull out the rack with the skillet and add the mussels and 1 tablespoon of the olive oil. Return to the oven. Every 3 minutes stir the mussels with a wooden spoon.
3. Mince the chilies, shallots and cilantro and put in a small bowl. Dribble in the remaining olive oil.
4. When the mussels are all open (usually 6–8 minutes), remove the hot skillet and pour in the dressing. Stir well. Pour all the mussels and juice with the dressing into a large bowl. Squeeze the lime over the mussels and serve very hot.

Serves 4–6

Vegetable *fritto misto*

This is my homage to a great Italian joint that happens to be in London.

River Café always makes me a bit jealous. It combines a weird but spectacular location, clever and comfortable design (its architect, Richard Rogers, is married to Ruthie, one of the co-owners), a wood-burning stove and a small but productive garden. One late spring afternoon, I arrived to much commotion. It was the day of the Henley Royal Regatta, Oxford vs. Cambridge. The walls had grown TV sets, the clientele were buzzing, and at 1:15, the joint emptied out. We all lined up on the bank of the Thames to watch as the sculls vied for the trophy. It lasted about two minutes, then we all returned to our tables, satisfied and ready to eat.

I always order the *fritto misto*. It's always anchored by a large, beautifully fried leaf (chard or similar), which is covered in a seasonal assortment of mushrooms, peppers, onions, artichokes, fennel or asparagus. It is a perfect, inspirational dish. I hope I can do it justice.

Wandering about Italy many years ago, Colman Andrews and I discovered the Ligurian method of making *fritto* batter. It is very simple: soft flour, sea salt and Ligurian white wine. I sometimes add sparkling water (for some reason Badoit works well). And that's it.

As at the River Café, I choose seasonal vegetables that I like fried. Enjoy!

4 cups peanut oil

1 cup lean white wine (*Roero Arneis, Sauvignon Blanc or Pinot Grigio*)

1¼ cups cold water

1 teaspoon baking soda

2 cups organic pastry flour

1 teaspoon sea salt, plus more to taste

2 pounds assorted vegetables (artichokes, carrots, Swiss chard, button mushrooms, onions, asparagus, eggplant)

1. Heat the oil in a deep pot to 325°.
2. To make the batter: In a large bowl, whisk together the wine, water and baking soda. Add the flour slowly, whisking until smooth. Add 1 teaspoon sea salt when the mixture is creamlike in texture.
3. Prepare each vegetable as if it were to be eaten raw. Cut off the leaves of the artichokes, scoop out the choke and cut into pieces. Peel the carrots and then peel into

long strips. Wash the Swiss chard and cut into leaves and stems. Wash and dry the mushrooms. Peel and slice the onions into rings. Break the woody stems off the asparagus and slice the eggplant.

4. Toss all the vegetables in the batter, lift them out and let the excess drip off. Fry in batches for 3–5 minutes each, till golden and cooked through. Drain the vegetables on paper towels. Serve hot, sprinkled with sea salt.

Serves 4–6

Fritto misto di mare

Chez Black is an amazing joint on the waterfront in Positano. The debonair proprietor has named his place for the color of his tan, and rightfully so. He is appreciative of everyone's patronage, and Chez Black is the place to go for a pizza and a beer, a four-course meal or a *dolce* and espresso. The owner loves to discuss your meal: Are you having the whole *orata*? Maybe some grilled octopus with roasted peppers? What about the *langosta* (which costs as much as a small Harley-Davidson)? My chum and I spent a lazy afternoon (soon evening) gazing out at the small group of islands close to shore, and we dreamed of a perfect restaurant/hotel in the fifteenth-century buildings there. Signore Black explained that the estate of Rudolf Nureyev owned them, they were available and the sum would stagger us. We dreamed on.

4 cups sunflower or corn oil

½ pound fresh squid, cleaned and the body cut into ringlets

½ pound baby shrimp, peeled

½ pound bay or sea scallops

½ pound white fish filet (you may use cod, halibut or bass), cut into 1-inch cubes

1 cup fine organic pastry flour

Sea salt to taste

1 recipe *fritto* batter (page 45)

1 lemon, cut into wedges

1. Heat the oil in a deep pot to 350°.
2. Toss all the seafood into a bag with the flour and season with sea salt.
3. Pour the *fritto* batter into another bowl and dip the floured seafood in the batter. Lift the seafood out of the batter and let the excess drip off.
4. Fry the seafood in batches until golden. Serve hot, garnished with lemon wedges.

Serves 4–6

Balsamic-marinated quail with hazelnuts and field greens

I love quail. So do the Italians, who treasure them and other small game birds. New machines remove most of the annoying bones, so you can enjoy the birds even more. I love the way this marinade tenderizes and flavors the birds. It will caramelize them nicely, giving them a beautiful mahogany exterior. Remember that a medium-rare quail, while edible, can taste gummy and bland; cooked through, the meat is succulent and delicious. I cook these on the grill, but a broiler works almost as well and is far more convenient. The added textures of the hazelnuts and field greens lend a good helping hand.

2 tablespoons *balsamico*

4 tablespoons hazelnut oil (optional)

2 cloves garlic, smashed

4 tablespoons plus 1 teaspoon extra-virgin olive oil

4 boneless fresh quail

¼ cup hazelnuts

Sea salt to taste

Freshly ground black pepper to taste

4 cups spinach, chard and arugula, washed, stemmed, dried and mixed together

1 tablespoon thyme blossoms (or rosemary blossoms or Johnny-jump-ups)

1. In a bowl, make a marinade with 1 tablespoon *balsamico,* the hazelnut oil if using, the garlic and 1 tablespoon of the olive oil. Toss the quail in the marinade and place it and the liquid in a resealable plastic bag in the fridge overnight.
2. The next day, crush the hazelnuts and toast in a sauté pan with 1 teaspoon of the olive oil until golden-bronze. Remove and season with sea salt.
3. Remove the quail from the marinade and season on both sides with sea salt and black pepper. (Discard the marinade.)
4. In a nonstick pan, heat 1 tablespoon of the olive oil, add the quail and cook for 5 minutes per side (they will turn very dark—that's good!). When cooked through, place in a bowl with the greens. Toss in the hazelnuts, the thyme blossoms, the remaining tablespoon of *balsamico* and the remaining 2 tablespoons of olive oil. Season and toss well, and serve on a platter.

Serves 4

Sautéed mushrooms on creamy polenta

This is the first dish I served at Barbuto. I wanted to evoke the Tuscan countryside. Near the Jewish town of Pitigliano are wonderful countryside restaurants that serve age-old Tuscan cuisine. Even though they are close to the sea, the earth is what inspires these places. One mainstay is porcini or chanterelles cooked in their own juices, with onion, garlic and usually a tart white wine, finished with a little butter and a bit of either rosemary or sage crisped in butter. The polenta is the yellow variety, coarse, creamy, cooked for an hour over a slow simmering stove, then enriched with Parmesan. All in all, a rather nice way to warm you after a brisk walk in those gorgeous hillsides and replenish a starved appetite from walking around Pitiliano. The area has some of the finest Etruscan ruins, and the cuisine, while not as ancient, fits well.

1 cup whole milk
6 cups water
2 cups organic stone-ground polenta
(white if possible)
Sea salt and freshly ground black
pepper to taste
¼ cup grated Parmesan

1 pound chanterelles, morels, *cèpes*,
shiitake or *hon-shimeji*
1 tablespoon extra-virgin olive oil
2 shallots, peeled and finely minced
1 tablespoon good Oloroso sherry
3 tablespoons unsalted butter
1 teaspoon fresh thyme leaves

1. To make polenta: Heat the milk and water to a simmer and slowly add the polenta. Stirring constantly, cook for 45–55 minutes or until creamy and cooked through. Season with sea salt and black pepper and add the Parmesan. Keep warm in a *bain-marie*: Fill a heavy pot halfway with hot water, put the polenta pot inside and place over low heat.
2. Slice or dice the mushrooms, wash in cold water and then air-dry.
3. Pour the olive oil into a sauté pan and turn the heat to high; add the mushrooms and cook until they are golden. Add the shallots and then the sherry, reduce the heat and whisk in the butter. Add the thyme at the last second. Spoon the polenta onto a platter and spread the mushrooms on top.

Serves 4–6

Baccalà on grilled toast with aioli

I admit to being a bit timid about *baccalà*. I've never really enjoyed the various versions I've had. The French was too potatoey, the Portuguese too fishy, the Spanish too garlicky. Even in Italy I've always felt the dish had a certain imbalance.

So to make my own, I've adapted the classic recipe.

First, the salt cod is rinsed in the usual manner, then it's cooked in milk flavored with garlic. Last, we poach the potatoes in this same liquid. To put together the *baccalà*, don't puree the potatoes, flake them with your hands. The cod should be carefully boned and flaked, again not puréed. The olive oil adds silkiness and flavor. *Baccalà* keeps for more than a week in the fridge and about a month in the freezer.

1 pound salt cod	Aioli (page 219)
2 cloves garlic	¼ cup extra-virgin olive oil
1 cup whole milk	4 slices *ciabatta*
1 cup cold water	
1 pound russet potatoes, peeled and sliced 1 inch thick	

1. Soak the cod in cold water in the fridge for 3 days, changing the water daily.
2. In a medium saucepan, combine the garlic cloves, milk and cold water. Heat to a simmer, add the cod and cook for 30 minutes, or until tender.
3. Remove the cod and poach the potatoes in the same liquid until they're tender.
4. Flake the cooled potatoes together with the cod. Add ½ cup aioli, mix well and form into 3-inch cakes.
5. Pour the olive oil into a sauté pan and cook the cakes over medium heat until golden brown on each side. Toast the bread, place a cake on top of each slice and garnish with additional aioli.

Serves 4

Moleche fritto (crispy fried soft-shell crab)

On Alice Water's fiftieth birthday, she came up with the typically Alice notion of inviting her friends to Venice to celebrate. Alice had rented a fifteenth-century palazzo steps away from the main section of the Grand Canale, the Hotel Gritti Palace, the Accademia gallery and other amazing edifices. As I was wandering along a small canal one afternoon, I came upon a little market: a few vegetable stands, a cheese purveyor and a couple of fishmongers. One was selling tiny brownish-yellow crabs, and I realized that they were the famous *moleche* or soft-shell variety, about the size of a silver dollar. That evening at Al Covo, the lovely restaurant known for its kindness to Americans and its affinity for seafood, I tasted them. The brownish fat exuded from within when they were cut open. Amazing.

Well, we have even better crabs in America. Our blue crabs are quite a bit larger. They range in fact from whales (three to a pound) to roaches (twelve to a pound). The latter are perfect in this dish, which replicates the one I consumed at Al Covo. They need to be properly dressed and prepared, but other than cooking them in good olive oil and lightly breading them, the recipe is quite simple, and the results are exquisite. Buy crabs that are very lively, and if you are in doubt, have your fishmonger prep them for you. They are also available frozen, and, strangely enough, are okay. The season varies from April to July depending on the region.

4 small soft-shell crabs (frozen are okay)	½ cup organic all-purpose flour
	2 teaspoons sea salt
½ cup organic stone-ground white polenta	2 cups extra-virgin olive oil
	Aioli (page 219)

1. Rinse the crabs but do not dry.
2. In a paper bag, combine the polenta, flour and sea salt and mix well.
3. Heat the olive oil in a skillet over medium-high heat. Place the crabs in the paper bag and shake thoroughly.
4. Carefully pan-fry the crabs, 2 at a time, for about 3 minutes per side. When the crabs are crispy, drain and place on a warmed platter.
5. Garnish with a dollop of aioli.

Serves 4

Sea scallop and cherry tomato skewers with spicy chilies

It has been many years since Ingrid Bengis, a magician from Maine, brought me my first diver sea scallops. The rubbery, tasteless, fishy sea scallops of old have been replaced with this moist, delicious shellfish, the royalty of the sea.

Here we cook sea scallops as simply as possible, on skewers (*a spiedini*). During the summer every seafoodmonger in Italy has these ready-made for the grill. The *spiedini* can range from salmon to swordfish to scallops. The skewers are easy to prepare the evening before. You can keep them in the fridge and pull them out when the grill is ready. The cherry tomatoes add juiciness and the chilies make a delicious, spicy sauce.

12 sea scallops, impeccably fresh
Juice of 1 orange (4 tablespoons)
Juice of 2 lemons (4 tablespoons)
3 tablespoons extra-virgin olive oil, plus more for coating the skewers
Sea salt and freshly ground black pepper to taste

1 jalapeño
2 cloves garlic
2 shallots, peeled and minced
24 firm cherry tomatoes
4–6 bamboo skewers, soaked in water for an hour

1. Wash and dry the scallops, toss them in a bowl with 2 tablespoons each of the orange and lemon juice. Add 1 tablespoon of the olive oil and season with sea salt and black pepper.
2. To make the dressing: Seed, stem and dice the jalapeño and mince the garlic and combine them with the remaining 2 tablespoons of olive oil, the shallots and 2 tablespoons each of the lemon and orange juice. Set aside.
3. Thread the scallops and tomatoes onto 4–6 bamboo skewers. Start with a tomato, then a scallop (make sure the scallop is pierced through the equator and lies flat), then repeat. Season with sea salt and black pepper and coat with olive oil.
4. Use a griddle or large cast-iron skillet or the broiler and cook the skewers for 3 minutes, or until the scallops are golden brown. If using a griddle or skillet, make sure the pan is very hot before you add the skewers so they will sear properly.
5. Serve with the dressing on the side.

Serves 4–6

Risotto pancakes with fontina

My business partner, Fabrizio Ferri, has lived in Milan for decades. One rainy Sunday night we hopped into his tiny Suzuki car with Gideon, his Irish wolfhound, and drove south of the city. We parked on a small town square and he guided us to a tiny restaurant. The pleasant room was partially filled.

We had a delightful meal, and perhaps the highlight was a risotto pancake, *riso al salta.* This traditional dish using leftover *risotto milanese* is profound in its simplicity. I loved it. The technique is a bit tricky; if the first pancake falls apart, don't despair. A proper pan is the key here. Use a Le Creuset enameled cast-iron pan or an ovenproof non-stick pan (see notes on pages 238 and 242). An old-fashioned griddle works well too; make sure it is seasoned well. The recipe does not work with fresh risotto; believe me, I've tried.

2 cups leftover risotto, chilled (use the recipe on page 95)
1 large egg
3 tablespoons grated fontina

Sea salt and freshly ground black pepper to taste
1 tablespoon extra-virgin olive oil

1. Preheat the oven to 400°.
2. In a bowl, mix the risotto with the egg, then add the cheese. Season with sea salt and black pepper.
3. In a 12-inch nonstick ovenproof pan, add ½ tablespoon of the olive oil and place over medium heat. Spoon in half of the risotto-egg mixture and flatten with a spoon. Cook for 2 minutes, then place in the oven. Cook for 5 minutes, then flip over the pancake and cook for 5 minutes more. Repeat with the remaining risotto. Serve hot.

Serves 4

Grilled or roasted prosciutto-wrapped figs with Gorgonzola

The origins of this dish come from my pal Michael Chiarello in Napa. I've known Michael for many years, and I admire his vigor and drive. He is passionate about all things Italian, and one hot and sultry summer night at his restaurant Tra Vigne in St. Helena, I tasted this dish. Just-ripe figs fresh from the local market, stuffed with young, firm Gorgonzola and wrapped with prosciutto, were charcoal-grilled over mesquite. These juicy, terrific packages of sin were amazing. I have adapted Michael's recipe and I hope I do it justice. Thanks again, Michael.

8 figs

½ cup (about 4 ounces) fresh
   Gorgonzola

8 slices prosciutto

2 tablespoons extra-virgin olive oil

Sea salt and freshly ground black
   pepper to taste

1. Preheat the oven to 350°.
2. Gently cut an X starting at the tip of each fig to about three-quarters of the way down. Divide the Gorgonzola into 8 pieces, insert 1 piece in each fig and then press the tips over them.
3. Wrap each fig with a slice of prosciutto and secure with a toothpick.
4. Drizzle with olive oil, season with sea salt and black pepper and then roast (or grill) for 10 minutes. Serve hot or at room temperature.

Serves 4

Gnocco fritto with griddled sausage

Here's a bit of Italian-restaurant sleuthing. I adore Slow Food International and one of the pleasures of membership is their interactive guides. One of the guides presents the small *osterias* (trattorias) of Italy where you get great food at reasonable prices. I had a layover in Milan with my pal Jimmy Bradley, and this window of opportunity allowed for a last lunch in Italy. We hired a taxi and found ourselves in a charming restaurant in an abandoned train station in a tiny village north of the airport. We had a spectacular lunch; among the many highlights were a risotto with *speck* and the use of Swiss cheese in a fonduelike preparation.

The dish I appreciated the most was the very simple house-made sausage, served raw! They also prepared griddled sausage with *gnocco fritto,* a pizzalike bread, to make little sandwiches, which were divine. I assure you, even if you make the sausage and fry your own fritters, the recipe is quite simple and easy to manage.

1 recipe JW pizza dough (page 75)	1 teaspoon dried oregano
1 cup diced pork shoulder	½ cup pomace olive oil (page 251)
½ cup chopped bacon	Sea salt to taste
¼ teaspoon red pepper flakes	2 tablespoons grated Parmesan

1. Roll out the dough into 4 thin rounds and keep chilled.
2. In a food processor fitted with a metal blade, combine the pork, bacon, red pepper flakes and oregano and process until coarsely blended. Remove and form into four 4 x ½-inch round patties.
3. Heat 1 tablespoon of the oil in a cast-iron skillet over medium-high heat and fry the patties for 3–4 minutes per side. Fry until golden and cooked through. Remove and keep warm. Wipe out the pan with paper towels.
4. Heat the remaining oil to 300° in the same skillet.
5. Fry the dough until puffed and golden brown, place on a tea towel and season with sea salt, then Parmesan. Serve with the sausage patties.

Serves 4

Calamari with wilted frisée and chili aioli

If you get a chance, visit the Marine Aquarium in Monterey, California. It is a small but almost perfect living museum, with live sea otters, sharks, jellyfish and other sea creatures. The squid tank amazes me. These delicate creatures dance, move in balletlike motions and act as if they own the ocean. They are extremely prolific and their importance as a food for many other species is tantamount to the ocean's survival.

In Monterey, the squid are a perfect size, with tentacles about six to eight inches in length. Bigger calamari tend to be tough and chewy. The griddle is a perfect cooking vessel. Fire-blasted on it, calamari exude their proteins, which caramelize and yield a taste of the sea. The calamari are easy to cook this way. This is a quick salad, and a lovely way to maximize this versatile seafood.

8–10 squid, freshly cleaned, enough to yield 2 cups chopped
4 tablespoons extra-virgin olive oil
¼ teaspoon red pepper flakes

Sea salt to taste
2 heads frisée, washed and dried
1 cup aioli (page 219)
¼ cup toasted bread crumbs

1. Heat a cast-iron griddle over medium-high heat.
2. Toss the calamari with 2 tablespoons of the olive oil and the red pepper flakes; season with sea salt.
3. Cook the calamari on the griddle for 2 minutes, or until golden, and transfer to a bowl.
4. Wilt the frisée on the griddle, drizzle with the remaining olive oil and toss with the calamari. Add the aioli, toss well and add the bread crumbs. Serve warm.

Serves 4

A true test of any cook is the ability to whip up a terrific soup. This sounds easier than it is. Few people in my opinion are well versed in the gentle art of soup making. It's somewhat of a lost cause. Soup should help create a harmonious bond at the table; it is the ultimate dish to strengthen any family. In Italy, soups can be magnificent, typically served as a ceremonial start to a grand meal or sometimes after the main course, as a coda to the meal.

Another test is if your children can make soup. My kids enjoy any soup with pasta, beans, tomatoes, pesto and chicken broth and they are very excited about the prospect of making their own. We make chicken stock at least once a week, so there is always some beautiful, clear delicious broth in the fridge. There is nothing better than a noodle soup on a cold, wintry day. My kids' take is simple: Cook some pasta, add the hot broth, some diced onion, pesto and *voilà*, instant cold-day remedy. The *borlotti* and lima bean soups are good examples of how kids can help and, when a little older, easily accomplish a masterful concoction. The real magic is sitting at the family table and doing some serious slurping.

Soups can have just three ingredients. The beauty is in the quality of ingredients and the use of perfectly compatible and ripe vegetables. My soups are almost always centered on onions. Their importance cannot be overstated. Onions provide more than just flavor; they form a chemical base that acts as a catalyst for any protein. Their slight acidity adds character, and the binding qualities of onions are miraculous. I am not a fan of flour or other traditional thickeners in soups. The Italians like tomatoes in addition to onions, as well as garlic and herbs. The liquid component is either cold water or stock. I am adamant that the stocks be well made and preferably fresh. Stale or poorly made stocks just make bad soup. When in doubt, cold water is hard to beat. It is up to us to provide the other ingredients.

Condiments make soups sing. They can be anything from a simple flip of good olive oil and Parmesan to a glorious, saffron-infused crème fraîche to *salsa verde.* I like to season judiciously. Good sea salt, red pepper flakes and fresh black pepper all guarantee a good product.

The right temperature is of supreme importance: A cold soup meant to be hot is insipid.

Borlotti bean minestrone

Here's a dish to warm the coldest of winter's evil nights. It is soup that will freeze well and, made in advance, actually tastes better after a day or two in the fridge. The ingredient list is standard but the flavors are not.

2 cups dried *borlotti* beans
12 cups cold water
3 onions
3 cloves garlic
1 Serrano chili
½ cup extra-virgin olive oil
Sea salt to taste

Bouquet garni: 2 bay leaves, stems from a small bunch of parsley, 2 sprigs thyme, 1 tablespoon black peppercorns and 2 cloves garlic, bound in cheesecloth
Freshly ground black pepper to taste

1. Wash the beans and soak overnight in 4 cups of water. Drain and dry.
2. Peel and slice the onions, smash the garlic, and mince the chili. Place in a deep pot with half of the olive oil. Heat to medium and season with sea salt. Cook gently for 10 minutes and add the beans and 8 cups of cold water. Heat to a boil; then reduce to a simmer. Add the bouquet garni and cook, uncovered, for 1 hour, or until the beans are tender and melt in your mouth. Remove the bouquet garni.
3. Season with sea salt and black pepper and serve with a drizzle of olive oil.

Serves 4

Nettle soup

Nettles are incredibly rich in vitamins, especially C and K. Therefore, they are not only delicious, but if you make this soup you have a chance of living longer—or, at the very least, having more fun. It will take forty-five minutes to make and the results are extraordinary.

Wash the nettles in cold water as you would spinach, rinsing four times to ensure there is no sand, and finely mince. Protect your hands by wearing cooks' rubber gloves.

The soup is vegetarian and soulful. I like to add some smoked paprika at the end for a bit of "outdoor" aroma and flavor.

2 bunches nettles (yielding 4 cups)
3 tablespoons extra-virgin olive oil
2 onions, peeled and sliced
2 cloves garlic, finely minced
2 tablespoons fresh parsley leaves

8 cups cold water
Sea salt and freshly ground black
    pepper to taste
½ teaspoon smoked paprika

1. Wash the nettles as described above. Dry in a spinner. Chop them fine.
2. In a heavy enameled casserole, heat the olive oil, onions and garlic and sweat for 10 minutes over medium heat. Add the nettles and the parsley and cook another 10 minutes.
3. Add the water, bring to a boil over high heat and then reduce to medium. Cook for 15 minutes. Let cool.
4. In a blender, liquefy the soup in batches and set aside. Clean the pot and return the puréed soup to the pot, heat to a simmer and season with sea salt, black pepper and paprika. Serve hot.

Serves 4

Guinea broth with fresh noodles

Guinea fowl makes a wonderful, rich broth. This soup, made with the bones from a roasted bird, can be made in just less than three to four hours.

This is a soothing broth, great to ward off colds and winter fever. The Guinea is a close relative of the partridge and pheasant, but it is less gamey and the meat is much more succulent. The result is a soup fit for a skiing trip or a state dinner.

The fresh noodles are simple—just water, flour and salt. The trick here is to use soda water; it makes the noodles sinuous and digestible. They take only about three minutes to make and you form them by pressing them through a sieve as you would *spaetzle*.

1 tablespoon extra-virgin olive oil

1 Guinea fowl carcass (or chicken)

2 red onions, peeled and sliced

6 cloves garlic, minced

8 cups cold water

1 small bunch parsley

3 carrots

3 turnips

1 small celery root

NOODLES

½ cup organic all-purpose flour

1½ teaspoons sea salt

1 cup soda water

———

Sea salt and freshly ground black
    pepper to taste

1 tablespoon grated Parmesan

1. In a casserole, heat the olive oil and sauté the carcass, onions and garlic until browned. Add the water and parsley and bring to a boil. Cook at a simmer for 3–4 hours. Strain, reserving only the liquid.

2. Peel and dice the carrots, turnips and celery root.

3. To make the noodles: Combine the flour and sea salt, then add the soda water and make a soft dough. Bring a pot of water to a simmer. Push the dough through a sieve and boil in the water for 1 minute. Strain and cool.

4. Bring the broth to a boil in a large pot, add the vegetables and cook for 8 minutes, until the vegetables are tender; add the noodles. Season with sea salt and black pepper and serve with Parmesan.

Serves 4–6

Cold tomato and tarragon soup

In the summer, when your appetite for heavy dishes fades, cold soups are a breath of fresh air. They are digestible, beautiful to behold and extract the essence of the tomatoes or other vegetables. Here I use bruised or irregular tomatoes. Bursting with juice, they make great soup. In fact a Bloody Mary made from the juice would be very good indeed.

This is a fast recipe; the tomatoes need no cooking to produce this delicious cold concoction.

6 heirloom tomatoes, bruised or irregular, but juicy and delicious

1 sweet white onion, peeled and minced

2 cloves garlic, smashed

24 fresh tarragon leaves, finely minced

Sea salt and freshly ground black pepper to taste

1 tablespoon extra-virgin olive oil (preferably a green Tuscan)

1. Cut the tomatoes into quarters and pass through a fine-mesh sieve (*tamis* or *mouli*) into a stainless-steel bowl.
2. Add the minced onions, garlic and tarragon to the tomatoes. Chill the soup in the refrigerator for about 1 hour.
3. Season with sea salt and black pepper and serve cold with a drizzle of olive oil.

Serves 4

Asparagus soup

The Italian way is always the most direct, simple and delicious. This soup epitomizes that philosophy. It also uses what we would normally discard, so it is economical as well. Remember those ugly ends of asparagus we saved in the recipe on page 4? Well, here is the way to maximize your purchase and enhance your repertoire. Asparagus ends, though bitter and fibrous raw, create a delicious soup—perhaps worthy of the gods—with just a little effort.

1 pound asparagus ends
3 tablespoons extra-virgin olive oil
2 onions, peeled and diced
3 Yukon gold or white potatoes, peeled and diced

4 cups vegetable broth
1 cup heavy cream
Sea salt and freshly ground black pepper to taste

1. Wash the asparagus, then chop into small pieces.
2. In a heavy pot, heat the olive oil and add the onions, potatoes and asparagus. Cook over high heat, stirring constantly, until all the vegetables are golden in color. This will take about 10 minutes. Add the broth, bring to a boil, reduce to a simmer and cook for an hour. Add the cream.
3. Let the soup cool. In a blender, in small batches, purée the soup, and then strain through a sieve to remove the fibrous bits. Season the soup with sea salt and black pepper and serve cold or hot.

Serves 4–6

Zuppa di mare

This soup is my personal favorite. You may use the leftover bones from a whole fish recipe or you can buy fresh bones from your fishmonger. I like shrimp and lobster shells. This soup is rustic and savory. It is well worth all the effort and has a flavor that will stay with you for a long time. It is kind of a poor man's bouillabaisse, spicy and rich.

4 quarts cold water

3 onions, peeled and sliced

12 cloves garlic, 6 left unpeeled,
   6 peeled

1 cup white wine

¼ jalapeño, seeded

Bouquet garni: 2 bay leaves, stems
   from a small bunch of parsley,
   2 sprigs thyme, 1 tablespoon
   black peppercorns and 2 cloves
   garlic, bound in cheesecloth

2 live lobsters

12 shrimp, shelled, reserve the shells

2 pounds fish bones, rinsed in cold
   water

¼ cup extra-virgin olive oil

Pinch of saffron

18 mussels, scrubbed and the beards
   removed

Sea salt and freshly ground black
   pepper to taste

1. Make a *court bouillon* with the water, 1 slice of the onion, 6 cloves unpeeled garlic, the wine, jalapeño and bouquet garni. Bring to a boil and cook the lobsters for 5 minutes; then remove and let cool. Shell the lobsters, save the shells and set the meat aside. Bring the *court bouillon* to a simmer and add the shells of the shrimp and lobsters and the fish bones.

2. Cook the broth for 45 minutes and then strain, reserving only the liquid.

3. In a large pot, heat the olive oil, the remaining onions and 6 cloves of garlic and cook for 5 minutes. Add the broth and bring to a boil. Add the saffron, the mussels and the shrimp and cook, covered, for 5 minutes or until the mussels open.

4. Divide the lobster meat equally among 6 bowls, taste the soup for seasoning and ladle it into each bowl. Serve hot.

Serves 6

Lima bean, corn and tomato soup with pesto

This is a late summer soup, when the limas are magnificent. They are called butter beans in the South and I think they may be the best beans on earth. Late summer corn has lost its intense sweetness, and the kernels have some good starchiness. Tomatoes are begging to be used and garlic and basil are at their best, with pesto at its apogee. Kids love to make this, but cutting the kernels requires some adult supervision. The corn cobs, the onions and the leftover bits of tomato make a nice vegetable stock. The stock cooks in an hour and adds a soothing viscosity to the finished soup.

2 large sweet onions

3 ears of corn

8 cups cold water

Pinch of sea salt, plus more to taste

2 cups shelled limas or butter beans
(frozen are okay)

2 large almost overripe tomatoes

2 tablespoons extra-virgin olive oil

2 cloves garlic, minced

½ cup pesto (page 224)

Freshly ground black pepper to taste

1. Peel and dice the onions; you should have 2 cups.
2. Shuck the corn and cut the kernels off the cob. Heat the water in a stockpot, add ½ cup of the onions and the cobs and bring to a boil. Add a pinch of sea salt and turn the heat to simmer.
3. Wash and dry the beans. Core the tomatoes and cut off the uglier bits, adding these to the soup stock. Dice the tomatoes, reserving all the juice, and set aside.
4. When the stock has cooked for an hour, strain it and set aside.
5. In a heavy pot, heat the olive oil, then add the remaining onions, the corn, beans and the garlic and sweat for 10 minutes on low. Add the strained stock, bring to a simmer and cook for 30 minutes. Add the tomatoes and simmer for 10 minutes. At the last second stir in the pesto and taste for seasoning. This is wonderful hot or cold.

Serves 4–6

San Francisco had some damn good pizza when I was growing up. I played in a lot of pizza joints as a trombone-playing rock 'n' roller, and Tommaso's in North Beach was way ahead of the curve. The restaurant has been offering wood-oven pizza since 1935, and hungry customers still line up around the clock to eat at this landmark.

I've eaten pizzas all over Italy, and one standout was in the old Milano train station many years ago. I noticed three things: a roaring wood fire, a reluctance to hurry the pie, and dough that was both tender and sticky. The image of that perfect pie has stayed with me, and over the years I have worked hard to replicate the dough. Flour is critical. I've tried bread flour, organic pizza flour and Italian hard wheat flour, and I have settled on one that is readily available: King Arthur white organic flour. It is perfect. It does change according to the season, and altitude is a huge factor, as is relative humidity.

I agree with the argument that fresh dough is not as delicious or as imbued with that certain tang as it is when enhanced by adding old dough. Therefore, I find that saving the dough for a day in the fridge helps achieve two things: a crisp crust and a better taste. I want bubbles to appear as the dough bakes, and day-old dough helps to promote those bubbles. Don't keep the dough in the fridge for longer than a day or it will look like pita.

Yeast is a major factor. I like fresh yeast, but it is sometimes hard to come by. Granular yeast is convenient but has a less interesting flavor. I add some organic unprocessed honey as a feeder for the dough. A little stale organic beer is good as well. Sea salt is important for texture and flavor, and last, the water needs to be fresh. If your water is hard, too warm from the tap or otherwise suspect, use bottled water.

Ovens are an exciting subject. I have used electric, wood-burning, grills, gas, gas/convection, and a new-fangled device with convection and microwave. I find that an oven with a tight seal is not as good as one that has a bit of a gap that allows it to breathe. The addition of a pizza stone is nice, but unnecessary. An old-fashioned perforated pizza pan is good, but a simple baking sheet works well, too. Your oven needs to have constant, regulated heat; always use a thermometer. I worry about the crust more than the top, and always check the pizza's bottom as it bakes. Timing can be erratic; the first pie is always a tester.

Serving a pizza you've made from scratch is exciting. At home, we tend to make Sunday night pizza night. Everyone makes his own version; some like it plain, others, complicated. But most important, making the dough is a group effort. My youngest son, Foster, adores opening the yeast package and mixing the warm water with the honey. Adding the flour and stirring, now that's fun!

After the dough has rested, we begin to make the pies. Foster stands on a stool (he's six) and insists that he can throw his pie into the "sky." He needs help, but he can form a nice round pie quickly. The other tricky part is spreading the sauce. I explain that it needs to stay within the boundaries of the crust, but he gets carried away. The pie is soon ready to be baked. Foster waits impatiently for his pie, ready to devour every last bite.

Alexander likes mozzarella, sauce and Parmesan; no basil, please. He also likes the overflow effect taught him by the great pizza master Charlie Hallowell of Pizzaiolo in Oakland, California. Overflow occurs when you push the sauce to the very edge of the dough so that it covers the crust. Alexander is a huge fan of this. Using the back of a spoon, he carefully nudges the sauce onto the edges.

Hannah is the connoisseur. She is the child who thinks boldly. Pesto, ham, salami, sausage, peppers, onions, four cheeses, mushrooms—in other words, the works. She likes to experiment, and her pizzas always taste great. I think kids of all ages love making pies.

JW pizza dough

Pizza dough is so idiosyncratic! Pizza is one of the finest achievements in cooking. Simple, perfect, satisfying to all. And probably the hardest thing to get right! I remember being admonished in cooking school for bragging about making puff pastry right the first time. "Make it a thousand times perfectly, and then we will talk!" Pizza dough might take many tries to get right. It is a living thing, and can be perky one day, sad the next. I alleviate its pain with honey and beer (to help it rise and for texture and flavor) and enough water to make it sticky to the touch. That water helps achieve a blistery, crispy, chewy crust.

1 tablespoon active dry yeast
2 tablespoons extra-virgin olive oil
2 tablespoons honey
¼ cup stale beer

1¾ cups warm water, plus more as needed
5 cups organic all-purpose flour
3 tablespoons sea salt

1. The day before you make your pizza, make the sponge: Combine the yeast, olive oil, honey, beer, 1¾ cups warm water and 1 cup of the flour in a large bowl. Cover with plastic wrap and leave out at room temperature for several hours, until the sponge has doubled in volume. Tap the bowl on the countertop to release the air (it's too sticky to punch) and refrigerate overnight.

2. The next day, add the remaining 4 cups of flour, the sea salt, and enough warm water to make a sticky dough. Turn out onto a well-floured countertop and knead for 10 minutes, or until the dough is satiny and smooth.

3. Place the dough in a greased bowl and cover with a clean kitchen towel. Let sit at room temperature for 2 hours, until the dough has doubled in size.

4. Divide into six 8-ounce portions. I prefer rustic pies to perfectly round ones. To form a pie, I dust a ball of dough with flour, and gently flatten it with my fist. Then, using my fingertips, I hold the dough on the edges and let gravity do its work. I gently squeeze the edges as I rotate the pie and it begins to take shape. After a couple rotations, I place it on the table. I dust it with more flour and pull it with my fingertips until it is about 10 inches around. Any shape is fine—just keep the dough uniformly thick. If holes form, squeeze the dough to fill them in. Any leftover dough can be frozen.

Makes enough dough for 6 10-inch pizzas

Pancetta, cherry tomato, *burrata* and scallion pizza

Here is a straightforward, yet lovely pie. The special ingredient is *burrata,* the king of mozzarella. This high-fat-content, luscious cheese is a work of art, handcrafted from water buffalo milk. The soft, fatty, wheylike texture is scrumptious on its own, but cooked on a pizza, it is mind-boggling. Only a master, who adds a good amount of heavy cream to the center of the mozzarella then wraps it with a native leaf, makes this cheese. It lasts only a week after it is made, then gradually turns hard, so use it the day you buy it.

Pancetta is a salt-cured, baconlike product that needs to be sliced thinly and used sparingly; too much and it will overwhelm the pie.

1 pint cherry tomatoes
1 bunch scallions
½ pound *burrata*
JW pizza dough for 2 pies (page 75)

½ cup pancetta diced into small
   pieces
¼ cup grated Parmesan
2 tablespoons extra-virgin olive oil

1. Preheat the oven to 450°.
2. Slice the tomatoes in half on the equator. Place the cut tomatoes in a bowl.
3. Wash the scallions, trim the roots and mince. Add to the tomatoes and toss well.
4. Dice the *burrata.*
5. Form the dough into 2 pies. Sprinkle each with the pancetta, then the scallions and tomatoes and finally the *burrata.* Spread the Parmesan evenly over the pies and then drizzle some oil on top. Bake for about 10 minutes, or until golden, top and bottom.

Makes 2 pies; serves 4–6

Eggplant, pepper, roasted tomato and Parmesan pizza

Here is a pizza that celebrates summer: delicate eggplant, heirloom tomatoes that have been fire-blasted to concentrate the juices, perky peppers that give great crunch and that zesty taste and a wee bit of Parmesan to help round out the flavors.

3 small elongated eggplants

2 tablespoons extra-virgin olive oil

Sea salt to taste

2 bell peppers, 1 red, 1 green

1 cup JW roasted tomato sauce
(page 232)

Freshly ground black pepper to taste

JW pizza dough for 2 pies (page 75)

2 tablespoons grated Parmesan

1. Wash, stem and dice the eggplants. Toss with 1 tablespoon of the olive oil. Season with sea salt and let sit for 1 hour. Seed and stem the bell peppers and slice into strips.
2. Preheat the oven to 450°.
3. In a heavy skillet, heat the remaining tablespoon of olive oil, and when it is smoking add the eggplant and peppers. Cook for 2 minutes over high heat. In a bowl, combine the tomato sauce and eggplant-pepper mixture; season with sea salt and black pepper.
4. Form the dough into 2 pies. Spread the eggplant-pepper-tomato mixture evenly over the two pies and then dust with Parmesan. Bake for 8 minutes, or until golden brown.

Makes 2 pies; serves 4–6

Clam pie

I like the current trend of nontraditional pizza toppings. I think there is room for many ideas, as long as they are sensible and taste good. In New Haven, Connecticut, there is a wildly popular pizzeria named Pepe's. Many years ago a dear friend, who loved all things Italian, and I made a trek to Pepe's just to eat a clam pie. It was closed, so we went to a rustic joint nearby. It was a bit seedy and, truthfully, the pies were just OK. Later that year on my own I went back to Pepe's and had a clam pie. Freshly minced littlenecks, garlic, olive oil and red pepper flakes with salt—it was a masterpiece!

Here is my humble version.

1 cup shucked clams (littlenecks are the best; Manilas will work, but not as well)
2 cloves garlic, minced
¼ teaspoon red pepper flakes

1 tablespoon minced fresh parsley
2 tablespoons extra-virgin olive oil
Sea salt to taste
JW pizza dough for 2 pies (page 75)

1. Preheat the oven to 450°.
2. Mince the clams and place in a bowl with the garlic, red pepper flakes, parsley and olive oil and toss to combine. Season with sea salt.
3. Form the dough into 2 pies. Spread the clam mixture evenly over both. Make sure it goes to the edge! Bake for 8–10 minutes and serve hot.

Makes 2 pies; serves 4–6

Pizza with chanterelle mushrooms, fontina, sweet onion and nettle purée

Here is an homage to my pal Charlie Hallowell of Pizzaiolo in Oakland, California, one of the maestros of pizza in America. In season he features nettle pizza. Now, we think of nettles as nasty stinging weeds, but they can be better than spinach or arugula. When washed, wilted and puréed, they make a delightful pizza topping, especially accompanied by some chanterelles, nutty fontina cheese and a bit of sweet onion.

1 bunch basil
1 cup nettles (if unavailable, use baby spinach)
1 tablespoon extra-virgin olive oil
½ pound very fresh chanterelles, washed and dried
1 sweet onion, peeled and sliced
¼ cup Prosecco
¼ cup water
Sea salt and freshly ground black pepper to taste
JW pizza dough for 2 pies (page 75)
½ cup diced fontina or *taleggio*

1. Preheat the oven to 450°.
2. Wash the basil, remove the stems and dry. Repeat with the nettles. Set aside.
3. In a skillet, heat the olive oil and sauté the mushrooms and onion for 1 minute; then add the Prosecco. Cook for 3 minutes or until unctuous. Turn off the heat and transfer the onion and mushrooms to a bowl. In small sauté pan, heat the water. Bring to a simmer, add the basil leaves and nettles and cook for 30 seconds. Season with sea salt and black pepper. Purée with a hand blender.
4. Form the dough into 2 pies. Spread the nettle purée evenly over the 2 pies, then top with the chanterelles and onion and the cheese.
5. Bake for 8–10 minutes.

Makes 2 pies; serves 4–6

Pizza with goat cheese, Swiss chard and picholine olives

Each summer my family treks to the Alps for a gorgeous vacation with dear friends. All the kids make pizza in the wood-burning oven and the results are fantastic.

The small cheese shop in the nearby mountain town of Annecy sells a fresh, fragrant goat cheese, which is fantastic on this pizza. It has just enough fat, but is delicate and crumbly and cooks well in the hot oven. A slice of this pizza makes for a perfect appetizer to munch on while sipping rosé from Liguria, say a Bisson Ciliegiolo, and watching the sun dip into the mountains.

8 ounces fresh goat cheese
  (preferably from a local farm)
¼ cup fresh chive blossoms
  (substitute any herb blossom)
3 tablespoons extra-virgin olive oil
Sea salt and freshly ground black
  pepper to taste

1 clove garlic, minced
1 bunch chard, washed and finely
  minced
JW pizza dough for 2 pies (page 75)
1 cup picholine olives, pitted

1. Preheat the oven to 450°.
2. Crumble the cheese into a bowl with the chive blossoms and 1 tablespoon of the olive oil. Season with sea salt and black pepper.
3. In a skillet, heat the remaining 2 tablespoons of olive oil, add the garlic and the chard and sweat for 10 minutes, or until the chard is wilted.
4. Form the dough into 2 pies. Spread the chard on the pies, then top with the goat cheese and the olives. Bake for 10 minutes.

Makes 2 pies; serves 4–6

Pizza with potato, green garlic, bacon and *robiola* cheese

When Pino Luongo opened Le Madri in New York's Chelsea district in 1988, he imported three women from Tuscany to cook and to ensure authenticity. He employed a very laid-back and casual service like that found in the Tuscan countryside, and the décor was homey and fun. It was a direct contrast to the staid, clubby feeling that many New York Italian restaurants had worn over the years. People flocked to Le Madri. It was here that I tasted *robiola* cheese for the first time. This soft, pliable and very versatile cow's milk cheese was sandwiched in the dough of a cooked pizza. The technique was to cook the formed dough plain in the oven, quickly split it open, sprinkle with the cheese and white truffle oil, then serve quickly. I think this was the first and last time I truly liked the oil; the next time it seemed artificial and flat (most truffle oils are artificially flavored). But the cheese was a masterpiece. Here I use it with precooked new potatoes, lovely pungent green garlic (use scallions if none is available) and bits of American bacon for crunch and smokiness. No tomatoes here; the acidity would be off-putting.

½ pound small white potatoes
1 stalk fresh green garlic, trimmed
    and minced (or substitute
    scallions)
3 tablespoons extra-virgin olive oil
½ cup diced smoky natural bacon

JW pizza dough for 2 pies (page 75)
½ cup diced *robiola* cheese
6 fresh basil leaves
Sea salt and freshly ground black
    pepper to taste

1. In a pot of simmering water, poach the potatoes for 10 minutes. Let cool in the water.
2. Drain the potatoes and slice thinly with a paring knife.
3. Preheat the oven to 450°.
4. Toss the garlic and 2 tablespoons of the olive oil with the potatoes, then add the bacon.
5. Form the dough into 2 pies. Dot each pie with half of the bacon-potato mixture. Scatter the cheese and tear the basil into strips over each pie. Drizzle with the remaining table-spoon of olive oil, season with sea salt and black pepper and bake for 8–10 minutes.

Makes 2 pies; serves 4–6

Margherita pizza

This is one of America's favorite pizzas. In Italy, especially in Naples, this is a thin-crusted pizza, very light and crispy, topped with canned tomato sauce, fresh mozzarella and a sprinkle of Parmesan, sometimes with basil leaves. The term "Margherita" originated in 1889, at a restaurant called Pietro e Basta Così, where a baker named Raffaele Esposito supposedly created a group of pizzas for King Umberto and Queen Margherita. The queen went for the buffalo (we assume) mozzarella, basil and tomato pizza and, *voilà,* pizza Margherita.

One variation I really like is the addition of arugula lightly tossed in olive oil and sea salt as a topping after the pizza has cooked. It makes the pizza much more refreshing.

1 cup fresh basil leaves plus 12 for garnish (optional)

3 tablespoons extra-virgin olive oil

1 teaspoon sea salt, plus more to taste

1 tablespoon boiling water

JW pizza dough for 2 pies (page 75)

1 cup JW roasted tomato sauce (page 232)

½ cup chopped *burrata*

¼ cup grated Parmesan

1. Preheat the oven to 450°.
2. To make the basil purée: Wash and dry the basil. Place 1 tablespoon of the olive oil, 1 teaspoon sea salt and the boiling water in a blender. Add ½ cup of the basil leaves and purée; add the remaining ½ cup basil and purée.
3. Form the dough into 2 pies. First, drizzle the dough with the remaining 2 tablespoons of olive oil and sprinkle with sea salt. Spread ½ cup of the tomato sauce on each. Sprinkle the *burrata,* then dab on 1 tablespoon of the basil purée. Finally sprinkle with the Parmesan. I like to garnish with fresh basil leaves.
4. Bake for 8–10 minutes.

Makes 2 pies; serves 4–6

Pizza with grilled *trevigiano* and fontina

I love grilled or baked *trevigiano.* I always find this member of the radicchio family to be a refreshing vegetable with any meat or poultry. It is a cinch to do right and requires little supervision. The technique is straightforward; the only caveat is to not overbake the *trevigiano,* but even when well cooked, it holds its flavor. The pizza uses baked *trevigiano,* which has been softened and whose flavor is luxurious. Serve with a chilled Valpolicella.

2 large heads *trevigiano*
1 teaspoon *balsamico*
4 tablespoons extra-virgin olive oil
1 cup chicken stock or water

Sea salt and freshly ground black pepper to taste
JW pizza dough for 2 pies (page 75)
½ cup grated or cubed fontina

1. Preheat the oven to 375°.
2. Cut the *trevigiano* in half, wash and dry.
3. Place the *trevigiano* in a Pyrex baking dish and drizzle with the *balsamico* and 1 tablespoon of the olive oil. Add the stock and sea salt and black pepper. Bake for 15 minutes. Let cool in the juices.
4. Increase the oven heat to 450°.
5. Form the dough into 2 pies. Chop the *trevigiano* and toss with the juices. Drizzle the remaining olive oil over the dough, then top with the chopped *trevigiano* and the fontina and bake for 8 minutes.

Makes 2 pies; serves 4–6

Pizza *ai frutti di mare*

This is a challenging pizza, but well worth the effort. You can experiment with different seafood: I like the combo of squid, shrimp, monkfish, clams and lobster, but you can use almost any seafood. The trick is to prepare the seafood in the morning and keep it chilled, which ensures that you can put the pizzas into the oven quickly with little fuss.

The garlic and saffron lend an exotic taste. Sicily was conquered by the Greeks, the Romans, the Phoenicians, Vandals, Normans, the Moors, the Spanish; even the British and the French had a hand in its affairs. Only recently has it emerged as an Italian stronghold. In the sixteenth century it was under the direct influence of the kingdom of Aragon of Catalonia, which controlled and influenced the culture. The food of Catalonia had a profound influence on Sicily, and we see it today in many subtle ways, the use of baked rice casseroles for instance, and the introduction of saffron.

4 sea scallops

8 mussels

8 clams

JW pizza dough for 2 pies (page 75)

1 cup JW roasted tomato sauce
   (page 232)

½ cup raw chopped calamari

2 tablespoons extra-virgin olive oil

Red pepper flakes

1. Preheat the oven to 450°.
2. Dice the scallops and wash the mussels and clams. Remove the beards from the mussels if necessary.
3. Form the dough into 2 pies. Spread half of the roasted tomato sauce over one pizza, then half of the calamari, scallops, mussels and clams and drizzle with 1 tablespoon of the olive oil.
4. Bake for 10 minutes, or until the pie is golden and the mussels and clams have opened. Serve with red pepper flakes. Repeat to make the second pizza.

Note: Resist the urge to bake both pizzas at the same time—you'll have rubbery shellfish.

Makes 2 pies; serves 4–6

Pizza with an egg, pancetta and tomatoes

Here is a perfect brunch pizza. A soft-cooked egg roasted on the pizza in a hot oven is dramatic and savory. The trick is not to overcook the egg, so timing is crucial.

4 eggs

JW pizza dough for 2 pies (page 75)

4 tomatoes, diced

2 tablespoons fresh oregano leaves

Sea salt to taste

2 tablespoons grated fontina

¼ cup pesto (page 224)

¼ pound pancetta, diced

1. Preheat the oven to 450°.
2. Crack the eggs into 4 small cups.
3. Form the dough into 2 pies. Toss the tomatoes with the oregano, sea salt and cheese and sprinkle the mixture over the two pies. Dot the tomatoes with pesto and then the pancetta. Bake for 4 minutes.
4. Pull the pizzas out and gently slide 2 eggs per pizza on top. Bake for another 4 minutes. Serve hot.

Makes 2 pies; serves 4–6

Alexander's overflow pie

I love teaching, especially young children. We often invite kids from a local school to make pie, pasta, salads and cupcakes. When the children arrive we fashion them aprons from napkins, and they get a set of gloves (like surgeons) and a ball of pizza dough. Then they go to town. Some pizzas are round, others square, some resemble Australia—no two are alike. Some kids favor sauce, some cheese, some both, and one kid wanted no topping at all.

My son Alexander likes his with simple, good sauce. (No green stuff!) He is very deliberate and delicate in his touch, as if he imagines how it will taste after it's been baked. I find it amazing that he sees the end product as he assembles the pie. He carefully rolls out the dough. Then, the exact amount of sauce, spread all the way to the edge. Then mozzarella, again not too much, and then a thin broadcasting of Parmesan and that's it. The result is perfection: crisp, crusty bottom, bubbly top, nice integration of sauce and cheese. Another great overflow.

JW pizza dough for 2 pies (page 75)
1 cup JW roasted tomato sauce
   (page 232)

½ cup grated Parmesan
1 cup diced mozzarella

1. Preheat the oven to 450°.
2. Form the dough into 2 pies.
3. Using the back of a spoon, spread the sauce evenly on the 2 pies, all the way to very edge.
4. Sprinkle with equal amounts of the Parmesan and mozzarella. Bake for about 8 minutes, or until golden brown and bubbly. Serve hot.

Makes 2 pies; serves 4–6

Justin's stromboli

How can I describe Justin Smillie? He is six feet eight inches, has worked for me for years and is as passionate about food as I am. He is a Jersey boy and grew up eating in New York City. Justin was the head chef at Barbuto a while ago, and for a special event, he promised his version of the stromboli. I haven't a clue about the name's origins, but rumor has it that the film, *Stromboli,* starring Ingrid Bergman, might be a source. I find this too far-fetched; more likely an immigrant from Stromboli named it for the island's volcano that erupts with regularity. It might also be the name of the eruption that can happen in a hot oven! The cousin of the stromboli is the calzone; I like the stromboli far more. It really is easy, the filling can be made ahead, the dough can be cold and the stromboli only needs twenty minutes out of the fridge before you bake it.

1 recipe JW pizza dough (page 75)
¼ cup grated mozzarella
½ pound portobello mushrooms
1 sweet onion, peeled and chopped
1 bell pepper, seeded and chopped
2 tablespoons basil purée
   (Margherita pizza, page 84)
2 tablespoons grated fontina
1 cup JW roasted tomato sauce
   (page 232)
Sea salt and freshly ground black
   pepper to taste
Extra-virgin olive oil for brushing

1. Preheat the oven to 400°.
2. Lightly oil a roasting pan that will accommodate the stromboli.
3. Roll out the dough to a 14-inch square.
4. Place the dough in the pan. (It's okay if it's too long one way. Let the end hang over the side, it will be folded over to make the top of the stromboli.)
5. Mix the remaining ingredients, except for the olive oil, together in a bowl and lay in the center of the dough. Fold the dough over the filling and crimp the edges.
6. Brush with the olive oil and bake for 30 minutes.
7. Let cool for 5 minutes and serve.

Makes 1 large stromboli; serves 4

The world revolves around pasta. It is the ultimate gift the Italians have bestowed upon us. Pasta can be fresh with or without eggs, dried in any shape imaginable, flavored or not, stuffed, rolled and baked, poached or even sautéed. You can make pasta to fit any mood. Dishes can be blindingly simple, prepared with only great olive oil and freshly crushed garlic or as refined as angel hair tossed with black caviar, chives and crème fraîche, extremely rustic with boar *ragù* and bread crumbs, spicy with seafood, or elaborate, with lobster, caviar and fresh cream. Sometimes I crave a late-night fisherman's linguine: grilled freshly caught sardines, chopped fennel, diced peppers and olive oil. *Trofie* (a tiny hand-rolled pasta) tossed with baby haricots verts, new potatoes, crushed hill-ripened tomatoes, and a peppery pesto from the slopes of Cinque Terre is sublime.

When choosing a pasta course, the first decision is a simple one: fresh or dried. Fresh pasta is a joy to make from scratch. Early in my career I was enthralled with Giuliano Bugialli's first book on Italian cookery, and I was determined to make a delicious handcrafted *tagliatelle*. I found it not only rewarding, but also easy to produce and truly satisfying.

Making fresh pasta by hand is not daunting; in point of fact, it is not work, but pleasure. I love creating a mountain of flour, submerging the egg yolks, salt and a touch of olive oil into the center and mixing it all together into an unctuous mass. This mound of dough is then transformed into silken strands of delicious noodles, sometimes with a bit of saffron or herb, other times plain and simple.

Early on the term "al dente" confused me, and I am sure I wasn't alone. Knowing exactly when a noodle is cooked can be an intimidating process. *Al dente* literally means "to the tooth," meaning there is a bit of resistance in the center. It does not mean raw. Nor does it mean cooked through. This is where cooking is magic. This is what separates good cooks from the ordinary: intuition.

The lore of pastas contains some fascinating stories. Some names are comical, such as *strozzapreti,* which literally means "to choke a priest." Or the rich classic, *spaghetti alla carbonara,* named after the sooty chimney sweepers because of the dish's copious use of black pepper. I must admit that I'm a simple pasta guy and some of the fancy shapes leave me a bit cold, but feel free to experiment. The basic categories that I use are as follows:

1. Freshly made semolina pasta with egg yolk only.
2. Store-bought dried pasta, usually from Italy, made from a hard semolina flour, sea salt and water. You'll be shocked how much of a difference there is between ordinary mass-produced spaghetti versus a handmade, hand-extruded, hundred-year-old brass die organic pasta from Napoli. The price usually reflects quality, so spend as much as you can for the finest pasta.
3. Flavored pastas made with a vegetable juice, herb, or purée.
4. Other flavors, including whole wheat, farro and spelt. They can be mind-blowing.

One pasta I love is ravioli that is stuffed with a whole egg yolk. Cooked gently, the tender ravioli exudes the golden yolk into the sauce.

A great job in the kitchen for budding young chefs is making their own noodles. When my daughter, Hannah, was three, she wanted to stand up on a stool and "help" Daddy. Her pasta skills progressed rapidly—neither machine nor rolling intimidated her. What she really loved was rolling out her own sheet of pasta and cutting it into edible shapes. I suggest you start them young, but at any age, the process is delightful.

When kids are tackling pasta, making the dough by creating a "volcano" of flour and then adding the eggs and salt to the caldera attenuates their excitement. They love massaging the dough into a rollable mass. The trickier part is using the machine. I suggest you start with small pieces of dough, let them get used to the machine's idiosyncrasies, then let them go to town.

Gnocchi with spring vegetables and basil

I've never liked the renditions of gnocchi that I've eaten in Italy and America. They were always gummy, covered with béchamel or another yucky sauce. One day my chef, Justin, knowing of my aversion to the classic preparation, froze a batch of raw gnocchi after he had rolled them out and cut them. We had a dinner party at my house and I took the gnocchi along as an afterthought. At home, I threw the gnocchi into a sizzling hot pan with butter and olive oil, while Justin looked at me with a crazy, quizzical expression. But the gnocchi turned into crisp pillows that were tender and fluffy on the inside and golden brown and crunchy on the outside. We served them with English peas, mint and a little fresh butter. They were a hit.

We prepare gnocchi at the restaurant the same way, but we do alter the vegetables, herbs and sauce occasionally.

3 large organic russet potatoes
2 tablespoons organic all-purpose
   flour
2 tablespoons extra-virgin olive oil
2 cups thumbelina carrots, washed
   and stemmed

6 tablespoons (¾ stick) unsalted
   butter
2 cups shelled English peas
12 fresh basil leaves
Sea salt and freshly ground black
   pepper to taste

1. Prepare the gnocchi: Steam the potatoes in a pot until cooked and tender (about 30 minutes). Remove and let cool for 2 hours. Peel the skin (this is very easy). If you have a food mill or ricer, rice the potatoes in it, or better yet, pass the potatoes through a fine-mesh sieve. Rice the potatoes onto a lightly floured marble or wood surface. Dust the potatoes with the flour and dribble 1 tablespoon of the olive oil on top. Very gently form a soft dough, making sure not to overwork it or it will be tough. Do this for 2–3 minutes and let the mass rest. Roll the dough into 1-inch-diameter tubes. With a paring knife cut the gnocchi into 1-inch lengths. Then roll each gnocchi over the tines of a fork to create slight grooves. When the gnocchi are finished, freeze them for at least 1 hour and up to 1 month.

2. Cook the carrots in simmering water for 20 minutes. Cool and cut into bite-size pieces.

3. Cook the gnocchi: Heat the butter and the remaining olive oil in a large skillet over medium-high heat. When the butter and oil are almost golden, add the frozen gnocchi and sauté for 3 minutes, moving them around so all sides start to darken.

4. Add the peas and carrots and continue to cook for 2 minutes. Toss in the basil leaves and season with sea salt and black pepper.

Serves 4 as a first course

Risotto with sweet peas, pea shoots and Parmesan

Risottos have intrigued me for years. Once, in 1979 at Valentino's in Santa Monica, I was served a spectacular risotto topped, of course, with white truffles; Michael McCarty, always known for his abject exuberance, had commandeered a baseball-size truffle for the slightly discombobulated owner Piero Selvaggio and proceeded to shower our risottos with an immense amount of truffle. The bill (after countless bottles of Le Salon Champagne, Barbaresco from Santo Stefano and other fantastic wines) came to $800. Later Piero, always a thoughtful and intellectual guide to all things Italian, kindly gave me the recipe. His first bit of advice was to use only the best rice, which, in his eyes, was Carnaroli rice from the Po River near Piedmont. Second, the broth should always be hot and not too reduced, flavorful but not sticky. And last, and perhaps most important, always deglaze the rice with a delicious white wine. I must admit I attempted many times to duplicate the perfection of that afternoon. But either the truffle or the rice was never right. I finally discovered the problem: I was trying to work too quickly. In my haste I created a glutinous mass, rather than a risotto of delicate creaminess.

So if you follow the steps here, I will reveal all my treasured tips and you will make perfect risotto from the get-go. This recipe is easily adapted to any other ingredient, so feel free to improvise, but as they say in Italy, it's all about the rice.

2 cups shelled fresh peas

4 quarts cold water, plus more as needed to cook the peas

2 tablespoons plus 1½ teaspoons extra-virgin olive oil

1 sweet onion (white or yellow), peeled and finely minced

Sea salt to taste

2 cups Carnaroli rice

2 cups good white wine (unoaked)

4 cups hot water

1 cup pea shoots

2 tablespoons unsalted butter

¼ cup grated Parmesan

¼ teaspoon coarsely ground black pepper

1 tablespoon fresh tarragon leaves, chopped

1. Bring a small pot of salted water to a boil. Blanch the peas for 1 minute, drain and rinse with cold water to halt the cooking.
2. Bring the 4 quarts of cold water to a simmer in an 8-quart stock pot. In a heavy casserole add the 2 tablespoons of olive oil and bring the heat to medium. Add the onion and sweat for 8 minutes; season with sea salt only. Add the rice and continue to stir for 5 minutes, then add the wine.
3. Cook the rice until the wine has reduced to ½ cup, then slowly add the hot water, ½ cup at a time. You want the risotto to remain loose, but not too soupy.
4. Continue to add more water until the rice is done (al dente). Add the peas, the pea shoots, butter and three-quarters of the Parmesan. Taste for seasoning and add the black pepper. To finish, drizzle with 1½ teaspoons olive oil and sprinkle with the remaining Parmesan and the chopped tarragon.

Serves 6

Fresh ravioli with pumpkin and sage butter

In our annual Thanksgiving dinner at Barbuto we do a lot of pumpkin. Here is a good starter recipe for anyone wishing to learn the basics of ravioli making. It is not only a lot of fun, but quite satisfying. Hand-rolled pasta is a bit chunkier and more rustic than the machine variety, but I love the result. This method for preparing the pumpkin can also be the beginnings for a great pumpkin pie. Sage is essential here, but please don't overdo it—the adage about the old devil sage is true.

The only other ingredients are pure Parmesan, sweet organic butter, fresh eggs and sea salt. Don't knead the dough too much. Overdoing it will yield a tough, noncompliant dough, and the ravioli will not be tender. Also, let the dough rest adequately, an hour at least.

PASTA

2 cups organic all-purpose flour, plus more for kneading

6 large egg yolks

1 tablespoon extra-virgin olive oil

1 teaspoon sea salt

FILLING

1 Hubbard squash (see Note)

4 tablespoons extra-virgin olive oil

Sea salt to taste

5 tablespoons grated Parmesan

3 tablespoons (¾ stick) unsalted butter

4 sage leaves, minced

2 cloves garlic, minced

———

2 large egg whites

1 tablespoon water

3 tablespoons butter

8 sage leaves, minced

4 tablespoons grated Parmesan

1. Preheat the oven to 375°.
2. To make the dough: In a large bowl, mix the flour with the egg yolks, olive oil and sea salt. Dump the dough onto a work surface and knead with some flour for 10 minutes. Let the dough rest for at least an hour. Then, using a pasta machine, roll out 3 sheets of pasta and let dry.
3. To make the filling: Split the squash into quarters, remove its seeds and sprinkle with

2 tablespoons of the olive oil and sea salt to taste. Place the pieces in a roasting pan and cover with aluminum foil. Roast for an hour, or until tender.

4. Scoop out 2 cups of the roasted squash and discard the skin. Add the Parmesan, the remaining olive oil, the butter, sage and garlic and mix well. Taste for seasoning.

5. Mix the egg whites and water to make a sealing solution and paint 1 sheet of dough with the egg wash. Place a heaping tablespoonful of filling every 4 inches on the dough. Fold the dough over the filling, making a square over each one. Crimp with a fluting tool, then cut uniform ravioli with a sharp knife or a circular cutting tool.

6. Repeat with the other 2 sheets of dough. You should have 30 to 40 ravioli.

7. Bring a pot of water to a rolling simmer and salt the water. Boil the ravioli for 5 minutes, or until they float to the surface. Heat the remaining 3 tablespoons of butter in a large sauté pan, add the remaining sage and then the ravioli. Sauté for 3 minutes and serve hot, garnished with the remaining 4 tablespoons Parmesan.

Serves 4–6

Note: Squashes include Hubbard, acorn, edible pumpkin and turban squash. All will work!

Spaghetti *cacio e pepe*

My dear friend Mauro Vincenti was a larger-than-life character. He was confident and knowledgeable about almost everything, but his true passion was food and wine. In 1980 he opened an amazing Italian restaurant called Rex il Ristorante in downtown Los Angeles.

There are two important things to know about that time. First, other than Valentino in Santa Monica, no one else in America was creating a stage for amazing pure Italian food; second, the cost must have been enormous. The Rex building, once the men's store of stores in LA, a haberdashery to the stars, had been dormant for many years. But huge decorative appointments were intact: Lalique glass, amazing mahogany built-in display cases, art deco light fixtures and marble terrazzo floors. Mauro used this amazing backdrop to present Italian food on a par with Michelin three-star restaurants of France. This noble adventure in a slightly offbeat site (downtown L.A. was not then on the rise) was mildly quixotic. Mauro loved every second.

One day in his very lovable and brusque fashion, he literally dragged me into the kitchen and told me to taste this spaghetti. It was wonderful but weird. What is that? I asked. *Cacio e pepe,* slang for pecorino cheese and black pepper. That's it? I thought. And Mauro, seeing my bewilderment jumped and said that's it—black pepper, pecorino cheese and al dente pasta. So here you go.

1 pound spaghetti	¼ cup freshly ground black pepper
¼ cup freshly grated aged pecorino	Sea salt (optional)

1. Bring a pot of salted water to a boil. Cook the pasta for 8 minutes, or until al dente, then drain.
2. Combine the pecorino and black pepper in a large bowl, then add the pasta and toss together. Add sea salt if necessary (it won't be—the pecorino is salty). Serve hot.

Serves 4

Whole-wheat pasta with walnut-garlic pesto

I got this pasta dish from the delightful Faith Willinger. She is an Italianophile, and quite a character. She makes it all sound like a party! She is also tough as nails and a stickler for detail. This winter pestolike sauce, redolent of garlic, parsley and crushed walnuts is very tasty, easy to make and keeps in the fridge for months.

The walnuts are the key here. Unfortunately, most shelled walnuts are rancid. The only ones I recommend are fresh, new-season whole walnuts. It's very easy to crack the shells and extract the nuts. The sauce should only be made with a mortar and pestle; otherwise it's not fluffy or smooth, but kind of granular.

1 pound walnuts (in the shell)
2 cloves garlic
2 tablespoons grated Parmesan
¼ cup extra-virgin olive oil
Sea salt and freshly ground black
    pepper to taste

1 pound whole-wheat pasta (linguine
    or spaghettini)
Juice of 1 lemon

1. To make the pesto: Shell the walnuts, spread on a baking sheet and toast in a preheated 350° oven for 8 minutes. Remove and let cool.
2. Using a mortar and pestle, mash the garlic and Parmesan with the walnuts to make a rough paste. Dribble in the olive oil. Taste and season with sea salt, if necessary, and black pepper.
3. Bring a pot of salted water to a boil. Add the pasta. Add some lemon juice to the pesto. When the pasta is al dente, drain and transfer it to a bowl. Add ¾ cup of the sauce, toss well and season with black pepper. Serve hot.

Serves 4

Bigoli al pomodoro

This is lovely pasta. It resembles large spaghetti with a tunnel through the center. To make it at home would be ridiculous, so the store-bought machine-made variety is the only way. The sauce is delightfully easy and you can use it on everything, so make a large batch and freeze it. The tip here is to fire-blast the tomatoes to build flavor, kill any bacteria and tenderize them. Studding the tomato centers allows the garlic to penetrate. After the sauce is made, it is quite easy to cook the pasta and toss it in the sauce, and *voilà*—a perfect pasta.

4 large heirloom tomatoes, cored

3 cloves garlic, 2 sliced into thin slivers, 1 smashed

3 tablespoons extra-virgin olive oil

Sea salt and freshly ground black pepper to taste

4 sprigs rosemary, leaves picked

1 onion, peeled and diced

1 bell pepper, stemmed, seeded and diced

1 pound *bigoli*

2 tablespoons grated pecorino

1. Preheat the oven to 475°.
2. Cut the tomatoes in half and arrange on a baking sheet. Stud with the slivers of garlic, sprinkle with 2 tablespoons of the olive oil and season with sea salt and black pepper. Bake for 20 minutes. When cool, chop and add the rosemary leaves.
3. In a large sauté pan, heat the remaining tablespoon of olive oil, add the onion, the smashed garlic and bell pepper and cook for 3 minutes over medium-high heat. Add the tomatoes, reduce the heat and cook for 10 minutes.
4. Bring a pot of salted water to a boil. Cook the pasta until al dente, drain and toss with the tomato sauce and pecorino. Serve hot.

Serves 4

Spaghetti *alla carbonara*

I have made this classic dish the same way for years: with olive oil, *guanciale* (cured jowl of pork), egg yolks and Parmesan. The tried and true is perfection, please believe me. I have had cooks add garlic and onions, peas and mushrooms. Blasphemy!

I have heard a couple different stories for the source of the name. Some people say it refers to miners (*carbonari*) because of the flecks of black pepper, but I like the story of Giuseppe Mazzini, the revolutionary from Genoa who was a member of a secret group called *carbonari,* who attempted for years to unify Italy. Regardless, this pasta dish is the world's richest and most decadent. A wonderfully gifted actress frequents Barbuto and always orders a double *carbonara*; God bless her!

¼ pound *guanciale*, diced
1 tablespoon extra-virgin olive oil
1 pound spaghetti
¼ cup grated Parmesan

4 egg yolks
Sea salt and freshly ground black
   pepper to taste

1. Cook the *guanciale* in the olive oil slowly for 10 minutes, or until cooked through. Keep warm.
2. Bring a pot of salted water to a boil. Cook the pasta for 8 minutes and drain, reserving ½ cup of the cooking water.
3. Add the pasta and water to the *guanciale* pan and bring to a boil. Add the cheese; turn off the heat. Add the yolks all at once and beat furiously for 1 minute. The eggs should not scramble but turn into a smooth sauce. Season with sea salt and black pepper and serve immediately.

Serves 4

Linguine with wild mushrooms

I adapted this recipe from Giuliano Bugialli many years ago. With blind faith I followed the recipe and rolled out the pasta myself. It worked. Over the years I've adapted his technique and made it my own. The recipe I use has more eggs, as it is made in Piedmont, and uses an organic flour and sea salt, but overall the dish hasn't changed much.

1 pound fresh morel mushrooms (you can substitute chanterelles, porcini or lobster mushrooms for the morels)

2 cups organic all-purpose flour, plus more if necessary

4 large egg yolks

1 teaspoon sea salt, plus more if necessary

¼ cup cold water, plus more if necessary

2 tablespoons extra-virgin olive oil

3 shallots, minced

¼ cup sherry

½ cup heavy cream

2 tablespoons grated Parmesan

Freshly ground black pepper to taste

1. Wash the mushrooms in cold water, dry and place on a towel.
2. To make the pasta: Pour the flour in a mound on the table and make a well in the center. In the well, place the yolks, 1 teaspoon sea salt and ¼ cup cold water. Mix the ingredients together and, if necessary, add more water or flour to make a smooth, elastic dough. Knead the dough for 2 minutes, then wrap in plastic wrap and let sit at room temperature for 2 hours.
3. Cut the dough into 4 pieces, flour a work surface, and, using a rolling pin, roll out the dough as thinly as possible. Dust each piece with flour and roll up into a cylinder. Using a sharp knife, cut the dough into ribbons about ¼ inch wide. Repeat the process until all the pasta is cut.
4. Fluff the pasta with some flour. If not using it today, freeze it.
5. In a sauté pan, heat the olive oil and cook the mushrooms over high heat. When browned, add the shallots and cook for 1 more minute, then add the sherry and cream. Bring to a boil, then turn off the heat.

6. Bring a pot of salted water to a boil. Add the pasta. Cook the pasta until it rises to the surface, drain, and add it to the pan with the mushrooms. Return the pan to the heat, toss the pasta and mushrooms together and taste for seasoning. Serve hot, sprinkled with the Parmesan and black pepper.

Serves 4

Tagliatelle *agli scampi*

Here is my version of a standard. "Scampi" is a loose term meaning shrimp in garlic butter. In Italy the Latin-named *Nodicus scampi* or langoustines are marvelous creatures. You can buy them in the United States, but the cost is daunting. To save your money and to be slightly P.C., I advise you use either frozen head-on shrimp from the Bahamas or fresh spot prawns (also called large shrimp!) from the West Coast. The preparation, however, is straightforward.

2 tablespoons extra-virgin olive oil

1 pound prawns, or 4 per person

1 clove garlic, minced

½ cup rosé wine

¾ pound tagliatelle

2 tablespoons unsalted butter

1 teaspoon lemon juice

Sea salt and freshly ground black
    pepper to taste

1. Bring a pot of salted water to a boil.
2. In a sauté pan over high heat, heat the olive oil and add the prawns. Cook for 2 minutes per side. Add the garlic and cook for another minute. Deglaze with the wine.
3. At the same time, cook the pasta for 6 minutes. When the pasta is done, add ¼ cup of the cooking water to the prawns, then drain the pasta. Toss the pasta with the shrimp, add the butter and toss well. Add the lemon juice, season with sea salt and black pepper and serve hot.

Serves 4

Kids' pasta with cream, Parmesan and butter

At Barbuto we call this the *bambini* (kids') pasta. It is spaghetti, cooked al dente, then tossed with sweet Vermont butter, Parmesan and just a touch of cream. No green stuff! Anyone under the age of twelve will second that, I'm sure. But this dish is a hit with adults as well.

½ pound spaghetti (or your favorite pasta)

6 tablespoons (¾ stick) unsalted butter

¼ cup heavy cream

Sea salt to taste

2 tablespoons grated Parmesan

1. Bring a pot of salted water to a boil. Boil the pasta for 7 minutes and drain.
2. In a 12-inch pan, heat the butter and cream and bring to a simmer. Add the pasta, turn the heat to medium and toss together. Season with sea salt only. Add the Parmesan, toss well and serve.

Serves 4 (kid-size appetites)

Rigatoni and spicy duck *ragù*

What is a *ragù*? A stew made into a sauce. This recipe is decadent—it requires a whole duck, stewed in red wine with carrots, onions, tomatoes, garlic, celery and other aromatics. The duck cooks for about three hours, or until the meat completely falls off the carcass. Sometimes I add a fresh batch of vegetables to augment the sauce if the stewed vegetables have disintegrated into the *ragù*. This will make a good amount of sauce, so either have a large party or freeze half.

1 Long Island duckling
Sea salt and freshly ground black
   pepper to taste
1 head garlic, cloves left whole
3 onions, peeled and diced
2 carrots, peeled and diced
1 stalk celery, diced

1 red Fresno or Serrano chili, seeded
   and minced
3 tomatoes, cored and diced
1 bottle red wine
1 pound rigatoni
½ cup fresh ricotta

1. Preheat the oven to 375°.
2. Place the duck in a roasting pan and season with sea salt and black pepper. Roast for 1½ hours. Remove from the oven, scoop out the fat and place it in a sauté pan. Sauté the garlic, onions, carrots, celery, chili and tomatoes in the duck fat until golden brown and add the wine.
3. Transfer the vegetables and wine back into the roasting pan with the duck and roast for another hour. Remove when the meat is falling off the bone.
4. Let the duck and vegetables cool. Scoop the vegetables into a bowl. Remove all the meat from the duck and add it to the vegetables. This is your sauce.
5. Bring a pot of salted water to a boil. Cook the rigatoni until al dente and drain.
6. Heat the *ragù* and season it. Add the rigatoni and sprinkle with fresh ricotta.

Serves 4–6

Pappardelle with meat *ragù* and poached egg

As in the preceding recipe, this *ragù* is essentially a stew that is cooked until it is sauce-like. I had it in a small place outside of Siena and was taken with it. I am reminded of the classic boeuf Bourguignon, but here the chunks of meat disappear, reduced to a succulent *ragù*. The poached egg is a capricious addition, but it is wonderful. Of course, one could omit the egg, but why?

2 tablespoons extra-virgin olive oil
2 pounds beef stew meat, cubed
½ cup chopped pancetta
3 onions, peeled and chopped
2 cloves garlic, chopped
1 bottle red wine
2 cups cold water
1 cup canned San Marzano tomatoes

Sea salt and freshly ground black
   pepper to taste
1 pound pappardelle
4 eggs
4 tablespoons (½ stick) unsalted
   butter
¼ cup grated Parmesan

1. In a large skillet, heat the olive oil and brown the beef and pancetta. Add the onions and garlic and cook until browned.
2. Add the wine and bring to a boil, then add the cold water and the tomatoes with their juice.
3. Braise for 3 hours, covered, on low heat.
4. When the meat is tender, mash with a fork and season with sea salt and black pepper.
5. Bring a pot of salted water to a boil. Cook the pappardelle until just tender. Drain, reserving 2 cups of the water.
6. Place the pasta water in a saucepan over low heat. Crack the eggs into a small bowl and gently slide them into the pot. Soft-poach the eggs—this will take about 3 minutes.
7. Place 3 cups of the sauce in a pan, add the butter, the Parmesan and the pappardelle and toss well. Season with sea salt and black pepper. Place onto a platter and carefully spoon the eggs on top. Serve hot.

Serves 4

Bucatini with artichokes, *cipolline* and fava beans

This is the quintessential spring pasta—entirely vegetarian. I love the wonderful flavors of the baby artichokes, small onions and the brilliant green fava beans. The vegetables are cooked until al dente, then gently stewed together with the vegetable broth, olive oil, a touch of sweet butter and lemon zest. A great way to start a spring dinner.

6 baby artichokes	1 pound *bucatini*
1 cup shelled fresh fava beans	4 tablespoons (½ stick) unsalted
4 *cipolline* (small flat onions originally	butter
from Umbria), peeled	1 pint cherry tomatoes
4 tablespoons extra-virgin olive oil	12 fresh basil leaves
Sea salt to taste	2 tablespoons grated Parmesan
2 spring onions	Zest of 1 lemon

1. Preheat the oven to 400°.
2. To clean the baby artichokes: Peel away the outside leaves and cut off the top ½ inch. Using a vegetable peeler, remove the tough outer skin from the stem. Cut the artichokes into quarters. Cook in simmering salted water until al dente. In a small pot, cook the fava beans until al dente, then peel them.
3. Place the *cipolline* in a square of aluminum foil, add 2 tablespoons of the olive oil, sprinkle with sea salt and close the foil. Roast for 30 minutes. Remove from the oven, peel and quarter. Wash and dry the spring onions and slice them into quarters.
4. Bring a pot of salted water to a boil. Cook the pasta until al dente, then drain. In a skillet, heat the butter and the remaining olive oil, add the artichokes, favas, *cipolline*, spring onions and the tomatoes and sauté for 5 minutes, then add the basil. Add the pasta to the vegetables and toss in the Parmesan. Season with the lemon zest and serve immediately.

Serves 4

Handkerchief pasta with pork meatballs

I adore this pasta shape. It is so easy to make that six-year-olds in my cooking classes can do it! The trick is to make the pasta as thin as possible without a lot of gluten; the gluten makes the dough tough and resilient. Use a cheap pasta machine and roll it out on the thinnest setting. Cut the pasta into precise squares. They should dry for a while so they will hold their shape.

The meatballs are fluffy and perfect; I use fresh bread as filling, not old, dry bread. The meat also has a bit of prosciutto or bacon, or better yet, both. I use an organic 70/30 beef (70 percent meat and 30 percent fat is a good ratio for meatballs, they will be quite tender), chopped veal and pork shoulder meat. The trick with meatballs is to soak the bread crumbs in the egg yolk and cream, then add the ground meat. Please don't knead the meat mixture; it will make the meatballs tough. The formed, uncooked meatballs freeze well.

PASTA

2 cups organic all-purpose flour

6 large egg yolks

½ teaspoon sea salt

MEATBALLS

1 loaf *ciabatta* (page 38), crust
    removed and bread made into
    crumbs

¼ cup heavy cream

1 cup each ground pork shoulder,
    veal and beef

½ cup chopped bacon

1 teaspoon dried oregano leaves

Sea salt and freshly ground black
    pepper to taste

¼ teaspoon red pepper flakes

2 tablespoons unsalted butter

2 tablespoons extra-virgin olive oil

2 cups cold water

SAUCE

2 tablespoons extra-virgin olive oil

2 cloves garlic, minced

2 tomatoes, cored and diced

2 tablespoons grated Parmesan

1 tablespoon chopped fresh parsley

Sea salt and freshly ground black
    pepper to taste

1. To make the pasta: Pile the flour in a mound on a work surface and make a well in the center. In the well, mix the egg yolks with the flour and sea salt. Knead for 10 minutes. Cover the dough with a towel and let rest for 1 hour.

2. With a rolling pin (or pasta machine), roll out the pasta as thinly as possible. Using a sharp knife, cut the pasta into 2-inch squares; then toss in flour. You can make and freeze these beforehand.

3. Preheat the oven to 375°.

4. To make the meatballs: In a large bowl, combine the bread crumbs, cream, ground meat, bacon and oregano. Mix until it just forms a ball. Season with sea salt, black pepper and red pepper flakes. Cook a small piece in a sauté pan to check the seasoning; adjust if necessary and then form into 36 meatballs, weighing about 1 ounce each.

5. In a sauté pan, heat the butter and olive oil and add the meatballs. When they are browned all over, transfer them to a roasting pan and carefully add the water. Place the roasting pan in the oven. Bake the meatballs for 30 minutes, or until they are cooked through. Remove from the oven and keep warm.

6. Ten minutes before the meatballs are done, make the sauce. In a large sauté pan, heat the olive oil, add the garlic and tomatoes and cook for 2 minutes.

7. While the meatballs are cooking, bring a pot of water to a boil, salt it and add the handkerchiefs. Cook until tender, or up to 5 minutes, then drain.

8. Add the meatballs and the cooked pasta. Toss with the Parmesan and parsley, season with sea salt, if necessary, and black pepper and serve.

Serves 4–6, but you'll have leftover meatballs

Trofie with peas, pancetta and spring onions

Here is the tiny hand-rolled pasta from the hills of Piedmont. *Trofie* look difficult but are really very easy, satisfying and quite fun to make. All you need is a bit of patience. That's it.

3 large egg yolks

2 cups organic all-purpose flour

Sea salt

¼ cup cold water

2 tablespoons unsalted butter

½ cup diced pancetta (if you can't find pancetta, substitute thick-sliced bacon)

2 cups spring peas

3 spring onions, diced

½ cup heavy cream

Freshly ground black pepper

¼ cup grated Gruyère cheese

1. Combine the egg yolks, flour and ½ teaspoon of the sea salt in a bowl and add the cold water. Mix with a wooden spoon until a nice ball forms. Flour a work surface and knead the dough until it feels resilient. Cover the dough with a towel and let rest for 1 hour.
2. To make the *trofie*: Roll off a pea-shaped piece of dough, mash it with your thumb (this is the *orecchiette* shape), then roll it to resemble a miniature croissant.
3. Bring a pot of salted water to a boil. Cook the *trofie* for 6–8 minutes, then drain.
4. In a saucepan, melt the butter over medium heat, add the pancetta and cook for 2 minutes. Add the peas, onions and cream, cook for 7 minutes and season with sea salt and black pepper to taste.
5. Toss with the cooked *trofie* and the cheese and serve.

Serves 4–6

Angel hair pasta with crabmeat, jalapeño and mint

I vaguely remember my pal Mario Batali once mentioning that his favorite pasta dish was Dungeness crabmeat with jalapeño chilies. I ripped off his idea and the dish is a bestseller at Barbuto. If I were in San Francisco I would cook my own crabs. As this is not always possible, you can easily substitute precooked Dungeness, blue crab, Jonah or stone. But only use "freshly cooked" crabmeat, never a package marked with the phrase "previously frozen." The spiciness of the jalapeño coupled with mint is intoxicating. People sometimes order two servings, one after the other.

½ pound cooked Dungeness crabmeat (or any good fresh crab), cleaned and picked through

1 jalapeño, stemmed, seeded and minced

1 clove garlic, minced

12 fresh mint leaves, torn

6 tablespoons (¾ stick) unsalted butter, cut into small dice

1 pound dried angel hair pasta

Juice of 1 lemon

Sea salt to taste

1. In a large bowl, combine the crabmeat, jalapeño, garlic, mint and butter.
2. Bring a pot of salted water to a boil and cook the pasta. It will take only 3 minutes.
3. When it's al dente, do not strain. Using a Chinese spider (see page 241), scoop out the pasta and toss it with the crab mixture. Add the lemon juice, season with sea salt and serve hot.

Serves 4

Tagliorini with shrimp and saffron

This delicious pasta is astoundingly easy to make. It does require peeling the shrimp, so buy fairly big ones, perhaps five per person. They should be very fresh or impeccably frozen and thawed. The sauce is a wonderful concoction of garlic, saffron and stock made from rosé wine and the shrimp shells. With the addition of some sweet butter, all is good.

1 pound fresh shrimp, shell on
⅓ cup water
1 cup rosé wine
1 pound *tagliorini*
2 tablespoons extra-virgin olive oil
Sea salt and freshly ground black
    pepper to taste

2 cloves garlic, smashed
6 tablespoons (¾ stick) unsalted
    butter
¼ teaspoon saffron

1. Peel the shrimp, reserving the shells. Heat the water, the wine and the shells in a saucepan and cook for 10 minutes. Strain, reserving the stock.
2. Bring a large pot of salted water to a boil. Add the pasta and cook for 8 minutes.
3. While the pasta is cooking, heat a sauté pan over medium-high and add the olive oil. When hot, tilt the pan and add the shrimp. Sauté for 3 minutes and add the sea salt and black pepper. When the shrimp is almost cooked, add the garlic and toss vigorously. Add the shrimp stock, the butter and saffron.
4. The pasta will be ready now. Drain the pasta and add to the shrimp. Toss well and serve.

Serves 4

Linguine with Manila clams, mussels and fennel

Here is my rendition of a classic. I add mussels and roasted fennel to the clams and toss the linguine in clam butter. Another fun addition (in season) would be fresh corn kernels. The best clams are farmed in Nova Scotia and Puget Sound. They are fresh, bright and superb.

2 pints mussels

24 clams (domestic Manilas)

2 bulbs fennel

10 tablespoons (1¼ sticks) unsalted butter

1 pound linguine

¼ teaspoon red pepper flakes (optional)

Juice of 1 lemon

1 cup corn kernels (optional)

½ cup dry white wine like a sauvignon from Alto Adige

Sea salt and freshly ground black pepper to taste

1. Wash the mussels and the clams. Trim and thinly slice the fennel.
2. In a sauté pan, heat 4 tablespoons of the butter and sauté the fennel for 10 minutes, or until tender (but not browned!).
3. Have two big pots ready, one with salted water for the pasta and an empty one for the mussels and clams.
4. When the pasta water boils, add the linguine. At the same time, in the other pot, combine the fennel, the red pepper flakes (if using), lemon juice, remaining butter, corn (if using), wine, mussels and clams, bring to a boil and cover until the mollusks are open.
5. When the linguine is just al dente, drain. In a large serving bowl, add the pasta, then the mussels and clams and their sauce with the fennel. It will take two people to toss—this is the fun part! Season with sea salt and black pepper and serve.

Serves 6–8

Strozzapreti with octopus, red wine and onions

How much do I love this pasta? According to folklore, priests, who are naturally hungry, loved this pasta shape so much that they would eat it until they strangled themselves. The genius who concocted this shape obviously wanted a pasta that would hold as much sauce as possible. It is only a dry pasta; I can't imagine trying to duplicate this by hand.

1 pound octopus (see Note)
1 cup red wine
2 cups cold water
3 red onions, peeled and sliced
¼ cup extra-virgin olive oil

Juice of 1 lemon
1 pound dried *strozzapreti*
Sea salt to taste
¼ teaspoon red pepper flakes

1. In a large pot, combine the octopus, wine, cold water and onions. Cook over gently simmering heat for 40–60 minutes or so until the octopus is tender.
2. Turn off the heat and let it cool. When cool, remove the octopus, reserving the liquid. Cut the octopus into even ¼-inch rounds.
3. Return the pot of wine and onions to the heat and reduce until 1 cup of liquid is left. Add the olive oil and lemon juice. Toss in the octopus and keep on a low flame.
4. Bring a pot of salted water to a boil and cook the *strozzapreti* until it is al dente. It will take about 11 minutes. When it is done, drain and add it to the octopus and bring the pot to a boil. Season with sea salt and red pepper flakes and serve.

Note: Generally octopus is sold frozen. That's okay, as the sauce helps to tenderize it.

Serves 4

The Italians do not garnish their plates with unnecessary artifice. Main courses are served simply with sauce, perhaps some herbs, good olive oil and lemon. I love the elegance of this; it shows off the main course and leaves the *contorni,* or vegetable course, to shine on its own. So accompanying vegetables need to be simple, straightforward and seasonal, gently flavored and quietly bold. I have included some of the most popular vegetables we serve at Barbuto and the ones I make only for friends and family. They are my secret passion.

Organically grown vegetables just taste better. If possible, vegetables should be picked, washed and cooked within one day. This is not always possible, but our local farmers' markets with their range of wonderful eggplants, onions, peppers, beets, corn and more make this an obtainable goal. I think a potato, while it can be put up in cold storage, is far better going straight from the ground to the pot. Asparagus and artichokes are more fragile than we imagine and deteriorate rapidly. As they sit in the fridge, vegetables lose their intrinsic value, their vitamins and minerals.

Hand selection is always the best. Spend some time sifting through the peas to find the best ones and your efforts will be rewarded. Looking at a hundred potatoes, perhaps twenty are worthy of your selection. The rest are either imperfect, browned, old or too large. Asparagus should be meaty, firm and crisp. Tomatoes should be bursting with liquid and have a tomato scent. Broccoli should not have any yellowing bits; cauliflower should be creamy white (or orange, purple, etc.). Greens like spinach should be healthy looking—don't be afraid of dirt that will wash off. Scallions should be squeaky; eggplant should be firm and pert.

On the subject of vegetables and children, start them young. Peeling carrots is a brilliant way to get them going. Shelling peas is also fun. Kids' knife skills can start with shallots. Instructing your child to use the tiniest paring knife, have them grasp it firmly on the handle. Holding the shallot as if it were a tennis ball, cut it in half with the noncutting fingers gripping that "ball" as tightly as possible. Cut firm, yet delicate, strokes, as thinly as possible. I like having my students practice on small onions, as it is easier to see the mistakes and they gradually get the hang of it. This skill is as important as any other. Cooks like razzle-dazzle; they adore flipping steaks and making flames with alcohol. But no skill is as important or valuable as slicing that shallot perfectly. It is the ultimate path to Buddha's hand. A perfectly cut vegetable is well on the way to becoming perfectly cooked or a gorgeous raw addition to any dish.

Marriage in the vegetable world is multirational; use good judgment and all will be well. A strange combo (asparagus with eggplant) is, well, strange and will taste that way. But couple the eggplant with onions, peppers and garlic, and the clouds will part. Greens, especially, benefit from crazy dance partners. I love mixing spinach with frisée, collards with *tat soi,* kale with chard. They play on their strengths as they gently cook, and the health benefits are extraordinary.

I could live on *contorni* alone—they rock my world!

Carrots with saffron and orange

Carrots can be tough when too small and only fit for donkeys if too large, but nowadays, we are blessed with a myriad of beautiful heirloom carrots in the farmers' market. I like them about ten inches in length, and about one and a half inches in diameter at the top. They need to be impeccably fresh, neither limp nor soft, and they should taste sweet, not bitter, when raw. There are white, yellow and burgundy-colored ones as well as the usual orange. I like blending the colors together. Here, the saffron adds delicacy and spice and a slightly exotic flavor. The orange enhances the flavor and brightens the colors and adds notes of acidity and mellowness.

2 pounds carrots

½ cup fresh orange juice

4 tablespoons (½ stick) unsalted
   butter

¼ cup cold water

½ teaspoon saffron

Sea salt and freshly ground black
   pepper to taste

1. Preheat the oven to 375°.
2. Top and peel the carrots. In a roasting pan with a lid, combine the carrots, orange juice, butter, and cold water and sprinkle with the saffron. Season with sea salt and black pepper.
3. Cover and bake in the oven for 30 minutes, until the carrots are tender. Serve hot.

Serves 4–6

Peas with pancetta and mint

This classic preparation can be adapted to any green vegetable, but I love peas. If you can't find peas that are sweet, use sugar snaps instead. The pancetta should be thin and not cooked too much or it will turn hard and chewy. The mint is essential, I prefer peppermint's fresh taste, and I am not a fan of spearmint. The flowers of mint are special. Use them!

2 cups freshly shelled peas
Sea salt to taste
6 tablespoons (¾ stick) unsalted
  butter

2 ounces diced pancetta
8 sprigs mint, leaves only, torn into
  small pieces

1. Wash and dry the peas. In a 4-quart pot, bring 2 quarts of cold water to a boil and add sea salt. Cook the peas for 4 minutes, then drain.
2. Heat the butter in a skillet over medium heat, add the pancetta and cook until golden. Add the warm peas and cook for 2 minutes more. Add the mint, season and serve.

Serves 4

Eggplant and oregano

I adore eggplants. In my youth the only ones in the marketplace were typically huge, black and gnarly. They were well suited for purées and salads, but for other dishes they were inadequate. Roll forward to the present day, when we are blessed with a thousand varieties. From Asia there are slender green, purple, lavender and black eggplants; these thin-skinned eggplants are great for grilling and sautéing. From Italy and other parts of Europe we have gorgeous ones that are purple and lavender, mottled, striated, and pure white and yellow—hence, the name "egg-plant." In our farmers' markets we see them all. For this dish I would recommend a thin-skinned variety, not too large—say eight inches long and two inches in diameter. The slender Japanese variety is perfect.

2 pounds lavender or purple elongated eggplants, weighing about 4 ounces each

Sea salt to taste
3 tablespoons extra-virgin olive oil
1 tablespoon fresh oregano leaves

1. Preheat the oven to 450°.
2. Split the eggplants in half lengthwise. Score them with a very sharp knife on the cut or flesh side only. Place the halves, cut side up, on a baking sheet and season with sea salt. Drizzle 2 tablespoons of the olive oil over them and then roast in the oven until they puff, about 8 minutes.
3. Remove and sprinkle with sea salt. Garnish with oregano leaves and a drizzle of olive oil.

Serves 4–6

Smashed new potatoes

Nothing is more pleasurable than reaching into a mound of soft dirt and yanking out some new potatoes. When I lived in Malibu I had that experience when I raided my neighbor's garden. It was quite sensual—the earth was warm, the potatoes firm to the touch—even if I got dirt in my shoes.

Potatoes are a curious lot; in Peru alone they must cultivate a thousand varietals. Italy did not begin its relationship with potatoes until the seventeenth century. They were not grown domestically until the nineteenth century, and even then, they were mainly an imported item.

But can you imagine gnocchi without potatoes, or venison in the mountains of the Dolomites without mashed potatoes? Potatoes are still not the most popular Italian starch; but at Barbuto, Americans love them. Here is a uniquely simple way of cooking them that is eye-catching and delicious. The first trick is to cook them twice, slow poaching them in simmering salted water, then frying them gently in butter and olive oil. The second trick is to gently squish the potatoes with a potato masher so they resemble a deflated football. This creates two flat cooking surfaces that will crisp perfectly.

2 pounds small white or rose potatoes (purple are fine but a bit weird)

2 tablespoons extra-virgin olive oil

3 tablespoons unsalted butter

Sea salt and freshly ground black pepper to taste

1. Wash and trim the potatoes. Place them in a pot and cover with 2 inches of cold, salted water. Bring to a boil, reduce to a simmer and cook for 45 minutes, or until tender. Drain.
2. In a large skillet, heat the olive oil and butter over medium heat, and when it sizzles, add the potatoes. They should all be touching. With a potato masher, gently press down on each one just to flatten. Cook until browned on the first side, flip over and repeat. Season with sea salt and black pepper and serve hot.

Serves 4

Broccoli rabe with red chili

Broccoli rabe was not a popular vegetable in America twenty years ago. But the Andy Boy farm in Watsonville, California, has been hell-bent on selling this healthy and delicious vegetable and has pushed the lowly broccoli rabe to at least a small place in many supermarkets. It is the easiest vegetable to cook, requiring but a few minutes to get to the table. You can just steam it or sauté it; it is really a matter of taste. Here I steam it, then sauté it with chili and garlic. I like the peppery kick of the peppers and garlic. The lemon is a mere accent; too much lemon will discolor the rabe and be too acidic. Too much butter and it will turn greasy. So the recipe is a precise one.

1 bunch broccoli rabe
1 red Fresno chili
4 cloves garlic
¼ cup extra-virgin olive oil
½ cup cold water
Sea salt and freshly ground black pepper to taste
2 tablespoons unsalted butter
1 teaspoon lemon juice

1. Wash and chop the broccoli rabe, seed and chop the chili, and smash the garlic.
2. In a large skillet, heat the oil; add the garlic and the chili and immediately add the rabe. Sauté for 2 minutes, then add the cold water.
3. Cook for 10 minutes; then cover, turn down the heat and cook slowly for 10 minutes more. Season with sea salt and black pepper; add the butter and lemon juice. Serve hot.

Serves 2–4

Cauliflower roasted with pine nuts and cream

Here is one the glories of Barbuto, a favorite dish almost from day one. Everyone who eats it remarks that they really disliked cauliflower until they had this dish. The trick is to arrive at a vegetable that is cooked through but still crunchy. A hot oven is a perfect means to produce this result. There is no steaming, just roasting. The whole cauliflower is used, including the stem, so it is very nutritious. The cream is minimal, so forgo it if you wish.

Many different types of cauliflower can be found at the market: the beautiful and weird conical-shaped romanesco, lovely purple, green and yellow varieties as well as the creamy white that is ubiquitous. I love mixing the colors together.

My former chef, Lynn McNeely, and I ate a version of cooked cauliflower at Babbo, Mario Batali's great restaurant. Intrigued by the simplicity, we were determined to find our own version. Cauliflower is quite versatile, but rarely does it shine. Along the way we tried poaching it, roasting it and sautéing the florets. This version is by far the easiest and tastiest. The cauliflower is fire-blasted at a high temperature and then allowed to rest so the heat circulates.

1 large cauliflower (about 2 pounds)
¼ cup extra-virgin olive oil
Sea salt and freshly ground black
    pepper to taste
2 cloves garlic, unpeeled and
    cracked slightly with a big knife or
    your fist

2 tablespoons heavy cream
2 tablespoons pine nuts or hazelnuts
1 ounce Parmesan, grated

1. Preheat the oven to 450°.
2. Wash the cauliflower and separate it into florets. Slice the florets in half.
3. Lightly coat a roasting pan with 1 teaspoon of the olive oil.
4. In a bowl, toss the cauliflower with the sea salt, black pepper, garlic and the remaining olive oil. Place the cauliflower in the pan and roast for 20 minutes. You'll need to stir

it once or twice. You want it to turn a nice golden brown. Stir in the cream during the last 5 minutes of roasting.

5. Meanwhile, in a small skillet, toast the pine nuts, stirring often so they brown evenly. This happens quickly, so watch the pan to be sure the nuts don't burn.

6. Remove the cauliflower and return it to the bowl; add the pine nuts and Parmesan and toss well. Taste for seasoning and serve.

Serves 4–6

Wilted kale and *pepperoncini*

1 tablespoon extra-virgin olive oil

3 cloves garlic, minced

1 small onion, peeled and diced

2 bunches kale, washed, stemmed
  and chopped (yielding 3 cups)

1 cup cold water

¼ cup roughly chopped
  pepperoncini

2 tablespoons unsalted butter

¼ teaspoon red pepper flakes

Sea salt and freshly ground black
  pepper to taste

1. In a large heavy casserole or a 2-handled pot, add the olive oil and garlic and cook over medium-high heat for 1 minute. Add the onion, stir and continue cooking for 3 minutes. Add the kale. Stir for 1 minute, then add 1 cup cold water. Cook until slightly wilted and reduce the heat. The cooking time depends on the kale; some cooks more quickly than others.

2. When the kale is tender, add the *pepperoncini*, butter and red pepper flakes and stir for 1 minute. Season with sea salt and black pepper and serve hot.

Serves 4

Cherry tomatoes with basil

This is perhaps the simplest dish in this book. Simple, but excellent. The tomatoes are meant to "burst" in the oven.

2 pints small farm-stand tomatoes

12 fresh basil leaves

2 tablespoons extra-virgin olive oil

Sea salt and freshly ground black pepper to taste

1. Preheat the oven to 350°.
2. Stem and wash the tomatoes. Wash, dry and julienne the basil.
3. Toss the tomatoes with the olive oil, sea salt and black pepper. Lay the tomatoes on a baking sheet.
4. Roast the tomatoes for 3–5 minutes, until the skins have split; then remove and toss in a bowl with the basil. Serve immediately or at room temperature.

Serves 4–6

Spaetzle with rosemary

Northern Italy shares a border with Switzerland and Austria, and the alpine cuisines of these nations meld together. One of the region's truly great dishes is *spaetzle,* loosely made free-form pasta that can be simply poached, or poached and fried. I like the former, with a good sprinkle of mountain cheese, garlic and parsley. It makes a great accompaniment for meat dishes, stews in particular. It is also good on its own. I love it on a cold winter's eve with some cool wine from Trentino or Valle d'Aosta.

2 cups organic all-purpose flour

1 cup sparkling water

1 teaspoon sea salt

4 tablespoons (½ stick) unsalted
   butter

1 teaspoon fresh rosemary leaves
   and blossoms, roughly chopped

Freshly ground black pepper to taste

1. Combine the flour, water and sea salt in a bowl. Mix with a wooden spoon.
2. Prepare a pot of simmering salted water. Put the batter in a colander, and holding it over the water, gently push the dough through the holes, using a knife to cut the *spaetzle* at 3-inch lengths. Boil them for 2 minutes and then transfer them to a serving dish. Add the butter and rosemary, season with black pepper, toss well and serve.

Serves 4–6

Grilled polenta with mascarpone

I grew up in a diverse neighborhood in Berkeley, California. Alan Ratto, a boyhood chum, came from the family that at the time ran the amazing Ratto's, a Victorian-era Italian food shop in downtown Oakland. Wood barrels of olives, capers and pickles lined the floor. Mortadella, *salumi* of all kinds and prosciutto filled the ceiling. Today Ratto's is not part of Alan's family, but my childhood memories linger.

I played music for many years and you could say that my music propelled me into cooking. One night the redheaded girlfriend of my band's piano player announced she was cooking polenta. I had been used to instant polenta, but here she spent an hour carefully stirring it with an old wooden spoon. She said that her grandmother from Sicily had taught her the technique: Slow is good, and fast is bad. I also believe that the right cornmeal is all-important. We use only old-fashioned stone-ground fine white polenta. The taste is otherworldly. It does take a full hour to cook, but you only need to stir every five minutes or so. The addition of Parmesan and butter near the end is important, as is sea salt, but no pepper.

Mascarpone can be made at home; it is very easy. I have included a brief recipe (page 233), so by all means try it. It will give you the giggles.

4 cups cold water

1 cup whole organic milk

3 cups organic stone-ground white
   polenta

4 tablespoons (½ stick) unsalted
   butter

½ cup plus 3 tablespoons grated
   Parmesan

Sea salt to taste

2 tablespoons extra-virgin olive oil

½ cup mascarpone

1. In a heavy stainless-steel or enamel pot, heat the cold water with the milk. When simmering, slowly add the polenta. Simmer, stirring constantly, for about 50 minutes, or until cooked. Add the butter, ½ cup of the Parmesan and sea salt. Coat a baking sheet with a bit of the olive oil and pour the polenta onto the sheet. Let it cool and place in the fridge overnight. Remove from the fridge and cut into rectangles.

2. Heat a charcoal grill or a griddle with grill ridges. Coat each polenta rectangle with the remaining olive oil and grill until golden.

3. Top with mascarpone and the remaining Parmesan and serve.

Serves 8–10

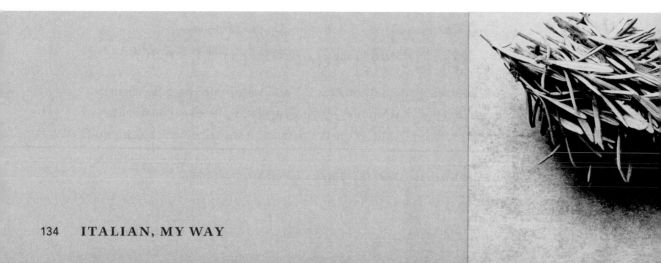

Fried polenta with rosemary

Using the polenta from the previous recipe—it's even better the next day—here is another method for cooking beautiful cornmeal. The polenta needs no coating and it will turn crispy and golden. If the amount of olive oil seems daunting, by all means use the second method, which cooks the polenta in a hot oven with a tiny amount of oil.

1 cup extra-virgin olive oil

1 rosemary branch

1 recipe polenta (page 133), chilled
and cut into 2-inch squares

Sea salt to taste

Frying Method:

1. Heat the olive oil in a cast-iron skillet to medium heat. Add the rosemary branch.
2. Fry the polenta until golden, then remove the rosemary. Salt the polenta and pull the rosemary leaves off the stem and garnish the squares. Serve hot or at room temperature.

Baking Method:

1. Preheat the oven to 400°. Coat a baking sheet with a liberal amount of olive oil.
2. Place the rosemary branch and the polenta squares on the pan, brush with olive oil and sprinkle with sea salt.
3. Bake until golden, about 20 minutes. Pull the rosemary leaves off the stem and garnish the squares. Serve hot or at room temperature.

Serves 6–8

Italians like their fish simple. Roasted, poached or, best of all, grilled. Served with little more than lemon and olive oil, the true flavor of the particular fish stands out.

Fish is a delicate, extremely perishable commodity and the best advice I can impart is to buy only the freshest possible. But the sad fact is that fishmongery is a lost art and even great fish restaurants are few and far between. The oldest urban markets—Billingsgate, Fulton and Les Halles—have disappeared, leaving behind supermarket fish. I am not a fan of fish that is packaged by a bulk-buying group.

One of the greatest places in Italy to eat fresh fish is in Porto Ercole, the port that supplies Rome. Here you can see the bounty of the Mediterranean. But the days of plenty are really gone. Sadly, we are facing a bleak fishing future. I am not sure if any regulatory commission can stop the plundering of the seas by fishing fleets with dragnets, and the dismal signs are everywhere. A truly fresh branzino, one that isn't farm raised, will cost about $200. *Orata* (sea bream), one the glories of Italian fish cookery, is scarce and equally expensive. The most drastic solution, of course, is to stop commercial fishing of all endangered fish. That might help, but permanent damage may have already occurred.

Best of all is to catch a fish at the beach, build a fire and roast it whole on an open grill. Another method I like is the paper bag treatment or *a cartoccio*. This cooking method is easy and entertaining. You can use whole or fileted fish, shrimp and scallops. The results are spectacular: the fish is moist and tender.

My experiences in Italy are by no means exhaustive, yet one truly stands out. When my partner, Fabrizio Ferri, and I first cemented our deal for Barbuto, he graciously invited my family to his island retreat on Pantelleria, a tiny rocky island off the coast of Tunisia. This remote and interesting place had been a pirate island for many years and before that, a Muslim stronghold. The Muslim influences are still apparent, particularly in the architecture. The houses are built of the local pumice stone and resemble strange igloos. The island is famous for three things: capers, sweet wine and seafood. When we arrived in August in hundred-degree heat, the sirocco was blowing sand and the water was brilliant blue. Fabrizio had promised that I would not have to cook, and his capable local chef prepared a different fish each evening. One night it was grilled swordfish, the next grouper, and another, spiny lobsters. But the crowning achievement was the typical Pantelleria fish stew with its trademark seven vegetables (one of which was French fries!). The rustic fish stew (kind of a pulverized bouillabaisse) was served first as two soups, one spicy with tomato, the second brothlike, then came the various fish in a mass surrounded by couscous, and finally the vegetables (zucchini, tomatoes, eggplant, onions, French fries, peppers and fennel). It was divine. It epitomized the way Italians like to eat fish—with bold strokes, no holds barred.

Pesce spada

At my business partner Fabrizio's house on Pantelleria he is also the fisherman of the group. One day he caught a lively hundred-pound swordfish, and we grilled it over local olive-wood cuttings. (His life-size photo of the fish hangs on the wall at Barbuto.) That was an amazing feast.

I love swordfish; it is a beautiful fish with a perfect texture. Some rare swordfish are very orange inside. The meat feels almost as if it has been tenderized, and the color is the result of the fish eating a tremendous amount of shrimp. Search these out; they are outstanding.

But there are disturbing issues regarding swordfish. First and foremost is its real scarcity—we have fished these magnificent creatures to near extinction. Second, we have polluted their breeding grounds, and the small fish they eat contain a good deal of mercury. Last, swordfish can be riddled with parasites (this only occurs in large specimens), so your butcher needs to be a specialist. I think much of what's on the market these days is frozen swordfish, which is often dry and bland. If I can't get line-caught, local swordfish that is certified by the local fisheries department, I will not buy it.

Four 6-ounce swordfish steaks
2 tablespoons extra-virgin olive oil
Juice of 1 lemon

2 very ripe and juicy tomatoes
Sea salt and freshly ground black
   pepper to taste

1. Rub the steaks with 1 tablespoon of the olive oil and lemon juice.
2. Prepare a grill.
3. Core the tomatoes and then slice in half; season with sea salt and black pepper.
4. Grill the swordfish over medium heat—no flames—for 3 minutes on one side, turn over and top each steak with a tomato half. Cook for another 4 minutes, then transfer the steaks to plates. Garnish with more olive oil and lemon juice.

Serves 4

Striped bass with new potatoes and picholine olives

My dear friend Colman Andrews, the cofounder of *Saveur* magazine, is always in the forefront of food. We have a long history and enjoy traveling the world together in search of new culinary treats. When he was amassing material for his definitive book on the food of the Riviera, he and I stopped for dinner at the restaurant da Puny in Portofino, Italy. This amazing portside restaurant takes full advantage of its perfect location. It is filled with glamorous diners, intent on enjoying fully the bounty of the Ligurian coast. Colman knew the dapper owner and let him pick our meal. The outstanding dish was a spectacular branzino cooked whole on a bed of Ligurian yellow potatoes, black olives and bay leaves. The extremely succulent meat was enhanced by a drizzle of Ligurian olive oil and local lemons. The crispy potatoes, faintly salty olives and magnificent fish were cooked to perfection. To sit in the center of town and eat some of the most wonderful food was an unparalleled delight. I've tried many times to duplicate the phenomenal dish we had that day, and finally I've succeeded. Here is my version with striped bass, which is more widely available in the United States.

4 large (½ pound each) Yukon gold
   potatoes
4 tablespoons extra-virgin olive oil
Sea salt and freshly ground black
   pepper to taste

1 striped bass filet (about 2 pounds
   with skin and bones)
1 cup picholine olives, pitted
8 bay leaves
2 lemons, cut into ¼-inch-thick slices

1. Preheat the oven to 400°.
2. Peel and slice the potatoes into large rounds about ⅛ inch thick. Place on a roasting pan and sprinkle with 2 tablespoons of the olive oil. Season with sea salt and black pepper and roast for 20 minutes. Remove from the oven and let cool.
3. Place the fish on top of the potatoes, sprinkle with the remaining olive oil, the olives and bay leaves, cover with parchment paper and cook for 20 minutes. Garnish with lemon and serve immediately.

Serves 4

Pompano in a paper bag

This dish came from my sojourn in the Florida Keys. I am a huge fan of Hemingway and had always longed for a visit to his home there. My chance came when I was asked to consult with a restaurant. (Ted Williams lived a mile away, but sadly, we never saw him.) I wanted to taste the local fare while I was there, and I found a time-warp joint in Isla Morada, which looked as if someone had designed it from an *Esquire* ad from the 1960s, complete with mounted swordfish and waitresses in nurses' outfits. They made simple, old-fashioned seafood and, of course, martinis. One of the dishes was the classic Keys favorite—pompano baked in a brown paper bag. The method is spectacular and almost foolproof. It seems Italian in spirit, so I've included it here.

1 large (about 2 pounds) pompano, cleaned and gutted	1 branch tarragon
	1 lemon, sliced
Sea salt	2 tablespoons extra-virgin olive oil

1. Preheat the oven to 400°.
2. Wash the pompano in cold running water. Season the inside with sea salt and then insert the tarragon and lemon slices. Drizzle with 1 tablespoon of the olive oil and sprinkle with sea salt.
3. Place the fish in a medium-size brown paper bag and fold up the opening. Put the bag on a baking sheet and bake for 20 minutes. Remove and cut the bag open with scissors. Scoop out the filets to a platter and drizzle with the remaining tablespoon of olive oil.

Serves 4

Scallops with preserved lemon and wilted spinach

The Italian name for scallops, *capasante,* has a wonderful, rich ring to it. "Scallops" just doesn't do justice to these gorgeous meaty white bivalves, especially those from Maine. The scallops caught in Europe are different from ours in America. There, the orange and white roe is delicious; here we discard it. There the meat is about half the size of our jumbo catch; ours, if very fresh, can have an abalone-like consistency.

The beauty of preserved lemons (I love the Meyer variety that grew in my yard in El Cerrito) is that they can be used in many dishes. The preserving process is quite simple. Left in a jar for a few days with just a little salt and sugar, the lemons yield an amazing taste.

16 large scallops (ask for U-10s—
    10 scallops per pound)
Sea salt and freshly ground black
    pepper
3 tablespoons extra-virgin olive oil
2 cloves garlic, minced

1 sweet onion, peeled and sliced
2 bunches very fresh spinach,
    washed and dried
2 tablespoons unsalted butter
1 tablespoon thinly slivered
    preserved lemons (page 234)

1. Clean the scallops and dry with paper towels. Sprinkle with sea salt and black pepper and coat with 1 tablespoon of the olive oil. Keep cold.
2. In a heavy skillet, heat 1 tablespoon of the olive oil; add the garlic, onion and spinach. Cook over medium heat until the spinach is wilted; season with sea salt and black pepper. Turn out onto a platter and keep warm. Wipe out the skillet with a paper towel.
3. Turn the heat to medium-high, add the remaining tablespoon of olive oil, and then the scallops, flat side down. Sear for 2 minutes, or until golden brown, and turn over. When golden brown on the other side—another 2 minutes—transfer to a warm platter. Put the spinach back in the pan, add the butter and turn off the heat. The residual heat will reheat the spinach and melt and incorporate the butter. Decorate the platter of scallops with the spinach and then dot with slivers of preserved lemon—a little goes a long way.

Serves 4–6

Lobster *alla piastra*

A *piastra* is a heavy cast-iron pan or griddle that can be heated to about 400°. It is a perfect medium for cooking seafood—especially shrimp, calamari and lobster. It makes cooking lobster, in particular, easy and fun and the results are outstanding. The trick is first to poach the lobster for five minutes. Then it can sit in the fridge for up to twenty-four hours. The hardest part is splitting the lobster—it takes a sure hand. The instructions are precise and simple, but bold. The *piastra* sears the lobster flesh so that it becomes crispy and sweet at the same time.

Two 1½-pound live lobsters
1 tablespoon sea salt, plus more to taste
Juice of 1 lemon
½ teaspoon paprika
1 tablespoon plus 1 teaspoon extra-virgin olive oil
1 bunch arugula, well washed and dried

1. Prepare the *piastra* by placing the empty pan over low heat for 30 minutes.
2. Have a large pot of boiling water ready to cook the lobsters. When the water comes to a boil, add 1 tablespoon sea salt, drop in the lobsters and cook them for 5 minutes, then plunge them into a sink filled with cold water. Remove and keep cold.
3. Place a lobster on a wooden board, head up. Using a 10-inch chef's knife, plunge the knife point directly into the lobster at the cross on its head. Split the lobster in half and crack the claws. Repeat with the second lobster. Place all the lobster pieces in a bowl and mix with the lemon juice, paprika and 1 tablespoon of the olive oil.
4. Cook the lobster halves on the *piastra,* flesh side down. Cover with a lid or a heatproof bowl. Cook for 5–8 minutes, or until the flesh is white, firm and springy to the touch.
5. Dress the arugula with the remaining teaspoon of olive oil and a pinch of sea salt and serve with the lobsters.

Serves 2–4

Grilled shrimp skewers with *cipolline* and *salsa verde*

A part of exploring the vast fish market in Porto Ercole is the daily perusal of the shrimp. There was a plethora of different varieties each day when I visited the market: striped or tiger, pink, gray, huge, small etc. It almost became a running joke: What type of shrimp spaghetti are we eating tonight? But of all the shrimp we had there, none was as good as the beautiful spot prawns from the Catalina Islands in California. Spot prawns are amazing, but fragile. They last only a day outside of water and don't last long even after they've been cooked. Their fragility, however, does not stand in the way of their almost spicy, briny flavor. They must have a delicious menu on the ocean floor.

Spot prawns, grilled whole and served with a grilled onion *salsa verde*, are perfection. If you can't find them or order them from your local fish store, shrimp make a worthy substitute.

8 *cipolline* (small flat onions originally from Umbria), peeled
2 tablespoons extra-virgin olive oil
Sea salt and freshly ground black pepper to taste

16 large shrimp, heads on
1 cup *salsa verde* (page 235)
4 bamboo skewers soaked in water for an hour

1. Preheat the oven to 375°.
2. Make a pouch out of aluminum foil and place the *cipolline*, 1 tablespoon of the olive oil and sea salt and black pepper inside. Seal and bake for 35 minutes. Let cool, peel the onions and save any juices from the pouch.
3. Thread each skewer with 4 shrimp.
4. Prepare a grill or broiler. Grill the shrimp about 3 minutes on each side. Serve with the onions and top with *salsa verde*.

Serves 4

Red snapper stuffed with olives and lemon

In the Mediterranean the closest fish to our red snapper is called an *orata.* There are other red snapper look-alikes and the rouget, if large, is similar. But *orata* is by far the closest cousin.

In America, red snapper is both an East Coast and Gulf fish. They love mangrove swamps. I was once out trolling near Islamorada when I spied fantastic schools of red snappers. They were the strawberry or rainbow variety, with beautiful markings. I don't know whether these markings have a culinary value, but they are gorgeous.

1 cup green olives, pitted
Juice of 2 Meyer lemons
4 tablespoons extra-virgin olive oil
Sea salt to taste

Two 2- to 3-pound red snappers,
    cleaned and gutted
2–4 bamboo skewers soaked in
    water for an hour

1. Preheat the oven to 375°.
2. Chop the olives and mix with the lemon juice, 1 tablespoon of the olive oil and sea salt. Fill the fish cavities with this mixture, and secure the openings with bamboo skewers.
3. Place the fish in a roasting pan, coat with the remaining 3 tablespoons of olive oil, season with sea salt and roast in the oven for 30 minutes.
4. Remove the pan from the oven and let the fish rest for 10 minutes. Remove the bamboo skewers. Serve the snappers whole. At the table, using a spoon, scoop out the filets. Spoon the olive stuffing over the filets and souse with the pan juices.

Serves 4

Skate with brown butter and *balsamico*

La razza (skate in Italian) is a wacky fish. We only consume the wings of a skate; the bodies have no value. The skin is tough, so it must be removed, and there is quite a bit of glutinous material that needs to trimmed, but the flesh itself is delicious. The main decision is whether to remove the bone. I tend to go by the size. If the wings are large, I remove the bone; if small (and because I'm a bit lazy), I leave them in.

There are two distinct cooking methods here. One is flour only; the other incorporates an egg wash as well. The batter remains the same: part organic stone-ground cornmeal and part good, wholesome King Arthur unbleached white flour. The corn creates the "crunch" factor, which I adore. If organic white stone-ground cornmeal is hard to find, by all means use a fine polenta, preferably white.

My lovely daughter at age three caught a beautiful ray in the intercoastal waters near Wrightsville, North Carolina, and exclaimed, "Daddy, he's too beautiful; let's let him go!" I would have liked to eat that beautiful ray, but she prevailed. In any case, the ray population is not in decline; in fact, with the overfishing of other species, it's in ascendance.

There is only a tiny amount of *balsamico* in this recipe. Please don't overdo it or the sauce will be cloying and sweet. A little goes a long way.

8 small skate wings (they will weigh about 2 pounds total)	½ teaspoon freshly ground black pepper
1 cup organic whole milk	2 large eggs
½ cup organic all-purpose flour	10 tablespoons (1¼ sticks) unsalted butter
½ cup organic stone-ground white polenta	½ cup extra-virgin olive oil
2 teaspoons sea salt	2 tablespoons *balsamico*

1. Wash and dry the wings and trim them if necessary. Keep cold. Have ready a 12-inch cast-iron skillet that will hold all the wings (or fry them in batches).
2. To prepare the crust mixture: You'll need 3 bowls. In one bowl, pour ½ cup of the milk. In another bowl, combine the flour and cornmeal plus 1 teaspoon of the sea salt and

the black pepper. In the third bowl, combine the 2 eggs with the remaining ½ cup of milk and the remaining teaspoon of sea salt and mix well.

3. Dip the wings in the milk, then place them in the flour mixture and coat well. Next, place them in the egg and milk mixture; then put them back in the flour for a second coating. Place them on a baking sheet.

4. Place the skillet over medium heat, add 4 tablespoons of the butter and ¼ cup of the olive oil. When the butter turns golden brown, add the wings skin side up and gently sauté until golden. Add the remaining olive oil, turn the wings over and cook until golden. Transfer the wings to a platter. Add the remaining butter and the *balsamico* to the pan. Off the heat, swirl together the butter and *balsamico* with the pan juices and pour over the skate.

Serves 4–6

Salmon steak, seared fennel and tarragon

The best wild salmon is the native American King salmon from Alaska. They appear around June each year. I pair them here with baby fennel, which grows wild at the same time. It is a good recipe for warm afternoons after school is out. Ask your butcher or fishmonger to cut the salmon into three-quarter-inch-thick steaks. They cook on the grill in about ten minutes.

2 pounds baby (or wild) fennel
Sea salt to taste
Eight ¾-inch-thick salmon steaks
1 tablespoon extra-virgin olive oil
Freshly ground black pepper to taste

8 tarragon sprigs
8 tablespoons (1 stick) unsalted butter
Juice of 1 lemon

1. Preheat the grill.
2. Wash, trim, core and shave the fennel. Place in a pot of cold water, season with sea salt and bring to a boil. Simmer for 5 minutes, then remove from the heat and drain.
3. Rub the salmon steaks with the olive oil, sea salt and black pepper.
4. Place the fennel, the tarragon leaves and butter in a saucepan.
5. Grill the steaks 3–4 minutes per side and, while they are cooking, heat the pan of fennel, tarragon and butter over the grill until the butter has melted to a saucelike consistency.
6. Remove the steaks to a platter, season with the lemon juice and add some to the fennel sauce. Garnish the steaks with the sauce.

Serves 8

Trout with hazelnuts

All the wonderful mountain regions of Italy—the Dolomites in the northeast, the Alps in the northwest, the Apennines in Abruzzi—have trout or *trota*. When I was an apprentice in the Vosges region of France, I had to secure live trout from the restaurant's freshwater pond upon command—not an easy task. Freshly caught trout are a revelation, but are extremely perishable, which is why smoked trout has become so popular. If you can buy fresh trout from a Chinese fish shop, they will do all the nasty cleaning for you.

These days it is quite easy to find trout filets, which are more acceptable to folks who hate those tiny bones.

This recipe is the essence of simplicity: trout, butter, hazelnuts, chives and lemon as a garnish. It is a terrific crowd-pleaser. I would serve a bit of warm polenta on the side and bottle of Pigato, the delicious white wine from Liguria.

4 small 10-ounce trout with heads on	2 cups raw hazelnuts
3 tablespoons extra-virgin olive oil	6 tablespoons (¾ stick) unsalted
Sea salt and freshly ground black	butter
pepper to taste	1 small bunch chives, minced
2 lemons	

1. Preheat the oven to 350°.
2. Wash the trout and pat dry with paper towels. Coat the trout with 1 tablespoon of the olive oil and season with sea salt and black pepper.
3. Cut 1 lemon into slices and juice the second lemon. Spread the hazelnuts on a baking sheet and roast for 6–8 minutes in the oven until golden brown. Remove them, then transfer to a clean kitchen towel and rub to remove the skins. Crush the hazelnuts lightly with a rolling pin or wine bottle so the pieces are crumbly.
4. In a large sauté pan, heat the remaining 2 tablespoons of olive oil and 4 tablespoons of the butter. Add the trout and cook for 3 minutes, then turn them over and cook 3 minutes more. Add the lemon slices to the pan so they absorb the fat and flavor the butter.
5. When the trout are done, transfer them to a platter. Add the remaining 2 tablespoons of butter and the hazelnuts and lemon juice to the pan. Stir in the chives, spoon the sauce over the trout and serve.

Serves 4

Char poached with aromatic vegetables and lemon dressing

Char is perhaps my favorite of all fishes. Called *Salmerino alpino* in Italy, it is a landlocked salmon that has evolved into a delicate, yet firm, fish, resembling an exceedingly elegant version of wild salmon. Wild char lives and feeds at great depths, so it has an amazing, earthy flavor. But it is now widely available as a farmed fish. I rail against fish farming, but the relatively small char industry has escaped the atrocities of farmed salmon so far. The fish feels strangely heavy and dense when you pick it up and has high omega-3 content. I recommend the wild version and have listed some sources on page 260. The main thing is how it's cooked. If it is very fresh, poaching is the only method that will do it justice. And because it is so meaty, poaching has an amazing effect. The meat becomes fork-tender, but not dry or cardboardlike. It can be poached and served cold (making it great for a really hot summer luncheon) and held in the poaching liquid until served. This is a noble fish.

2 carrots, peeled and diced
2 turnips, peeled and diced
4 new potatoes, peeled and diced
2 spring onions, sliced
4 radishes, trimmed and diced
1 cup white wine
2 cups cold water

2 sprigs parsley
4 char filets
Sea salt and freshly ground black
    pepper to taste
Juice of 1 lemon
4 tablespoons (½ stick) cold unsalted
    butter

1. Cook the carrots, turnips, potatoes, spring onions and radishes in simmering salted water until al dente, about 8 minutes. Drain and set aside.
2. Make a *court bouillon* with the wine, water and parsley. Boil for a minute, then simmer for 15 minutes. Strain out the parsley, reserving the liquid.
3. Place the vegetables and the filets in a poaching pan, add the *court bouillon,* season with sea salt and black pepper and cook gently for 8 minutes, or until the fish is done. Place the fish in a warm bowl.
4. Add the lemon juice and butter to the poaching liquid and bring to a boil. When the butter is melted and incorporated, pour over the fish and serve.

Serves 4

Halibut *alla milanese*

I love the cooking sensibility of northern Italy. One of the more ubiquitous techniques, especially in Lombardy and Piedmont, is coating foods with bread crumbs and eggs. That coating, which becomes second nature once you get the hang of it, is incredibly versatile. You can use it to cook anything from zucchini to a pig's foot. (I've always envied Mario Batali's pig's foot Milanese.)

Halibut has the perfect texture and meatiness to stand up to a coating of bread crumbs. Other fish might be overwhelmed or simply lost in the crunch, but halibut remains very moist even with a bit of overcooking. It can even be cooked ahead, then flash heated for a second before serving. Here's a chef's tip: Dip the steaks twice. Once in flour, then twice in the egg bath and bread crumbs. The coating will be crunchier and more substantial, the filets will be incredibly moist and the crust divine.

2 cups organic all-purpose flour

3 egg yolks

½ cup heavy cream

Sea salt to taste

Four 1-inch-thick halibut steaks (have your fishmonger cut the steaks across the whole fish)

2 cups fresh bread crumbs

8 tablespoons (1 stick) unsalted butter

¼ cup extra-virgin olive oil

Juice of 1 lemon

1. Pour the flour onto a plate. In a shallow bowl, mix the egg yolks with the cream and season with sea salt.
2. Dredge the steaks in the flour, then dip them in the egg yolk mixture (they can sit in the mixture for up to an hour), then dredge them in the bread crumbs. When fully coated, place them on a plate.
3. In a skillet large enough to hold the 4 steaks in a single layer, melt 4 tablespoons of the butter with the olive oil over medium heat, then add the steaks and cook until the coating is crispy and golden brown. Turn them over with a fish spatula. Add the remaining 4 tablespoons of butter and cook until crispy on the other side.
4. Put the steaks on a platter, swirl the lemon juice in the pan and drizzle the steaks with the cooking juices. Serve immediately.

Serves 4

Wild salmon baked in rock salt with tarragon and lemon

Salmon is an amazing creature. Freshwater fingerlings wander into the treacherous open ocean and fend against countless odds; then three years later, their life cycle finished, they return to the streams where they were hatched. I grew up hearing many myths of giant salmon leaping twenty feet over man-made dams to get to their spawning grounds. Those myths turned out to be mostly true, but we have fished the poor salmon into near extinction. To compensate, we have created penned farm salmon, which on paper seems a great idea, but in reality is science unchecked. I do not defend farmed salmon, organic or otherwise. With careful planning and a reduction of dams (or better, their removal), the noble salmon might return.

This recipe is based upon the rare appearance of a wild salmon at your market. Better yet, if you or someone you know goes fishing and brings back a salmon, well, that is the greatest glory.

Salmon has an amazing amount of fat. Good fat. So to exploit this, I love to roast salmon in rock salt. Bake it and then serve it with just lemon and great olive oil. The salmon is stuffed with beautiful herbs and lemons, plus some spices that create an aromatic balance that is intoxicating.

4 egg whites	1 orange, sliced
Two 1-pound boxes kosher salt	3 lemons, 1 sliced, 2 cut into wedges
One 4- to 5-pound salmon, salmon trout or char, cleaned and gutted	4 sprigs parsley
	1 small bunch basil
Sea salt and freshly ground black pepper to taste	4 tarragon sprigs
	Extra-virgin olive oil to taste

1. Preheat the oven to 375°.
2. In a very large bowl, whip the whites to soft peaks, add the kosher salt and mix well. Pour half the mixture into a large roasting pan.
3. Wash and dry the salmon. Season the interior with sea salt and black pepper and stuff with the sliced orange and lemon and the parsley, basil and tarragon.

4. Place the salmon on the salt in the roasting pan, then cover with the remaining salt and egg white mixture. Using your hands, pack the salmon so that it is completely covered. Place the salmon in the oven and roast for 40 minutes.

5. Remove the salmon and let it rest for 10 minutes. Gently lift off the salt shell using a spatula. Remove the top skin of the salmon (it will be too salty) exposing the salmon filet. Use a spoon and scoop out the salmon. When you reach the spine, remove it carefully. Continue lifting out the bottom filet. Serve with the lemon wedges and a dash of olive oil.

Serves 4–6

The neighborhood around Barbuto is the location of New York's wholesale meat markets, which for almost one hundred and twenty years have been operated mainly by Italian families. They hail from all over Italy and have thrived despite the influx of sleazy late-night activity, fashion houses, nightclubs and, yes, Italian restaurants. I love the fact that my daily order of meat arrives five minutes after master butcher Pat La Frieda has carefully carved, chopped and wrapped it up. If I need something in a hurry, I walk the few blocks and pick it up myself. While it is true that butchers, like fishmongers, are disappearing from the urban landscape, it is nice to see these guys operate as they have always done, moving whole sides of pork, lamb and beef on giant hooks to the craftsmen who carve the meat into our desired cuts.

Lately there has been a call for naturally raised grass-fed beef. I am all for it. I had naively pretended that all cattle were raised in beautiful open fields, grazing till the end of their days peacefully and without much human intervention. Not until recently did I become aware of the practices of large ranching conglomerates who use growth hormones, massive amounts of antibiotics, and weird feed (soybeans and other nonsense). I think we all need to purchase carefully—only from honest, old-fashioned ranchers who believe in hard work, natural grazing and humane butchery. In Italy, the small, regal herds of Chianina, Piemontese and Maremmana cows provide a naturally grass-fed product that is rich in heritage and long on taste. My first taste of that beef was in Florence many years ago when I sampled the very famous *bistecca fiorentina*. I went to Sabatini, the essential spot for this celebrated dish. And it was good, though not as good as I imagined it to be, nor as good as a T-bone from Grison's back home in San Francisco.

Over the years I have come to understand how to cook grass-fed beef.

American meat can be more marbled and tender, but European prime cuts similar to ours (rib eye, T-bone, strip steak) tend to be chewy and quite different in taste. European prime cuts need to be cooked rare, rather than medium, which will toughen the meat and render it inedible.

Lamb, too, is very different in America. We like our lamb chops big; in Europe they are about half the size, and in my opinion, sweeter and far more delicious.

A few years ago I spent a delightful spring holiday in Porto Ercole. My pal Craig and I decided to cook lamb one evening. We traipsed to the local butcher and quite unexpectedly he told us, "No lamb today, please come back next Wednesday!" Wednesday arrived, we hurried back and he handed us our package containing the lamb leg; my first thought was, "What the hell?" The package weighed about a pound (actually it was eight hundred grams). We paid our money and took it home. It had enough meat for one, and we were four hungry adults! The whole "baby" lamb probably had weighed about twelve pounds dressed. Laughing at our stupidity, I was reminded of how different food cultures can be. Perhaps more precisely, the American standard is different from the rest of the world. I adore our large T-bone steaks from corn-fed four-year-old cattle, but they are simply not the same thing as the Italian Piemontese two-year-old cattle raised solely on grass. England is probably closer to us than any other meat-producing nation, but Italy continues to do things as they have done for centuries. Not wishing to be a purist or a snob, I have tried to understand and create recipes that reflect my own experiences and tastes. These meat recipes are an amalgam of ideas and experiences from both sides of the Atlantic. And since I consider California a lost state of Italy, it is a very important part of the mix.

Leg of lamb braised for seven hours

We have a special table at Barbuto, the chef's table. It is made from two-hundred-year-old oak planks from a barn in Pennsylvania. The table was handmade on the spot so that we could fit it precisely to the space. It has an old church pew as a seat and a rough-hewn finish. People flock to it. We have one simple rule for diners at the table: the menu is up to us. One dish that we started serving early on was this leg of lamb. Braised for seven hours in a very slow oven, it has the consistency of butter. I think it is one the best ways to serve a lot of people easily without slaving your day away in the kitchen. It is a straightforward recipe, requiring little maintenance once it's in the oven. I like serving the lamb with wilted greens, polenta, cauliflower and fried potatoes. The sauce is divine! It can be used as a lamb *ragù* for pasta or for another lamb dish.

One 3- to 5-pound leg of lamb
Sea salt and freshly ground black
  pepper to taste
2 tablespoons extra-virgin olive oil
2 cups robust red wine

1 head garlic, broken into cloves
1 branch rosemary
3 cups cold water
3 tablespoons unsalted butter
2 tablespoons chopped fresh parsley

1. Preheat the oven to 350°.
2. Season both sides of the lamb with sea salt and black pepper.
3. In a roasting pan over high heat, heat the olive oil and then sear the lamb for 3 minutes on each side.
4. Add the wine, garlic, rosemary branch and water. Place in the oven, cover with aluminum foil and bake for 7 hours.
5. Remove the lamb. Place the meat on a cutting board. Strain the sauce through a mesh strainer into a small saucepan and add the butter and parsley. Season the sauce with sea salt and black pepper, if necessary. Slice the lamb and serve hot with the sauce.

Serves 4

Grilled T-bone lamb chops with rosemary and garlic

When I was growing up in Cotati, California, we raised lambs. The rich land is suitable for all types of crops, livestock and poultry, and since the late '60s, vineyards as well. Our little farm was mainly about chickens, but my grandparents always had a steer and thirty head of sheep. The lambs from this fantastic region are equal to any other in the world, though I don't remember ever having eaten one as a child.

A true spring lamb weighs about thirty pounds "dressed" or about sixty pounds in the pasture. I love to cook lamb whole, but roasting a leg is the closest thing to it in our home kitchen. The T-bones that are cut from the loin portion contain a little piece of the filet, the backbone and a nice meaty piece of the loin. Seek cuts at least two inches wide; any smaller and they will dry out on the grill or in the sauté pan. Here the T-bones are marinated in a simple red wine and garlic-rosemary marinade; this helps tenderize them and adds a nice flavor component.

In my years as a chef, I have been able to eat lamb around the world. I can unequivocally state that in Italy it is the simplest and perhaps the best. On my honeymoon, I researched a remote hotel near Assisi. It was just before the earthquake and my wife, Sally, and I visited the Duomo and were overwhelmed by the beauty of the Giottos. I hope the fates have been kind to those frescoes. Driving to the hotel we found ourselves on a steep dirt track. I thought we would pitch over the edge of the road any minute. We arrived late, and dinner was almost over. After being shown to our lovely room overlooking that narrow valley, we hurried to have a bite. The waitress asked us for our order and I said lamb. After unmemorable *primi* we were served sizzling crispy shoulder lamb chops, with rosemary butter and French fries. I have not had a better meal.

1 cup red wine

4 cloves garlic, 2 crushed, 2 minced

1 sprig rosemary plus 1 tablespoon chopped rosemary leaves

¼ cup plus 2 tablespoons extra-virgin olive oil

8 T-bone lamb chops

1 bunch spinach, stemmed and rinsed

Sea salt and freshly ground black pepper to taste

1. To make the marinade: Combine the wine, crushed garlic, rosemary sprig and ¼ cup of the olive oil. Marinate the chops for 2–4 hours in the refrigerator.
2. Prepare a grill.
3. In a skillet, heat the remaining 2 tablespoons of olive oil, the minced garlic and the spinach. Turn the heat to medium and cook slowly for 10 minutes, stirring occasionally. Season with sea salt and black pepper.
4. Brush the marinade off the chops, season with sea salt and black pepper and grill (I think 3–5 minutes per side, but you need not overcook! Test doneness by pressing with your index finger: raw=mushy; rare=soft but resilient; medium-rare=firm but still somewhat pliable; medium=firm; well done=dead). Serve with the spinach.

Serves 4

Hanger steak with *salsa piccante*

Ah, the kick-ass sauce! A grilled steak needs some kick and I love chilies. I like using Hatch chilies from New Mexico; their season is rather short but worth it. Fresno chilies also work well. I find they have a nice round flavor, medium heat and marry well with the sweet onions, *balsamico* and garlic. Hanger steak is sometimes called the "butcher's cut." It is an earthy, meaty steak that appeals to everyone who likes meat with texture. Skirt steak is a viable substitute, but rib eye is not (though I love rib eyes, they can be a bit fatty). The steaks are simply rubbed with sea salt and a generous amount of freshly ground black pepper. The trick is to sear the hell out them. No timidity here; let the cast-iron skillet do its duty. If it's summer, by all means use a charcoal grill. For a wine that sucks up the heat, choose a Barbera from Piedmont.

One 24-ounce hanger steak	1 sweet onion, peeled and chopped
Sea salt and freshly ground black	2 Hatch or red Fresno chilies
pepper to taste	1 tablespoon extra-virgin olive oil
3 cloves garlic	2 tablespoons *balsamico*

1. Preheat the oven to 375°.
2. Trim the steak and season with sea salt and black pepper. Bring it to room temperature.
3. To make the salsa: Put the garlic, onion, chilies and olive oil into a cast-iron skillet. Roast in the oven for about 10 minutes. Remove from the oven, deglaze with the *balsamico* and then purée everything in a food processor fitted with a metal blade until chunky.
4. Prepare a medium-hot grill. Sear the hanger until dark mahogany in color and crispy on all sides—this takes vigilance, but only about 8 minutes total. Hanger should be rare to medium-rare. Let the steak rest for 5 minutes, then slice.
5. Serve with the salsa.

Serves 4–6

Pork chops with *salsa rossa*

The world of pork has changed dramatically in my thirty-odd years of cooking. I remember the taste of pork chops of my youth—crispy, with luscious, crusty fat and tender at the bone. Then came the dark ages, from 1970 to about 1990, when all of a sudden, pork was lean, mean and nasty. Pork chops looked great but were dry, with little or no fat, and they had no flavor. Slowly, as the '90s progressed, I started seeing what we now call heritage farm pigs, which were raised on small farms and looked and tasted like pigs of old.

I have even sponsored some local pigs in Napa, and the 4-H boys proudly presented me with two one-thousand-pound pigs (for which I paid $3,000, all for a good and noble cause).

Now fantastic heritage pigs are more widely available. Tiny suckling pigs come in at one to twenty-five pounds; the thousand-pound behemoths are their giant cousins.

Four 10-ounce pork chops, cut from the rib section or called "center cut"

Sea salt and freshly ground black pepper to taste

2 tomatoes, diced

1 onion, peeled and diced

2 cloves garlic, smashed

¼ cup red wine vinegar

¼ cup extra-virgin olive oil

1 red Fresno chili

8 tablespoons (1 stick) unsalted butter

1. Season the pork chops with sea salt and black pepper. Place in the fridge for 2 hours or overnight. The salt will cure the meat slightly and the pepper will add flavor.

2. To make the salsa: Place the tomatoes, onion, garlic, vinegar, olive oil and chili in a food processor fitted with a metal blade and pulse until you have a nice, chunky sauce. Taste for seasoning and set aside.

3. Remove the pork chops from the refrigerator and bring them to room temperature. Melt 4 tablespoons of the butter in a heavy cast-iron skillet over medium-high heat and cook the chops for 6 minutes per side, until they're golden brown, register 150° in the interior and are pink, not gray, in color.

4. Remove the chops to a platter and keep warm. Add the salsa to the pan and heat through. Swirl in the remaining 4 tablespoons of butter and then pour 2 tablespoons of the salsa over each chop.

Serves 4

Porchetta

In the spring, festivals all over Italy celebrate this wonderful dish. I love to cook suckling pigs, but they're not widely available in America. So here is a nice compromise: pork loin that is cooked in the style of suckling pig. The trick is to use a nice piece of pancetta to moisten and flavor the meat. I like to add portobello mushrooms and garlic, which give amazing texture and flavor. Polenta makes a luscious accompaniment to this dish.

Two 12-ounce boneless pork loins,
    each with fat layer attached
Freshly ground black pepper to taste
2 cups whole milk
1 head garlic, broken into cloves
1 pound portobello mushrooms
1 shallot

1 tablespoon fresh thyme leaves
6 tablespoons (¾ stick) unsalted
    butter, at room temperature
½ pound diced pancetta
Sea salt to taste
Polenta (page 49), prepared without
    the mushrooms

1. The night before you make the dish, make a lateral incision to lift the fat cap of each pork loin. Season each loin liberally under the flap with black pepper and refrigerate overnight (this will flavor and tenderize the meat). The next day, preheat the oven to 400°.

2. Bring the milk to a simmer over medium heat and poach the garlic cloves for 5 minutes. This will eliminate their astringency. Let the garlic cool in the milk; then strain, reserving the milk and garlic separately.

3. Wash, dry and dice the portobellos. Peel and dice the shallot. Combine the mushrooms, shallot and garlic cloves in a bowl. Add the thyme and butter and mix well.

4. Add the diced pancetta to the portobello mixture. Remove the pork loins from the fridge and stuff the portobello mixture under the flaps. To secure the flaps, use toothpicks as anchors or use metal skewers (which are easier to remove).

5. Place the pork in a roasting pan and roast in the oven, basting often, for 1 hour, or until the center reaches 150°. The loins will turn a glorious brown. Remove from the oven, place the loins on a cutting board and let rest. Add the milk to the pan and deglaze the juices over low heat. Whisk the mixture until it makes a nice gravy. Taste for seasoning. Carve the loins at the table and serve with some polenta and the gravy.

Serves 4–6

Pork chop *alla milanese*

Veal *alla milanese,* that ubiquitous dish in Lombardy, is a hard commodity to find in America. Not only rare, but expensive and usually not organic or hormone free. Here I suggest using our magnificent heritage pork. It is meatier, moister and has great texture. If one doesn't know, they will think it's veal. I love anything cooked this way, so feel free to substitute chicken breasts, turkey, eggplant, etc. It's a fabulous cooking method.

Four 10-ounce bone-in pork chops
7 tablespoons plus 1 teaspoon
    extra-virgin olive oil
Sea salt
Freshly ground black pepper
1 loaf fresh country bread
1 cup organic all-purpose flour

3 large eggs
4 tablespoons (½ stick) unsalted
    butter
Juice of 2 lemons
3 cups arugula, washed and dried
2 tablespoons grated Parmesan

1. Place each pork chop in a separate large resealable plastic bag and, using a rolling pin, gently pound each chop until it is 8 inches in diameter. Coat each one with 1 teaspoon of the olive oil and season with sea salt and black pepper.

2. Remove the crust from the bread and cut the bread into 1-inch cubes. Using a blender or food processor fitted with a metal blade, pulse the cubes of bread into fine crumbs. Pour the crumbs into a paper bag.

3. Pour the flour in a large bowl and season with sea salt and black pepper. In another large bowl, beat the eggs with 1 teaspoon of sea salt and 1 tablespoon of the olive oil. Place the chops in the flour, dust them well and then dip each one into the egg mixture. Let the chops marinate in the egg for 1 hour, refrigerated.

4. Transfer the chops, one at a time, to the bread crumb bag. Close the bag and shake well to coat each chop thoroughly.

5. Place a cast-iron skillet large enough to hold 2 chops in a single layer over medium heat. Add 2 tablespoons of the olive oil and 2 tablespoons of the butter. When the mixture is golden brown, place 2 chops into it. Cook for 4 to 5 minutes on the first side. Using a thin spatula, gently turn over each chop. You may need to add another tablespoon or so of oil. Cook for 3 more minutes. Remove from the heat and transfer the chops to a

platter. Add the juice of 1 lemon to the fat in the pan, stir to deglaze and pour the juices over the chops. Wipe out the pan and repeat this process for the remaining chops.

6. In a serving bowl, toss the arugula with the Parmesan and 1 tablespoon of the olive oil. Add sea salt to taste. Serve a small mound on top of each chop.

Serves 4

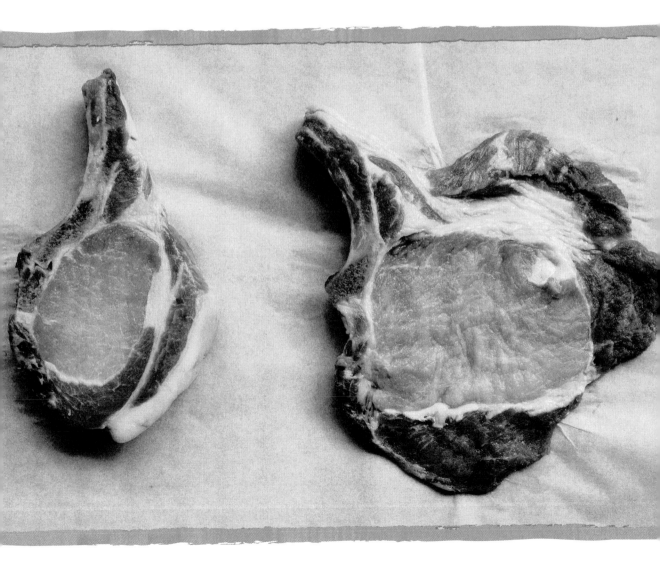

T-bone steak *ai ferri*

Everyone adores Florence—the museums, the architecture and of course the food. One restaurant loved by many is Cibrèo. It has two seating areas: one formal, the other casual. I enjoy the communal seating of the latter; it is my favorite way of eating in Italy. The dishes are contemporary in that the portions are sensible, not huge, and they have the right amount of seasoning.

The dish that always floors me is the T-bone. The unique flavor of the Chianina beef is hard to duplicate in America. It is a grass-fed cow, but it is still tender and juicy. The trick is to crisp the hell out of the steak quickly. *Ferri* means "grill" in Italian, literally the iron over the fire. The grill is the best cooking method, but the *piastra*, or griddle, is good as well. The broiler, too, is frankly the cleanest and least chancy—no splattered arms or hands. It is hot, absorbs all the grease and is the best method for making a steak crusty.

The natural *contorni* would be broccoli rabe and potatoes, but French fries work well, and I am partial to wilted greens. The sauce is simply good olive oil, sea salt and lemon; the beef needs nothing else.

Two 18-ounce T-bone steaks
3 cloves garlic, 1 split, 2 smashed
Sea salt and freshly ground black
 pepper to taste
1 pound Italian-style (square-leafed)
 spinach
¼ cup extra-virgin olive oil, plus
 more for serving

1 onion, peeled and diced
1 red Fresno chili, minced
¼ cup cold water
3 tablespoons unsalted butter
1 lemon

1. Rub the steaks with the split clove of garlic, sea salt and lots of black pepper. Let them sit at room temperature for an hour.
2. Prepare a charcoal grill.
3. Rinse the spinach 4 times and dry.
4. Heat the olive oil, onion, the 2 cloves of smashed garlic, the chili and spinach in a

large skillet over medium heat. Add the cold water and butter. Cook the spinach for 3 minutes, until wilted, and turn off the heat. Do not cover (it will go gray and lifeless).

5. Cook the steaks on the grill until they have a good crust on each side (in Florence they are always rare).

6. Serve with a bit of olive oil and the lemon cut into wedges, the spinach and black pepper.

Serves 2–4

Fegato di vitello con arancia

Venetian-style sautéed veal's liver is a dish that has quietly gone out of fashion, but I love it. Properly prepared it represents the soul of sophisticated Italian cookery. The exotic infusion is subtle, a touch of saffron and turmeric, raisins, garlic and orange zest. The spice of the red chilies is spectacular here.

The chef's trick is to slice the meat as thinly as possible. It really helps. If you are squeamish, have the butcher do it. The other trick is to keep the meat ice cold until you cook it.

Prepare the sauce ahead, almost as a condiment, then cook the liver and heat the sauce on the side. The onions are the foil here; they help lift the *fegato* into a mellifluous, soulful dish.

2 pounds fresh, not frozen, calf's liver

½ teaspoon saffron

½ teaspoon ground turmeric

½ teaspoon ground cinnamon

1 tablespoon raisins

1 blood orange

1 clove garlic, smashed

½ cup organic stone-ground white polenta

½ cup organic all-purpose flour

Sea salt and freshly ground black pepper to taste

1 teaspoon red pepper flakes

2 tablespoons unsalted butter

1 tablespoon extra-virgin olive oil

1 sweet onion, peeled and thinly sliced

1. If you are a complete novice, have a butcher show you how to peel the liver. It isn't hard; it is just a matter of practice (see Note).
2. Mix together the saffron, turmeric, cinnamon and raisins.
3. Zest the orange, then juice it.
4. In a small bowl, mix together the zest and juice of the orange and add the spices, raisins and garlic. Set aside.
5. Slice the liver into 6 very thin, 5-ounce pieces. In a paper bag, mix together the polenta and flour with the sea salt, some black pepper and the red pepper flakes. Toss the liver in the bag and dust off any excess coating.

6. In a large skillet, heat the butter and olive oil. Heat to medium-high, then sauté the liver until it is golden on each side (about 2 minutes per side). Remove the liver to a platter, add the onion and cook for 1 minute. Add the spice and orange mixture and cook another minute. Taste for seasoning and spoon over the liver. Scrumptious!

Note: Peeling a liver is akin to peeling the plastic off a child's toy—start at one end and gently tug off the filmy layer.

Serves 4–6

Lombardia-style pork ribs

On a soft autumnal night, in a gentle rain, my partner, Fabrizio Ferri, Gideon (his Irish wolfhound and Barbuto's mascot) and I traipsed to the Lombardia countryside just a few miles south of Milan. As is true in much of Italy, ten miles from the huge, bustling city, the relative tranquility of the pastoral rural neighborhood became the norm. We stopped at a country restaurant to have dinner. A table fit for ten (which suited Gideon just fine as he is about seven feet long stretched out) was ours for the night. We started with local *salumi*, then I had *riso al salto*. The *riso* was without parallel, but the ribs were magnificent. The chef explained that they were marinated, poached in a court bouillon, then reheated. He kind of lied, and it took me a year to replicate the recipe. Here is my rendition.

1 tablespoon each whole black peppercorns, anise seed, star anise, salt, cumin seed and red pepper flakes
2 cloves garlic
2 full pork spareribs (8 bones each)
¼ cup extra-virgin olive oil

2 heads Savoy cabbage
2 sweet onions
4 large carrots
8 cups chicken stock
Sea salt and freshly ground black pepper to taste

1. Three days before you serve the dish, grind all the dry spices and the garlic in a spice mill or blender.
2. Pat the pork dry with paper towels and rub with the spice mixture. Cover, place in the fridge and marinate for 3 days.
3. Prepare a grill.
4. Brush the spice rub off the ribs, pat dry, and brush them with the olive oil. Grill for 20 minutes on each side. Let cool.
5. Trim the cabbage and peel the onions and carrots and cut them into large chunks. Place the onions, carrots and ribs in a large pan and cover with the chicken stock. Bring to a simmer over low heat and cook for 1 hour. Add the cabbage and continue cooking until the meat is tender, about 1 hour more.
6. Taste for seasoning and serve hot!

Serves 6

My maternal grandmother spent her later years caring for chickens, ducks and other farm animals. She wore a bandanna wrapped around her head as she polished eggs for the market. I would help sometimes, holding eggs up to the light to ensure that there were no double zygotes or large flecks of blood. She would carefully sand the shells to remove any imperfections, and carefully pack them into the waiting cases.

She was a product of Brooklyn, the Bedford-Stuyvesant neighborhood. It had always been a diverse neighborhood; my mother's classmates in elementary school were like salt and pepper. She and her husband, Leo (a graduate of Cooper Union and an Army Corps engineer), were sent to the dusty fields of Sonoma after doctors discovered his eyesight was failing. In Sonoma they were promised a small farm for little money and a fast education in farming and animal (specifically chicken) husbandry. Their existence was sufficient to procure a simple car, a TV and some small creature comforts. They never went on vacation because there was no one else to care for the animals. They were farm-locked, yet they seemed happy.

But my grandmother was a terrible cook. Her idea of a well-cooked chicken was something reduced to scraps and bones. Maybe this is what influenced me to create my simple yet pure rendition of chicken.

The poultry dishes of Italy are the essence of simplicity, whether it is a duck roasted with black olives and kumquats and served with roasted rutabaga; a quail, gently grilled and served with fresh wine grapes; or a goose treated with an elegant rusticity. I discovered a delicious Guinea fowl in a small village outside of Florence many years ago that had been first roasted and then braised in a lovely cabbage and bean casserole. It was a nearly perfect dish, served in a little *agriturismo* (a small country house in Italy with a few rooms, where you dined with the family). That bird had flavor. The chickens of my youth had been okay, a bit stringy, certainly inoffensive, and yet they possessed nothing magical. I have re-created some recipes based on my travels in Italy, but more important, I think I am most influenced by the vision of my grandmother's bandanna.

JW chicken *al forno* with *salsa verde*

In the light of full disclosure, my JW chicken is neither one recipe, nor one dish. I have achieved a certain acclaim for it, but truth be told, the variations are many. The chicken that propelled the whole myth started at Jams in New York City. I was under the influence of my good friend Larry Forgione, one of the masterminds of the American culinary revolution. His desire to seek out small farmers has blossomed into a movement. Among the people he has cultivated was a biologist turned chicken farmer named Paul Kayser. Paul's passion for raising a bird equal to the noble *poularde de Bresse* in France was infectious. And his chickens were fantastic.

A major component of my success is the esoteric wood oven we use at Barbuto. I designed it with a pizza oven on top and a massive grill below. It's very versatile; we cook anything from fish to desserts in it, and the oven is the perfect place to roast the JW chicken. We use a Pennsylvania natural chicken, butterfly it (that is, we remove the backbone with kitchen shears), then spread it with olive oil and roast at a high temperature. These steps are easy to duplicate at home. The only extra piece of equipment you might want is an oval sizzle platter. You can order these at any good kitchen-supply house. They are standard restaurant equipment and enable you to fire-blast the chicken, giving it a crispy skin and succulent, perfectly moist meat.

The last bit of good news is the *salsa verde,* which is incredible. We serve it on scallops, lamb, pizza, and with vegetables. It is addictive!

One 4-pound free-range organic
   chicken (fresh only)
Sea salt and freshly ground black
   pepper to taste

¼ cup extra-virgin olive oil
1 lemon
Salsa verde (page 235)

1. Preheat the oven to 450°.
2. Wash the bird in hot water (this will remove any nasty juices that collect in the plastic wrap that all chickens seem to come in). Dry with paper towels.
3. Using kitchen shears, cut out the backbone of the chicken and remove any fat (these can be added to a chicken stock, page 218). Then, using a heavy chef's knife, cut out the breastbone. Season the 2 halves with sea salt and black pepper.

4. Place the chicken halves, skin side up, on 2 sizzle platters and dab with the olive oil. Cut the lemon in half and place a half, cut side down, next to the chicken on each platter.

5. Roast the chicken for 35 minutes, basting every 10 minutes. If it is not browning well, turn it over after 15 minutes, and then right it for the last 5 minutes. When it is done, remove the chicken to a platter and pour off the excess fat. Cut each breast in half and cut the thigh from the leg. Serve with *salsa verde* and garnish with the roasted lemon.

Serves 4

Quail with Concord grapes

The season for Concord grapes is late August and September. These gorgeous purple beauties are native to New York. They are extremely juicy (beware—the juice will stain) and taste phenomenal. I love roasting them for a couple of minutes to burst the skins and marry the juice with the quail's natural juices.

Callipepla californica (quail) is the state bird of California. They require some work to taste really great (they can be a bit bland), and a marinade works wonders.

4 semi-boneless quail (frozen are okay)

¼ cup white wine

1 tablespoon walnut oil

2 tablespoons extra-virgin olive oil

3 cloves garlic, smashed

2 bunches grapes (Concord are preferable, but seedless green or red grapes can be substituted)

Sea salt and freshly ground black pepper to taste

½ cup chicken stock

6 tablespoons (¾ stick) unsalted butter

1. The day before you make the dish, marinate the quail. In a bowl, combine the wine, walnut oil, olive oil, garlic and 10 grapes that you have crushed slightly. Add the quail, cover and refrigerate overnight.
2. The next day, preheat the broiler.
3. Remove the quail from the fridge and discard the marinade. Pick and wash the remaining grapes, place in a bowl and set aside.
4. Place the quail in a broiling pan and season them on all sides with sea salt and black pepper. Broil the quail 3 minutes per side, or until very browned and cooked through. Put the pan on the stovetop, remove the quail to a platter and keep warm. Add the grapes and the chicken stock to the roasting pan and cook over high heat for 2 minutes, then add the butter. Season with sea salt and black pepper and then pour the sauce over the quail and serve.

Serves 4

Squab with soft polenta and game sauce

I love squabs, which are immature pigeons. They have a truly wonderful skin, with a good amount of fat that crisps beautifully. I have cooked squabs many ways; here they are roasted whole at high temperature. The heat browns the skin, and after a good fifteen-minute rest, the meat is tender and moist. Soft polenta is a traditional accompaniment.

The game sauce is enriched by the addition of Saba, a syrup derived from wine grapes. The sauce is delicious and quite easy to make. The croutons added at the last minute add crunch and flavor.

1 loaf *ciabatta* (page 38)

4 cloves garlic

1 tablespoon extra-virgin olive oil

Sea salt and freshly ground black pepper to taste

Four 1-pound squabs

2 onions, peeled and chopped

¼ pound button mushrooms

8 tablespoons (1 stick) unsalted butter

¼ cup *balsamico*

¼ cup Saba

½ cup red wine

Polenta (page 49), prepared without the mushrooms

1. Preheat the oven to 325°.
2. To make the croutons: Cut the bread into ½-inch cubes and put on a rimmed baking sheet with the garlic cloves. Toast in the oven until golden. Place the croutons in a bowl with the olive oil and toss well. Season with sea salt and black pepper and set aside.
3. Wash and dry the squabs with paper towels. Season with sea salt and black pepper.
4. To make the sauce: Cook the onions and mushrooms in a saucepan with 2 table-spoons of the butter until nicely browned. Deglaze the pan with the *balsamico*, stir in the Saba, season and swirl in 4 tablespoons of the butter.
5. Increase the oven temperature to 450°.
6. In a roasting pan on the stovetop, heat the remaining 2 tablespoons of butter and

brown the birds, breast side down, until golden, turn them over and place them in the oven. Roast for 10 minutes. Take the squabs out of the oven, transfer to a platter and keep them warm.

7. Deglaze the pan with the red wine, stirring and scraping up any browned bits. Add this mixture to the mushroom sauce. Cut the squabs into quarters and coat with the sauce. Sprinkle with the garlic croutons and serve with polenta.

Serves 4–6

Guinea fowl braised with cannellini beans and Savoy cabbage

Here is a dish that I found in an *agriturismo* one lonely night in a tiny village near Florence. The fowl had been roasted and braised, then refrigerated and they were reheated while I nibbled on almonds and olives, drank a simple Sangiovese and read a book. It arrived, cut up into small pieces with the soft, succulent beans. I had some fresh goat's milk cheese and then I was off to recover the trail to my friends' house. The next day we headed to Grosseto di Mare to enjoy the beach and pizza. But the taste of that dish lingered. I couldn't wait to try to duplicate it at home.

2 cups cannellini beans	2 carrots, peeled and cubed
One 3-pound Guinea fowl	2 stalks celery, diced
1 tablespoon extra-virgin olive oil	3 ounces pancetta, diced
Sea salt and freshly ground black	7 cups cold water
pepper to taste	1 bay leaf
1 onion, peeled and cubed	2 tomatoes, diced
3 cloves garlic	1 head Savoy cabbage, sliced

1. Place the beans in a large pot, cover with 2 inches of cold water and soak overnight.
2. Wash and dry the Guinea fowl and cut into 10 small pieces using a cleaver or large knife: Split the Guinea fowl in half. Separate the breast from the leg. Separate the thigh from the leg. Cut both breasts into 3 equal pieces.
3. Heat the olive oil in a large heavy pan. Season the pieces with sea salt and black pepper and sauté until dark golden brown.
4. Remove the fowl to a platter and add the onion, garlic, carrots, celery and pancetta to the pan. Brown lightly, then add 2 cups of the cold water and return the bird to the pan. Bring to a boil, then reduce to barely a simmer, cover and cook for an hour. Remove from the heat and cool.
5. While the Guinea fowl is cooking, make the beans. Drain the beans and discard the soaking liquid, place them in a large pot with the bay leaf and cover with 5 cups of

cold water. Bring to a boil, then reduce to a bare simmer and cook for 25 minutes, or until tender.

6. When the beans are tender, add the tomatoes and cabbage. Cook until the cabbage is wilted. Season well with sea salt and black pepper.

7. Reheat the Guinea fowl stew. Spoon the beans and cabbage onto a platter, then spoon the stew on top. Serve hot.

Serves 4–6

Guinea fowl with chestnuts

Italians have been cultivating these delicious birds since the days of Rome, when they were more popular than their cousins, chickens and ducks. I find them richer and better tasting than chickens. They have a much gamier flavor, which you can lessen simply by aging them for two days in the fridge. They weigh only about one and a half to two pounds so they cook quickly. They also make a tremendous stock, which you can use for many things. It is hearty and soulful, and the sauce made from it, exquisite.

1 pound fresh chestnuts
1 onion, peeled and diced
2 carrots, peeled and diced
1 stalk celery, diced
6 cloves garlic
11 tablespoons unsalted butter

1 Guinea fowl
Sea salt and freshly ground black
   pepper to taste
1 cup Barbera wine

1. Preheat the oven to 400°.
2. Make a crosshatched incision on the bottom of each chestnut. Place the chestnuts in a roasting pan and roast for about 15 minutes, or until the peel comes off easily.
3. Place the onion, carrots, celery, garlic and the chestnuts in a stovetop-safe roasting pan or a casserole. Add 3 tablespoons of the butter and sauté over medium heat for 5 minutes, or until the vegetables are just cooked. Make a space in the pan and place the Guinea fowl in the middle of the vegetables. Top the Guinea fowl with 2 tablespoons of the butter and season with sea salt and black pepper.
4. Pour the wine into the pan, add 2 tablespoons of the butter and place it in the oven for 45 minutes; you will need to baste every 10 minutes. When the bird is golden brown, remove it from the oven and place on a serving platter or cutting board. If the pan juices are runny, place the roasting pan over medium heat to reduce the liquid. If not, add the remaining 4 tablespoons of butter and season with sea salt and black pepper. Carve the fowl and serve with the sauce and vegetables.

Serves 4

Chicken Piedmont-style

Here is a classic breading that I love. The crispiness of the finished product is really amazing. This is an adult version of chicken fingers. A nice *contorni* would be fried polenta.

4 large, very fresh boneless, skinless
    chicken breasts
6 tablespoons extra-virgin olive oil
Sea salt
Freshly ground black pepper to taste
1 loaf fresh country bread

1 cup organic all-purpose flour
3 large eggs
2 pomegranates
1 head red cabbage
6 tablespoons (¾ stick) butter

1. Coat the breasts with 1 tablespoon of the olive oil. Season with sea salt and black pepper.

2. Remove the crust from the bread and cut the bread into 1-inch cubes. Let dry for 1 hour at room temperature. Place in a blender or food processor and pulse into fine crumbs. Pour about 3 cups into a paper bag.

3. Pour the flour into a large bowl. Season with sea salt and black pepper. In another large bowl, beat the eggs, 1 teaspoon sea salt and 1 tablespoon of the olive oil. Dredge the breasts in the flour, then place them in the egg mixture and marinate for 1 hour in the fridge.

4. Transfer the chicken breasts, one at a time, to the bread crumb bag. Close the bag and shake well to coat the breasts thoroughly. Repeat with the remaining 3 breasts. Transfer to a plate.

5. Seed the pomegranates into a bowl. Core and finely slice the cabbage.

6. Place a heavy skillet large enough to hold the breasts in a single layer over medium heat. Add 2 tablespoons of the olive oil and 4 tablespoons of the butter. When the mixture is golden brown, add the chicken breasts. Cook 4–5 minutes, then turn over. Cook for 3 more minutes, until golden brown. Transfer the breasts to a platter.

7. Add the remaining 2 tablespoons of olive oil and 2 tablespoons of butter to the pan and cook the cabbage for a few minutes until tender. Stir in three-quarters of the pomegranate seeds.

8. Place the breasts in a warm oven for 3 minutes to reheat. Put the cabbage on the platter and put the breasts on top. Decorate with the remaining pomegranate seeds and serve.

Serves 4

Coniglio al vino bianco

Rabbit is well-known in Italian cookery. The taste is mild and delicious. It has started to be more popular in the United States, but a certain social stigma prevents more people from enjoying it. The bones make an incredible sauce, the meat is hard to overcook and it roasts quickly and beautifully. Marinate the rabbit overnight, which helps bring out its intrinsic flavor and imbues the meat with a bit of acidity and the aroma of garlic and wine. I like to serve this dish with polenta (page 49) and arugula salad (page 10).

1 large fresh rabbit
1¼ cups white wine
2 tablespoons extra-virgin olive oil
4 fresh sage leaves
4 sprigs parsley
2 carrots, peeled and diced
2 onions, peeled and diced
4 cloves garlic
8 tablespoons (1 stick) unsalted butter

Sea salt and freshly ground black pepper to taste
1 cup cold water
Bouquet garni: 2 bay leaves, stems from 1 small bunch of parsley, 2 sprigs thyme, 1 tablespoon black peppercorns and 2 cloves garlic, bound in cheesecloth

1. With a cleaver, cut the rabbit into 8 pieces or have your butcher do it for you. Place in a bowl and add ¼ cup of the wine, the olive oil, sage, parsley, ¼ cup each of the carrots and onions, and 2 cloves of the garlic. Toss well, cover with plastic wrap and refrigerate overnight.
2. The next day, remove the rabbit pieces and dry them. Discard the marinade.
3. In a large skillet or casserole, heat 6 tablespoons of the butter. Season the rabbit with sea salt and black pepper, and sauté the pieces until golden. Add the remaining carrots, onions and garlic and continue to cook until the vegetables are colored. Add the remaining cup of wine, the water and the bouquet garni. Cook, covered, for 1 hour.
4. The rabbit should be perfectly cooked, or tender, at this point. Cut off a small piece to taste. Remove the bouquet garni. Add the remaining 2 tablespoons of butter and taste for seasoning. Serve.

Serves 4

Roast duckling with dates, black olives, small onions and kumquats

Here is a simple and effective method for extracting the great flavors of a duck and not sweating the details. At Chez Panisse many years ago, Jean-Pierre Moullé would laboriously fuss over sixty fat-laden ducks in the ovens, while they furiously spat fat and grease. He always wore short pants and was as determined a cook as I have ever seen. After roasting, he would carefully dump out all their collected fat. He would carve the ducks beautifully and garnish them with a fantastic red wine elixir he had prepared over the previous few days from duck bones and good red wine. I was mesmerized.

Here is a much simpler version of Jean-Pierre's mastery. I like the ducks from Bell & Evans; they remind me of the Nantais strain from the Loire Valley, perhaps the best ducks in the world. A nice *contorni* would be wilted kale and *pepperoncini* (page 130).

One 5-pound Bell & Evans duckling, fresh if possible
Sea salt and freshly ground black pepper to taste
1 pound *cipolline* (small flat onions originally from Umbria), peeled

½ cup fresh pitted dates
½ cup pitted black olives
½ cup kumquats
2 cups good red wine
2 cups chicken stock
2 tablespoons unsalted butter

1. Preheat the oven to 400°.
2. Wash the duck in hot water, remove the innards and the excess fat from the cavity and pat dry with paper towels. Season with sea salt and black pepper.
3. Bring a 2-quart pot of water to a simmer and gently poach the onions for 3 minutes.
4. In a roasting pan, place the duck, breast side up, and roast for 20 minutes, basting frequently.
5. Add the poached onions, the dates, olives and kumquats to the pan and continue cooking for about 30 minutes.
6. Place the duck on a warm platter and cover. With a slotted spoon, scoop the fruit

and onions out of the roasting pan and set aside. Carefully pour off the excess grease. Place the roasting pan on the stovetop, add the wine and stir, scraping up any brown bits that have adhered to the bottom of the pan.

7. When the wine has reduced to half its original volume, add the stock and cook until it has been reduced to about ¾ cup. Return the dates, olives, kumquats and onions to the pan. Stir in the butter and add some black pepper.

8. Carve the duck or cut with poultry shears. Place the cut pieces in the roasting pan and heat for 3 minutes. Serve in the roasting pan with the sauce.

Serves 4–6

Stewed chicken with Meyer lemon, garlic and white wine

Here is a New York City chicken dish that is ubiquitous in the old-time Italian joints, from Rao's to Carmine's, from Patsy's to Tommaso's. The dish varies from house to house; some call it *pollo scarpariello,* others call it *cacciatore* (hunter's style)—whatever the name, the dish should be clean, heartwarming and simple. Here is a very quick, delicious version.

1 large roasting chicken
3 tablespoons extra-virgin olive oil
Sea salt and freshly ground black
   pepper to taste
1 sweet onion, peeled and sliced
8 cloves garlic, sliced

1 cup Vermentino or similar dry
   white wine
Juice of 2 Meyer lemons
3 tablespoons unsalted butter
Poached Arborio rice (page 236), to
   serve

1. To cut up the chicken: Remove the legs and, using a cleaver, cut the legs from the thighs and cut the thighs in half, following the thighbone. Remove the breast and cut it into 3 sections.
2. In a very large ovenproof skillet, heat 2 tablespoons of the olive oil to medium. Season the chicken pieces with sea salt and black pepper and sauté, skin side down, until very well browned (about 10 minutes). Turn them over, and when all the pieces are browned, remove them and keep warm.
3. Add the onion and garlic and brown them, then add the wine and the juice of 1 lemon. Return the chicken to the pot, cover, and cook over low heat for 40 minutes. The chicken will have absorbed most of the pan juices.
4. Place the chicken pieces on a platter. Add the butter and the remaining lemon juice to the pan juices and scrape up any browned bits. Taste for seasoning, then spoon the sauce over the chicken. Serve hot with the poached Arborio rice.

Serves 4

Goose for Christmas

Here is a really scary beast. Most cooks have never cooked a goose, but we all secretly desire to try. I attempted to cook my first one in Paris with some expats one really cold and miserable Christmas in 1976. I had waited too long to procure one from the Saint-Sulpice market, so I went to a butcher in Les Halles. A little, grimy, sad fellow returned with the sorriest excuse for a goose I'd ever seen. "Oh well," I sighed, and paid way too many francs. I left somewhat disheartened. And, no, it was not good.

One gray day a few years ago in the hills near Barbaresco, in Piedmont, I was with a group of Slow Food wine tasters. We stopped to taste some wine with the dapper Moccagatta brothers. The house was a large, conventional Piedmontese structure with a terracotta roof, yet one would never have expected a winery lurking inside. I walked around the back to check the grapes and vineyards, and discovered two old farts. One was holding a tremendous goose in his chubby arms and the other was attempting, quite unsuccessfully, to sever its head from the body. At that moment the girls in our group arrived; the shrieks, mixed with the sorry bleeping of the goose, made for a dreadful but funny scene. Later on that trip we had some deep-fried and breaded goose liver and some lovely roasted goose.

Here is my version of the dish. One could substitute two large chickens, but it's not the same, is it?

One 8-pound fresh goose	1 tablespoon extra-virgin olive oil
1 onion, peeled and sliced	2 tablespoons unsalted butter
6 cloves garlic	2 tablespoons grated Parmesan
2 cups red wine	Freshly ground black pepper to taste
Sea salt to taste	4 russet potatoes
4 cups cold water	4 branches tarragon
1 butternut squash	

1. Remove the fat from the neck and cavity of the goose. Place the fat into a 2-quart pot and cover with cold water. Bring to a simmer and cook for 1 hour, then skim off the fat and discard the water. Put the fat in the refrigerator until ready to use.
2. Remove the gizzards and place them in another saucepan with the onion and garlic. Add the wine and simmer for 1 hour. Strain and set aside.

3. Preheat the oven to 375°.

4. Wash and dry the goose and rub the skin with sea salt. Place in a roasting pan and pour 1 cup of the water over the goose. Roast for 8 minutes per pound, or about 1 hour; turn the heat down to 325° and roast for another hour, basting often. The goose will be a lovely brown.

5. Cut the squash in half. Rub with olive oil and sea salt, and roast, cut side down, beside the goose for the remaining hour at 325°. When the squash is tender, remove from the pan and let cool. Scoop out the flesh and place in a pot over medium heat. Add the butter and Parmesan and season with black pepper.

6. Peel and dice the potatoes. Place in a saucepan with 3 cups of water and boil for 10 minutes. Drain and pat dry.

7. In a large skillet, melt the reserved goose fat. Add the potatoes and sauté for about 35 minutes, or until golden brown. Remove, season and keep warm.

8. Remove the goose from the oven and let rest for 30 minutes to 1 hour before carving. Pour off the fat (for later). Deglaze the pan with the red wine stock, stirring and scraping up any browned bits from the bottom of the pan. Add the branches of tarragon and reduce the sauce to 1 cup. Strain and place in a sauceboat.

9. Carve the goose and serve with the sauce, potatoes and squash.

Serves 6–8

Ah, sweet Italy! *La dolce vita di Italia.* Picture a ripe peach, split in two, drizzled with peach-blossom honey and served with a dollop of peach *sorbetto.* Or a red wine–flavored cannoli filled with sheep's milk ricotta studded with bitter chocolate. The best dessert I can imagine is a bowl of freshly picked wild raspberries, a dollop of mascarpone sweetened with a bit of sugar and a sprinkle of amaretti.

The beauty of desserts, Italian style, is their intrinsic simplicity. The Italian markets hold a bounty of gorgeous raw products, from chestnuts and amazing eggs to wild blueberries, strawberries and sumptuous melons. Occasionally in some of the older *pasticcerie* you'll find candied fruits galore or 1950s-era pastries, but on the whole, Italians prefer the rustic. Their desserts are never elaborate or silly.

The art of pastry in Italy is ancient. In the guilds established in Italy, most importantly in Florence in the twelfth to eighteenth centuries, the baker's art was coupled with that of master artists such as painters and sculptors. The de' Medicis threw lavish banquets and parties at which the crowning glories were huge masterpieces of marzipan, fresh fruit, ice creams, flowers and even live birds.

Under all this excess was a sound basis in technique. As Giuliano Bugialli correctly points out, the ethereally light cake named *génoise* in French is a Ligurian concoction. Soufflés probably originated in Italy, and elaborate sugar work was most likely a product of those guilds.

What does this have to do with my food? The sheer magnitude and density of this culinary history can leave one with a sense of awe, but better yet, one can glean contemporary ideas from the past. The glory of gelato, which has been handed down to us and refined to perfection, is something we take for granted. But the history of gelato reveals that it took five hundred years to achieve the scrumptious *gianduja* gelato that you find everywhere in Italy. The intensity of flavor is unlike anything in America. Why? We use too many eggs. Italian gelaterias have the right proportions of cream and milk, so the flavor of the fresh fruit shines through. Perhaps that ripe peach sums it all up: Search out the best sugar, flour, eggs, chocolate, nuts and fruits, treat them simply and well and you will be rewarded.

Budino

Chocolate pudding is one of the most satisfying American desserts, and the Italians have been producing an intense bittersweet chocolate *budino* for centuries. I think that sometimes people eat at Barbuto solely for the *budino*: we serve literally thousands a year. It is drop-dead easy. Feel free to experiment with flavorings. A dash of grappa makes it sparkle, a touch of Grand Marnier applies a bit of elegance and a sprinkle of lemon zest brightens the flavor. I like to add a bit of cinnamon and anise to perk up the chocolate. Served with whipped cream and a cookie, it is almost nirvana.

8 ounces bittersweet chocolate	1½ teaspoons unsalted butter
1 ounce milk chocolate	Pinch of sea salt
2 cups heavy cream	¼ teaspoon pure vanilla extract
6 large egg yolks	Unsweetened whipped cream, for
6 tablespoons sugar	serving

1. In a bowl, over simmering water or in a double boiler, melt the chocolates. Set aside.
2. In a heavy stainless-steel saucepan set over medium heat, warm the cream, but don't let it boil. In a small bowl, whisk together the yolks and sugar. Pour about half of the hot cream into the yolks, whisking constantly.
3. Pour the cream and yolk mixture into the saucepan of hot cream and cook over medium-low heat, stirring constantly with a rubber spatula, until the custard coats the spatula, about 10 minutes. Strain through a fine-mesh sieve, stir in the butter and chill in the refrigerator for 30 minutes to cool slightly.
4. Whisk the custard into the melted chocolate, a little at a time. The mixture will seize up and become a bit lumpy at first, but as you add more of the custard it will smooth out to a puddinglike consistency. Whisk in the sea salt and vanilla. Add any additional flavorings at this point, if you like.
5. Pour the pudding into a serving bowl. Place a piece of plastic wrap directly on top of the *budino* to prevent a skin from forming as it cools. Chill in the refrigerator for several hours. Serve with unsweetened whipped cream.

Serves 4–6

Torta al limone

Here is a recipe adapted by my first chef at Barbuto, Lynn McNeely, from a recipe by master baker Flo Braker. I love the cake's incredibly moist and vibrant texture and healthy amount of acidity. The addition of marzipan lends a nutty-sweet flavor that is delicious and elusive. I like serving the cake with whipped cream and a little lemon-flavored syrup. It keeps well for two weeks in the fridge and freezes well. It also makes great toast in the morning and is a wonderful base for strawberry shortcake.

CAKE

1 cup cake flour

1 teaspoon baking powder

¼ teaspoon sea salt

2½ ounces almond paste

1 cup (2 sticks) unsalted butter,
    at room temperature

¾ cup sugar

2 large eggs, at room temperature

1 tablespoon lemon zest

1½ teaspoons pure vanilla extract

LEMON SYRUP

½ cup lemon juice

1 cup sugar

Zest of 1 lemon

———

Whipped cream, to serve

Fresh fruit, to serve

1. Preheat the oven to 350°. Butter and flour an 8-inch round cake pan.
2. Sift the flour, baking powder and sea salt into a large mixing bowl.
3. In the bowl of an electric mixer, using the paddle attachment, break up the almond paste on medium-low speed. Alternate adding the butter and sugar, a little at a time, stopping frequently to scrape down the sides of the bowl with a rubber spatula. When all the butter and sugar have been added, increase the speed to medium-high and cream the mixture until light and fluffy. Add the eggs very slowly, so the batter doesn't break, and beat in the lemon zest and vanilla. Remove the bowl from the mixer and stir in the dry ingredients.
4. Pour the batter into the prepared pan. Bake for 30–40 minutes, or until the surface is deep golden brown and the edges have shrunk away from the pan slightly. Let

cool, then tap the bottom and sides to loosen the cake, and invert to remove from the pan.

5. To make the syrup: Combine the lemon juice and sugar in a small saucepan. Bring just to a boil, then remove from the heat and strain through a fine-mesh sieve. Stir in the lemon zest and set aside.

6. Serve the cake with whipped cream, a drizzle of lemon syrup and fresh fruit.

Serves 6–8

Zuppa inglese

"English soup" is a classic vanilla cream custard topped with gorgeous little floating islands of meringue. It is a very easy recipe that can be made in advance. In fact, I prefer to let the "soup" sit overnight; it develops a superior texture and flavor in the fridge. The vanilla custard is also a master recipe for ice cream. It will keep for a week in the fridge, and you can add your favorite ice cream flavorings directly to the custard.

8 large eggs, separated	3 tablespoons cold water
1½ cups plus 2 tablespoons sugar	Pinch of sea salt
1 vanilla bean, split	¼ cup toasted slivered almonds
1 cup whole milk	1 pint raspberries
½ cup heavy cream	

1. To make the custard: Briskly whisk together the 8 egg yolks and ½ cup of the sugar in a stainless-steel saucepan. Scrape the seeds from the vanilla bean and place the seeds, pod, milk and cream into another pan over medium heat. When the mixture is hot, slowly whisk it into the yolks. Turn on the heat under the yolk mixture and cook gently for 4–5 minutes, stirring constantly. As soon as the custard thickens, turn off the heat. Do not allow the custard to boil. Strain through a fine-mesh sieve and refrigerate until ready to use.

2. To make the caramel: Combine 1 cup of the sugar and the 3 tablespoons of cold water in a small copper saucepan. Without stirring, bring to a boil and cook until the syrup is light gold in color; then turn off the heat and set aside.

3. Bring a large pot of water to a simmer.

4. To make the floating islands: In a copper bowl using a whisk, or with an electric mixer, whip the 8 egg whites with the sea salt. When soft peaks form, slowly add the 2 tablespoons of sugar and whip until stiff. With a large spoon, form the meringue into quenelles, carefully float the quenelles in the simmering water and poach for about 2 minutes. Pour the chilled custard into a large bowl, top with the meringue quenelles and drizzle the quenelles with the caramel. If the caramel has thickened too much to pour, return the pan to the heat for a few minutes.

5. Top with toasted almonds and raspberries.

Serves 6–8

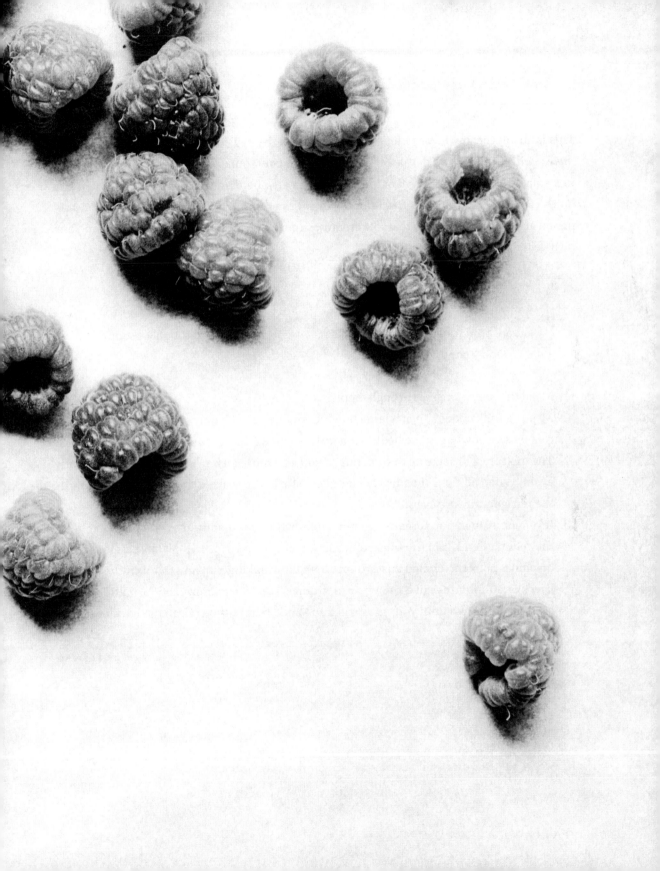

Gelato *gianduja*

This is absolutely my favorite ice cream. Its base is the egg custard recipe from the *zuppa inglese* with the addition of toasted hazelnuts and good milk chocolate. It can be churned in a small-batch home ice cream maker, but can also be made in a freezer tray if you stir up the cooling custard every five minutes or so, as you would for granita. You will be surprised at how much fun it is to make creamy, superior ice cream. You'll want to open your own gelateria!

1 recipe *zuppa inglese*, warm (page 197)

6 ounces high-quality milk chocolate, roughly chopped

⅛ teaspoon sea salt

1 cup hazelnuts (or almonds), toasted and roughly chopped

1. Make the *zuppa inglese* through step 1.
2. Melt the milk chocolate in a large bowl set over a pot of barely simmering water; then remove the bowl from the heat. Stir a little of the warm *zuppa* into the milk chocolate. The mixture will seize up at first, but as you add more custard, it will become smooth again. When all the *zuppa* has been added, stir in the sea salt and chill the mixture in the refrigerator for several hours.
3. If you are using an ice cream machine, follow the manufacturer's directions to churn the gelato, then stir in the toasted hazelnuts at the end. If you don't have an ice cream machine, pour the chilled custard into a shallow baking pan and put it in the freezer. Every 5–10 minutes, give the custard a quick stir to minimize the formation of ice crystals. Continue until your gelato is thick and creamy, then stir in the hazelnuts and allow to harden.

Serves 4–6

Brutti malfatti

The name means "ill formed" and "ugly," and that sums up its appearance. But the taste is spectacular! Egg whites keep well. Two weeks is the maximum in the fridge, but they can also be frozen.

1 cup plus 1 tablespoon hazelnuts

¼ cup plus 2 tablespoons sugar

1 large egg white

Pinch of sea salt

1 teaspoon pure vanilla extract

1. Preheat the oven to 350°. Line 2 baking sheets with parchment paper.
2. Spread the hazelnuts on a third baking sheet and toast in the oven for 8–10 minutes; let cool. Chop roughly and combine with the sugar in a large mixing bowl.
3. Reduce the oven temperature to 300°.
4. Using a whisk, whip the egg white until stiff but not dry and lumpy looking, add the sea salt and vanilla and gently fold into the hazelnuts and sugar.
5. Drop quarter-size spoonfuls of batter onto the parchment-paper-lined baking sheets. Bake for 20 minutes, or until golden brown. The cookies should be crispy throughout. If they are still soft inside, return to the oven for another 10 minutes.

Makes 2 dozen cookies

Blueberry crisp

Mirtillo (wild blueberries) grow all over Italy. The season, late summer and fall, produces an amazing crop of crisp, sweet and tart berries. Nutritionists believe that blueberries are a fantastic antioxidant and that the juice may aid in longevity. Perhaps bears understand this innately, because they are always in the blueberry fields, gorging on the wild fruit. In the Pacific Northwest the great, wild huckleberry is very much like the Italian *mirtillo*. I think they are the world's best berry. If these are available in late fall, try them (they are also available frozen). Crisps are not a typical Italian dessert, but the ingredients—polenta, butter, berries and sugar—seem to create something Italian-like.

½ cup plus 1 tablespoon organic stone-ground white polenta

½ cup organic pastry flour

¼ cup plus 2 tablespoons granulated sugar

2 tablespoons brown sugar

¼ teaspoon ground cinnamon

¼ teaspoon ground allspice

½ teaspoon sea salt

8 tablespoons (1 stick) unsalted butter

3 cups wild blueberries

Juice of 1 lemon

1. Preheat the oven to 375° and butter an 8-inch pie pan.
2. To make the topping: In a large bowl, mix ½ cup of the polenta with the flour, ¼ cup granulated sugar, brown sugar, cinnamon, allspice and sea salt. Dice the butter and add to the flour mixture. Using your fingers, crumble the butter and flour until the mixture resembles coarse cornmeal. Set aside.
3. In a bowl, mix the blueberries with the remaining 1 tablespoon polenta, 2 tablespoons granulated sugar and the lemon juice. Pack the pie dish with the blueberries and then cover with the topping. Bake for 40 minutes, or until bubbly and golden brown.

Serves 6–8

Lemon raspberry *crostata*

This rustic tart has a sweet crust, almost like a sugar cookie. It is filled halfway with almond frangipane—almond paste, butter and egg—and baked. The frangipane is then topped with a Meyer lemon custard and fresh raspberries and baked again. It is served at room temperature with a dollop of whipped cream and some chopped toasted almonds.

CRUST

1 cup (2 sticks) unsalted butter, at room temperature
½ cup plus 3 tablespoons granulated sugar
3 large egg yolks
½ teaspoon pure vanilla extract
3 cups organic all-purpose flour
½ teaspoon sea salt

ALMOND FRANGIPANE

1¾ ounces almond paste
3½ tablespoons unsalted butter
½ cup confectioners' sugar
1 large egg, at room temperature
¼ teaspoon pure vanilla extract
1 heaping tablespoon organic all-purpose flour
Pinch of sea salt

LEMON CUSTARD

⅓ cup granulated sugar
1 teaspoon organic all-purpose flour
¼ cup Meyer lemon juice
1 large egg
2 large egg yolks
¼ cup heavy cream
Pinch of sea salt
1½ teaspoons Meyer lemon zest

---

1 pint fresh raspberries
1 cup heavy cream, whipped to soft peaks
½ cup almonds, toasted and roughly chopped

1. To make the dough: In the bowl of an electric mixer, using the paddle attachment, cream the butter and sugar on medium speed. Beat in the egg yolks, one at a time. Add the vanilla. Add the flour and sea salt and mix until the dough just comes together. Form the dough into a disk, wrap in plastic wrap and chill for at least 1 hour or up to 2 days.
2. To make the frangipane: In the bowl of an electric mixer, using the paddle attachment,

beat the almond paste on medium speed. Alternate adding the butter and confectioners' sugar, a little at a time, and scrape down the sides of the bowl with a rubber spatula frequently; this will help to break up any lumps of almond paste. Beat in the egg and vanilla. When the mixture is light and fluffy, add the flour and sea salt and mix until just combined. This can be made a few days ahead and chilled until needed.

3. To make the lemon custard: In a mixing bowl, whisk together the sugar and flour. Whisk in the lemon juice, egg and egg yolks, then the cream and sea salt. Strain through a fine-mesh sieve, stir in the lemon zest and set aside.

4. Preheat the oven to 375°.

5. To make the tart: Tear off small pieces of dough and press them into the sides and bottom of an 8-inch fluted tart pan with a removable bottom. Keep pressing in pieces until the entire pan is covered with a ¼-inch-thick layer of dough. Bake for 10–12 minutes, until the crust is just golden. Remove and let cool.

6. Spread the bottom of the tart shell with a ½-inch-thick layer of frangipane. Return the tart to the oven and bake for another 10–15 minutes, until the frangipane is set.

7. Turn the oven temperature down to 325°. Sprinkle the raspberries on top of the frangipane. Stir the lemon custard and carefully pour it over the frangipane. Bake the tart until the custard does not wiggle when you gently nudge the pan, about 20 minutes. Remove and cool to room temperature. Serve each piece with a dollop of whipped cream and sprinkle with toasted almonds.

Serves 8

Caramel panna cotta

This is an eggless custard made with cream, milk and caramelized sugar and set with gelatin. At Barbuto it is served in a bowl with a little whipped cream, some chopped toasted hazelnuts and thin cocoa meringue wafers. Sheet gelatin can be purchased at a gourmet food shop.

1½ cups sugar
½ cup water
2½ cups heavy cream
4 gelatin sheets
2 cups whole milk

¼ teaspoon pure vanilla extract
Pinch of sea salt
½ cup hazelnuts, toasted and
 chopped
Cocoa meringues (page 208)

1. Combine the sugar and water in a 4-quart saucepan, cover and bring to a boil over medium heat. Let boil for 2–3 minutes, then uncover and turn up the heat to high.

2. Cook until the sugar begins to caramelize. Swirl the pot so the sugar caramelizes evenly—do not stir or the sugar will crystallize. When the sugar turns deep brown, turn the heat down to low and slowly and carefully add 2 cups of the cream, a little at a time. The sugar will splatter, so use a very long-handled spoon or whisk to stir in the cream. When all the cream is incorporated, remove the mixture from the heat and set aside.

3. Soak the gelatin sheets in ice water until they are soft (3–5 minutes). Squeeze out as much water as you can; then stir them into the hot caramel cream. When all the gelatin has dissolved, stir in the milk, vanilla and sea salt. Strain through a fine-mesh sieve and pour into eight 4-ounce ramekins. (You could also use a 1-quart mold.) Chill for several hours or overnight, until set.

4. Just before serving, unmold the panna cottas. Dip the molds in hot water, then turn them out onto serving plates. Whip the remaining ½ cup of cream to soft peaks and spoon a dollop on top of each panna cotta. Serve with a sprinkle of toasted hazelnuts and a piece of cocoa meringue.

Serves 8

Cocoa meringues

I adore meringue. In La Varenne cooking school, I first discovered the technique of making egg whites into an exquisite dessert. Here I use cocoa powder to produce an ethereal concoction.

¼ cup unsweetened cocoa powder

½ cup confectioners' sugar

¼ cup plus 3 tablespoons granulated sugar

Pinch of sea salt

⅓ cup egg whites

¼ teaspoon pure vanilla extract

1. Preheat the oven to 300°. Line a half-sheet pan with parchment paper.
2. Sift together the cocoa, confectioners' sugar, 2 tablespoons of the granulated sugar and the sea salt.
3. In the bowl of an electric mixer, using the whisk attachment, whip the whites on medium-high speed until they are frothy. Add 1 tablespoon of granulated sugar and whip to soft peaks. Very slowly, while the mixer is still running, add the remaining ¼ cup sugar and whip until the whites hold stiff peaks. Beat in the vanilla.
4. Gently fold the dry ingredients into the whites. Spread as thinly as possible onto the parchment paper in the pan using an offset spatula.
5. Bake for 15–20 minutes, or until the meringue is completely crispy. To test, remove a piece from the oven and let it cool, then break off a bit. If the meringue bends instead of breaking, return it to the oven.
6. When cool, break the meringue sheet into cookie-size shards.

Makes about 15 cookie-size shards

Semifreddo

Semifreddo means "half-frozen" in English. This is a vanilla parfait, or mousse, which has been spiked with a little rum, to which chopped dark chocolate and pistachio *torrone* have been added. (*Torrone* is a nougat candy made with egg whites, honey, sugar, pistachios, almonds and candied orange. You can find it in most Italian-food stores.) The mousse is frozen in a loaf shape, then cut and served with chocolate sauce.

8 large egg yolks

½ cup sugar

¼ cup water

3 cups heavy cream

2 teaspoons pure vanilla extract

Pinch of sea salt

¼ cup dark rum

2 cups chopped *torrone*

½ cup chopped bittersweet
  chocolate

Chocolate sauce (page 210)

1. Line an 8 x 4 x 4-inch loaf pan with 2 long layers of plastic wrap that overlap the sides of the pan.
2. In the bowl of an electric mixer, whip the yolks on high speed until they are very thick and pale. Meanwhile, combine the sugar and water in a small pot and bring to a boil. Do not stir. Cook to the soft ball stage (240° on a candy thermometer); remove from the heat and, with the mixer still running, very carefully pour the sugar syrup down the side of the mixer bowl. When all the syrup has been added, turn the machine to high speed and whip until the bowl is cool to the touch, approximately 5 minutes.
3. In a large bowl, whip 2 cups of the cream to soft peaks and fold in the yolk mixture. Add the vanilla, sea salt and rum, then fold in the chopped *torrone* and chocolate. Pour the mixture into the prepared loaf pan, cover with plastic wrap and freeze overnight.
4. When ready to serve, gently tug on the plastic wrap until the loaf lifts out. If the *semifreddo* doesn't come out easily, turn the loaf pan upside down on a plate and run it under hot water for a few seconds. Peel off the plastic wrap and quickly slice the loaf into 1-inch slices. Whip the remaining cup of cream and serve each slice with a dollop of cream and a drizzle of chocolate sauce.

Serves 6–8

Chocolate sauce

This is a foolproof recipe for chocolate sauce. You can keep it in the refrigerator for sundaes or to serve with a slice of cake. It's best served warm.

8 tablespoons (1 stick) unsalted
   butter
¾ cup plus 2 tablespoons sugar
2 tablespoons unsweetened cocoa
   powder
1¼ cups heavy cream

½ cup corn syrup
5 ounces dark chocolate, chopped
5 ounces milk chocolate, chopped
¾ teaspoon pure vanilla extract
Pinch of sea salt

1. Melt the butter in a 4-quart saucepan. Whisk together the sugar and cocoa, then whisk into the butter.
2. Add the cream and corn syrup and bring to a boil.
3. Turn off the heat and stir in the chocolates. Add the vanilla and sea salt and stir until all the chocolate has melted.
4. Set aside to cool, then refrigerate. To use, warm in a *bain-marie* until the sauce has reached a pourable consistency.

Makes about 1 quart

Tiramisù

This classic is made with ladyfingers (dry sponge cookies) that are soaked with espresso and Kahlúa, and layered with sweetened mascarpone. Although this dessert is ubiquitous in most Italian joints, it is delicious if made well. I first encountered a version that was worthy at Mezzaluna in New York City. Aldo Bazzi, whom I had known briefly from my days selling Alfa Romeos (he was the president of Alfa Romeo America) had a pizzeria. The only desserts were tiramisù and gelati. My pastry chef, Heather Miller, developed this recipe, and it makes the garden variety taste ordinary.

FILLING

1½ cups mascarpone
¼ cup sugar
Seeds of ½ vanilla bean
1¼ cups heavy cream
Pinch of sea salt

SYRUP

½ cup espresso or very strong coffee
¼ cup water
¾ cup Kahlúa

2 dozen *savoiardi* biscuits or
    ladyfingers, available at Italian
    import stores
Chocolate shavings for garnish

1. To make the filling: In the bowl of an electric mixer, combine the mascarpone, sugar and vanilla bean seeds. Using the paddle attachment, mix on low speed for just a few seconds to remove any lumps; then very gradually add the cream and sea salt, stopping occasionally to scrape down the sides of the bowl with a rubber spatula. This will ensure that you have a smooth, creamy filling. When all the cream is added, increase the speed to medium and beat until thick but still satiny. Don't overmix—too much beating and your mascarpone will seize up like overwhipped cream.

2. To assemble the tiramisù: Make the syrup by pouring the espresso, water and Kahlúa into a shallow bowl or pan and stir to combine. Quickly dunk 2 ladyfingers in the syrup, turning to allow them to absorb some of the syrup, then line them up tightly in the bottom of a 9-inch square baking dish. Repeat until the entire bottom of the pan is

covered. Spread half the filling over the ladyfingers, then repeat the layering process. Drizzle any leftover syrup over the second layer of ladyfingers before covering them with the last layer of cream.

3. Cover the tiramisù with plastic wrap and refrigerate for several hours. To serve, scoop out 6 portions and place each into a bowl; sprinkle with chocolate shavings.

Serves 6

Biscotti al cioccolato

My grandmother, who hailed from Russia or Poland depending on who was telling the tale, made a type of biscotti. It was a traditional twice-cooked batter, infused with a little hard liquor and almonds. It was delicious. I have always fantasized about them, and I have augmented them here with chocolate. The biscotti need to "age," so plan to make them a week before using. They also last a long time. Keeping them around is good thing, perfect for that impromptu party.

1 teaspoon ground cinnamon	2 cups sugar
4 cups organic all-purpose flour	3 large eggs
1½ teaspoons baking soda	1 teaspoon pure vanilla extract
1 tablespoon baking powder	¾ teaspoon almond extract
1 teaspoon sea salt	3 cups almonds or hazelnuts or both,
4 tablespoons (½ stick) unsalted	roughly chopped
butter	2 cups chopped dark chocolate

1. Preheat the oven to 325°. Line a baking sheet with parchment paper.
2. In a mixing bowl, combine the cinnamon, flour, baking soda, baking powder and sea salt. In the bowl of an electric mixer, using the paddle attachment, cream the butter and sugar together. Slowly beat in the eggs and vanilla and almond extracts.
3. Add the flour mixture and mix until just combined. Fold in the nuts and the chocolate. Form the dough into a 12 x 3-inch flattened log. Place on the prepared baking sheet and bake for 25 minutes.
4. Remove from the oven and let cool. Lower the oven temperature to 300°. Slice into ½-inch rounds and bake for 15 minutes more.
5. Store in an airtight container.

Makes about 2 dozen

Torta al cioccolato con pignoli

I've had this recipe in my repertoire for ages. I wanted to emulate the flourless chocolate cakes so popular a few years ago, but with my own twist. The pine nuts are extraordinary with the bittersweet chocolate. The crust is a mixture of ground almonds and pine nuts. The dough is light, fluffy and sinuous, easy to make and freeze. I like this with chocolate *sorbetto*.

DOUGH

1 cup organic all-purpose flour

½ cup unsweetened cocoa powder

1 cup almond meal

½ cup ground pine nuts

½ teaspoon sea salt

1 cup (2 sticks) unsalted butter, at
   room temperature

¾ cup sugar

FILLING

6 ounces bittersweet chocolate

4 large eggs

⅓ cup sugar

½ teaspoon pure vanilla extract

Pinch of sea salt

1. Make the dough: In a bowl, combine the flour, cocoa, almond meal, pine nuts and sea salt. In the bowl of an electric mixer, using the paddle attachment, cream the butter and sugar on medium speed until fluffy. Reduce the speed to low, add the dry ingredients and mix until just combined. Roll out the dough ⅛ inch thick between sheets of parchment paper and chill for 2 hours or overnight.

2. Preheat the oven to 350°. Spray a 10-inch tart pan with a removable bottom with nonstick cooking spray. Press the dough onto the bottom and sides of the pan. Bake for 10–15 minutes, until firm to the touch. Remove and cool. Don't worry if the crust slides down the edges of the pan as it bakes.

4. Make the filling: Melt the chocolate in a large bowl set over a pot of barely simmering water. Let cool. In the bowl of an electric mixer, using the whisk attachment, whip the eggs and sugar on high speed until very pale and thick, about 5 minutes. Whip in the vanilla and sea salt. Fold a third of the egg mixture into the chocolate to lighten it, then fold in the remainder.

5. Immediately pour the filling over the crust and bake for 20–25 minutes, or until puffed and set. A skewer poked into the center of the tart will show some crumbs, but not a runny filling. Remove and cool before serving.

Serves 10

Chicken stock

Carcass of a roast chicken

2 onions

4 cloves garlic

8 sprigs parsley

2 carrots

1 teaspoon freshly ground black
  pepper

1. In an 8-quart pot, heat 6 quarts of water and add all the ingredients. Bring to a boil, then reduce to a bare simmer.
2. Skim the fat and scum off the top.
3. Cook, uncovered, for 6 hours.
4. Strain and discard the chicken and vegetables. Let cool.

Makes 3–4 quarts

Aioli

Aglio ("garlic") and *olio* ("olive oil") are the bricks and mortar of Mediterranean cuisines. I could not imagine a world without the two. They are frequently abused, but when treated well they can elevate any dish (except for desserts). The key here is to not bruise the garlic, remove any green stems and use a mild blended olive oil (or blend your own). If the oil is too peppery or strong, the sauce will be too bitter.

3 cloves pure white garlic with no
    blemishes
¼ teaspoon sea salt
5 turns black pepper from a
    pepper mill

2 egg yolks (optional; see Note)
1 cup mild olive oil
1 teaspoon hot water

1. Using a mortar and pestle, crush the garlic with the sea salt and black pepper.
2. Add the egg yolks, if using, to the garlic.
3. Dribble in a tiny bit of olive oil; keep crushing and stirring, adding drips of oil (this is tedious but efficacious). The process will take about 15 minutes until all the oil is absorbed. Add the hot water and keep at room temperature.

Note: If you add the egg yolks at the beginning, before adding the oil, the process will take a shorter time, but the result is not as authentic.

Makes 1 cup

Bolognese sauce

1 pound veal shoulder meat devoid
    of sinew and fat
1 pound pork shoulder meat devoid
    of sinew and fat
1 pound beef shoulder chuck or
    blade roast devoid of sinew
    and fat
Sea salt to taste
4 tablespoons extra-virgin olive oil
3 medium carrots, peeled and finely
    diced

2 medium stalks celery, minced
2 large white or yellow onions,
    peeled and diced
4 cloves garlic, smashed
2 cups white wine (Gavi or similar)
1 cup canned San Marzano tomatoes
1 bay leaf
Parsley
1 cup heavy cream

1. Cut the veal, pork and beef into tiny dice and season with sea salt.

2. In a heavy skillet, heat 2 tablespoons of the olive oil. Add the carrots, celery and onions and cook slowly over medium heat until soft. Add the garlic, cook 3 minutes, and then scoop out the vegetables. Turn up the heat to high; add the remaining 2 tablespoons of olive oil and the meat. Cook, stirring occasionally, until lightly browned, about 20 minutes. Return the cooked vegetables to the pot, add the wine and tomatoes and enough cold water to give a souplike consistency. Add the bay leaf and parsley and simmer slowly for 3 hours.

3. When the sauce is cooked, remove the bay leaf and add the cream. The *ragù* is ready for any use. It can be kept in the refrigerator for up to 2 weeks or frozen for up to 1 month.

Makes 3–4 quarts

Romesco sauce

4 ripe tomatoes or 1 pint ripe cherry
   tomatoes
5 tablespoons extra-virgin olive oil
Sea salt to taste
½ cup almonds
½ cup hazelnuts

1 cup cubed stale bread
2 red Fresno chilies
1 onion, peeled and quartered
2 cloves garlic
3 tablespoons red wine vinegar

1. Preheat the oven to 475°.
2. Wash and core the tomatoes (or stem the cherry tomatoes) and cut them in half. Sprinkle with 1 tablespoon of the olive oil and the sea salt and roast for 15 minutes. Let cool.
3. Lower the oven temperature to 350°. Spread the almonds, hazelnuts, bread, chilies, onion and garlic on a baking sheet and roast until golden brown. Let cool.
4. Place all the cooled ingredients in a food processor fitted with a metal blade, add the vinegar and the remaining 4 tablespoons of olive oil and purée. You will have a rich, crumbly sauce.

Makes about 1 quart

Gremolata

Typically served with *osso buco*, this is more a condiment than a sauce. It goes together in a second and can perk up any heavy meat dish, but I especially like it spread on toast topped with *burrata* mozzarella.

3 cloves garlic

1 cup fresh parsley leaves, chopped

3 tablespoons extra-virgin olive oil

1 teaspoon lemon zest

1 teaspoon orange zest

Juice of 1 lemon

Sea salt and freshly ground black
  pepper to taste

1. Mince the garlic and mix with the parsley and olive oil.
2. Add the lemon and orange zests and the lemon juice. Season with sea salt and black pepper. Serve at room temperature.

Makes 2 cups

My salad dressing

Here is my basic dressing, but please, feel free to improvise. The basis is simply shallots, mustard, red wine vinegar and olive oil. One could use walnut or hazelnut oil, sherry vinegar or omit the mustard and use crème fraîche instead. One could add tarragon, chives, basil or a combo thereof. A touch of soy is good too. Have fun!

1 shallot, peeled and minced
2 tablespoons Dijon mustard
1½ tablespoons red wine vinegar
¼ teaspoon lemon juice
Pinch of cayenne

¼ teaspoon sea salt
⅛ teaspoon freshly ground black
  pepper
6 tablespoons green extra-virgin
  Tuscan olive oil

1. In a 4-ounce jar with a lid, combine all the ingredients, cover tightly and shake well.

Makes 1 cup

Pesto

One can make a pesto with other herbs, but this sauce, which is the salsa of choice in Liguria, depends entirely on good basil. Basil, especially the Genovese variety, is really important. Equally important is the methodology: Use a mortar and pestle; the sauce is just better. A machine-made pesto is fun but lacks the gorgeous, unctuous quality of a mortared sauce.

2 cloves garlic

½ cup toasted pine nuts

4 cups fresh basil leaves, washed
　　and dried

½ cup grated Parmesan

1½ cups extra-virgin olive oil

1. Using a mortar and pestle, smash the garlic until smooth. Add the toasted pine nuts and mash until smooth and incorporated. Transfer to a large bowl.
2. In batches, smash the basil using the mortar and pestle until it reaches a smooth consistency. Place it in the bowl with the garlic and pine nuts.
3. Add the Parmesan to the basil mixture and continue to work the mixture while slowly drizzling in the olive oil. The consistency should be smooth and not oily; add more Parmesan if necessary.
4. Serve immediately with your favorite pasta.

Makes about 3 cups

Walnut and winter pestos

Here is another example of a sauce used as a "mother" or base. In winter, when parsley is always available, we make a delicious winter pesto. In Liguria, the gorgeous walnuts are harvested in the fall and keep well into the long winter. Scrumptious!

2 tablespoons grated Parmesan

4 cloves garlic

½ teaspoon sea salt

½ cup fresh parsley leaves, washed and chopped

1 tablespoon or ½ cup walnuts (see Note)

1 cup extra-virgin olive oil

1. Using a mortar and pestle, mash together the Parmesan, garlic and sea salt.
2. Add the parsley, reduce to a purée and then slowly add the walnuts. Slowly drizzle in the olive oil while continuing to work the mixture.

Note: Add only 1 tablespoon of walnuts for winter pesto and ½ cup for walnut pesto.

Makes 2 cups

Roasted chili salsa

This is a seductive, piquant sauce that will last for a long time. It does wonders for steaks, especially grilled meat. It is an addictive salsa.

4 tablespoons extra-virgin olive oil

Sea salt to taste

8 cloves garlic, halved

6 shallots, peeled and halved

1 sweet onion, peeled and quartered

3 red Fresno chilies, topped, seeded and quartered

1 poblano chili, topped, seeded and quartered

¼ cup sherry vinegar

1. Heat a griddle over medium heat with 1 tablespoon of the olive oil and a little sea salt. Add the garlic, shallots, onion and chilies and cook until golden brown, turning often.
2. Place the ingredients in a bowl, add the remaining 3 tablespoons of olive oil and the vinegar, and toss well. Let cool and use as a sauce or condiment.

Makes approximately 4 cups

Blood orange dressing

How perfectly simple! You take dazzlingly ripe oranges, juice half and section the others, toss with a good olive oil and orange zest, add some sea salt and bang—a great sauce. Amazing with fish, salads and vegetables, especially carrots, and even with meat.

4 blood oranges

1 shallot, peeled and minced

¼ cup extra-virgin olive oil

2 tablespoons red wine vinegar

¼ teaspoon sea salt

⅛ teaspoon freshly ground black
  pepper

1. Zest and juice 2 of the oranges in a bowl.
2. Add the minced shallot, olive oil, vinegar, sea salt and black pepper and mix well.
3. Section the 2 remaining oranges and mix with the sauce. Keep at room temperature.

Makes 2 cups

Roasted garlic sauce

There is a lot of garlic in this book for good reason. It is incredibly versatile, and when cooked correctly it makes anything taste better, is very healthful and has a distinctive flavor. I could not live without it. Here is a sauce that could seduce the most adamant of garlic haters to love it.

3 heads garlic

5 tablespoons unsalted butter

1 sweet onion, peeled and sliced

1 cup tart white wine

2 cups chicken stock

2 bay leaves

2 tablespoons grappa

3 tablespoons heavy cream

Sea salt and freshly ground black
    pepper to taste

1. Separate the garlic into cloves and peel but leave whole. In a skillet set over medium heat, melt 3 tablespoons of the butter and sweat the garlic and onion. Cook until golden. Add the wine, bring to a boil and then add the chicken stock, bay leaves and grappa. Cook for 15 minutes, remove the garlic with a slotted spoon and set aside.
2. Raise the heat and reduce the sauce by half.
3. When the sauce is reduced and thickened, add the cream and the remaining 2 tablespoons of butter and return the garlic to the pan. Season to taste with sea salt and black pepper.

Makes 3 cups

Lobster dressing

An incredibly useful dressing and very easy to make. With shrimp shells, this makes shrimp dressing.

4 tablespoons extra-virgin olive oil

2 cups fresh lobster or shrimp shells

1 onion, peeled and diced

4 cloves garlic, lightly crushed

Pinch of saffron

2 tomatoes, cored and diced

2 cups white wine

Juice of 1 lemon

Sea salt to taste (optional)

1. To make the lobster stock: In a large pan, heat 1 tablespoon of the olive oil and the lobster shells, onion and garlic and sauté for 10 minutes. Add the saffron, tomatoes and wine. Bring to a simmer and cook for 30 minutes. Strain into a saucepan. Over low heat, reduce the sauce to ½ cup. When it is reduced, set aside to cool.

2. To make the dressing: Mix the reduced lobster stock with the remaining 3 tablespoons of olive oil, the lemon juice and a touch of sea salt if necessary. This will keep a week in the fridge.

Makes 1½–2 cups

Lamb jus

2 pounds lamb scraps, bones and
   fatty pieces
2 onions
1 head garlic
Sea salt to taste

1 sprig fresh rosemary
2 cups white wine
6 quarts water or chicken stock
4 sprigs fresh thyme
1 small bunch parsley

1. Preheat the oven to 375°.
2. Place the bones in a heavy casserole or roasting pan with the onions and garlic, sprinkle with a little sea salt and add the rosemary. Bake until golden. Don't overbake or the bones will make a bitter stock.
3. Transfer the contents of the pan to a stockpot, set it over medium heat, douse the bones with the wine and reduce until almost dry. Add the water or stock and the thyme and parsley and simmer for about 4 hours. Skim off the scum that rises to the top from time to time. Strain into a saucepan and reduce the liquid by half.

Makes about 6 cups

Pork braising sauce

A fantastic liquid in which to immerse your beloved pork products. It can be used for loin chops, tenderloins, pork butt and, of course, the ultimate: a whole pork leg.

10 pounds pork or veal bones

6 tablespoons extra-virgin olive oil

10 onions, peeled and quartered

2 heads garlic

8 quarts chicken stock

2 bay leaves

1 bunch parsley

1. Preheat the oven to 350°.
2. In a roasting pan, toss the bones with olive oil and roast for 45 minutes, then add the onions and garlic and roast until everything is golden.
3. Transfer the ingredients to a stockpot and add the chicken stock, bay leaves and parsley. Bring to a boil, reduce to a simmer, skim well and simmer, uncovered, for 8 hours.
4. Strain the sauce into a large container and let cool. Chill overnight. The next day, remove the fat that has collected on top.
5. Place the sauce in a heavy saucepan and reduce by half.

Makes about 3 quarts

JW roasted tomato sauce

I should bottle this stuff. It is the easiest sauce to make and dazzles everyone who tries it. The important notes are to have ripe tomatoes, a hot oven and not to burn the garlic. Other than that, this is quite easy and long-lasting. It improves with age.

3 tablespoons extra-virgin olive oil

4 very ripe beefsteak or heirloom tomatoes

2 cloves garlic, finely chopped

2 sprigs rosemary, leaves finely chopped

2 sprigs lavender, leaves finely chopped

1 teaspoon sea salt

1. Preheat the oven to 450°.
2. Coat a heavy casserole or roasting pan with 1 tablespoon of the olive oil.
3. Cut the tomatoes in half and place in a large bowl. Add the garlic, rosemary, lavender, the remaining olive oil and the sea salt and toss well. Place in the casserole and bake for 25 minutes, checking halfway to make sure the garlic isn't burning. If the garlic burns, discard it.
4. Remove and let cool. Transfer the contents to a blender and purée until smooth. The sauce can be used cold, at room temperature or hot.

Makes 4 cups

Mascarpone

This recipe is adapted from Giuliano Bugialli's *Classic Techniques of Italian Cooking.*

> 1 quart organic heavy cream
> ¼ teaspoon tartaric acid

1. Pour the cream into a large bowl and place it over a pot of simmering water. When the cream reaches 180° on a kitchen thermometer, turn off the heat and add the tartaric acid. Stir for 30 seconds, then remove the bowl from the hot water and continue stirring for 2 minutes.
2. Line another bowl with 2 layers of cheesecloth and pour in the cream. Cover and refrigerate for 12 hours.
3. Divide the mascarpone into 4 portions and wrap each in cheesecloth. Refrigerate for another 12 hours before using.

Makes about 1½ cups

Preserved lemons

A staple of Sicily, these lemons are bold, exciting and delicious.

6 lemons
½ cup coarse kosher or sea salt
2 tablespoons sugar

1. Cut the lemons in quarters. Place in a big bowl, add the kosher or sea salt and sugar and toss well.
2. Bring a pot of water to a boil and completely submerge a jar big enough to hold the lemons along with a tight-fitting lid. Boil for 30 minutes. Remove the jar from the water using tongs. Place the lemons in the sterilized jar. Place the jar in a cool spot for 3 days. After the lemons have cured, use ½ lemon at a time. Cut into rough pieces before adding to your recipe.

Makes about 3 cups

Salsa verde

If there is one sauce that is ubiquitous in my kitchen, this is it. We put it on everything except desserts. It is wonderful on fish and seafood, terrific on meats, scintillating on poultry. It is also great with eggs, pizza, pasta, etc. It is a "mother" sauce to which you can add anything you like: tomato sauce, peppers, roasted onions and more. It is truly a cornerstone of my cooking.

¼ cup capers in salt

4 anchovy filets

3 cloves garlic

½ cup chopped fresh parsley

½ cup chopped arugula

½ cup chopped fresh basil

½ cup chopped fresh cilantro

¼ cup chopped fresh tarragon

¼ cup chopped fresh chives

¼ cup chopped fresh sage

¼ teaspoon red pepper flakes

1 cup extra-virgin olive oil

¼ teaspoon sea salt, or to taste

1. Soak the capers in cold water for 1 hour, then drain.
2. Soak the anchovies in cold water for 15 minutes, then pat dry and remove the bones using tweezers.
3. Using a mortar and pestle, smash the capers, anchovies and garlic until smooth, then transfer to a large bowl.
4. Add the parsley, arugula, basil, cilantro, tarragon, chives, sage, red pepper flakes and olive oil. Season with the sea salt. The consistency should be chunky but not oily.

Makes 3 cups

Poached Arborio rice

A simple but extremely useful recipe. It forms the beginnings of rice pudding and seafood salad, and is a perfect accompaniment to main courses and a filler for terrines. The goal of eliminating all traces of starch and the desire to create chewy, delicate globes of rice are the opposite aim of making traditional rice.

2 cups Arborio rice
2 teaspoons sea salt
1 tablespoon extra-virgin olive oil

1. In a heavy stockpot, bring 6 quarts of water to a boil. Add the rice and sea salt. Reduce to a rolling simmer (not gentle) and cook for about 12 minutes.
2. Pour the oil onto a baking sheet. Test the rice (it should be just cooked—neither al dente nor mushy) and remove from the heat. Drain off the liquid and pour the rice onto the oiled baking sheet. Let cool and season if necessary.

Makes 4 cups

KITCHEN TOOLS

The Simple Kitchen

If your kitchen is small, all you really need are two forks, a spatula, a whisk, a French spatula, two wooden spoons, a sauté pan, a 2-quart saucepan, a wok, a braiser, a baking sheet and a mixing bowl.

BAMBOO SKEWERS

These are important: They are handy for roasting, grilling, sautéing, etc., and they work well for closing up a stuffed fish or chicken. I love them as toothpicks! Make sure to soak them in cold water before using. I like three sizes: 5 inches, 8 inches and 12 inches.

BLENDERS

We use a Vita-Mix commercial model at Barbuto. It is a work of art and American engineering. It goes from zero to a hundred quickly, is strong and spins on a dime. The Waring we use at home is archaic but lovely; I love the thick glass container. I use blenders for a multitude of things: pesto, bread crumbs, milkshakes, dressings, salsa, jams, etc.

BOWLS

It sounds obvious, but good bowls are important. I have six sizes of stainless-steel ones (the restaurant weight are far better, last forever and are quite affordable). My venerable copper bowl was designed for egg whites; somehow the molecular structure of copper creates a more stable foam—egg whites are harder to overwhip. I quite like the feel of my heavy ceramic bowl (a hundred years old from my wife's great-grandmother). I use decorative ones to let bread dough rise or to store fruits and vegetables, and tiny ceramic ones for salt, spices and my son's pennies. Wooden bowls are beautiful (I love cherry and apple wood; olive wood is for salads); they don't conduct heat and they stack neatly. I scour flea markets for old bowls; they clean up well, and bowls that are worn with age are always attractive.

CAKE AND BREAD PANS

I have rectangular ones, round ones, square ones and deep ones. I have cast iron, aluminum, Pyrex and stainless steel and use different ones for different recipes. I have not tried the new Thermolon ones, but they make sense—no seasoning or oiling before baking. The pans I reach for most are aluminum rounds 8 inches and 9 inches in diameter and 3 inches deep; 8-inch-square cast iron; 9 x 13-inch Pyrex; and my aluminized-steel 9 x 5 x 3-inch loaf pans.

CAST-IRON PANS, POTS AND GRIDDLES

Iron is important to our health and well-being, and using a cast-iron skillet is a good way to add iron to your diet. I adore my plain, ugly 8-inch griddle at home; the reverse side has a good ersatz grill. I have the world's greatest cast-iron pan. It comes from Finland. It has a cool-to-the-touch handle, weighs a ton, is perfectly flat and cooks beautifully. It was very expensive but will last three lifetimes. I use the black French iron pans for sautéing and the heavy enamel LeCreuset casserole for long braises and stews. Cleaning cast iron is a bit tricky. If you burn something or forget to clean it right away, it takes some serious effort to clean, but refrain from using soap or cleanser. Hot water and one of those green scrubbing pads work well. I always put a couple inches of water in the pan after cooking and bring it to a boil, which also aids in the cleaning process. Nothing cooks a pork chop better than an old Lodge 12-inch well-seasoned, cast-iron pan! To season the pan, mix 1 cup of oil (any kind) with 1 cup of coarse salt in the pan and bake it for 2 hours in a 350° oven. Let cool; wipe the pan clean and use.

CHEESE GRATERS

At Barbuto we grate vast quantities of Parmesan in a Cuisinart; hand graters would be too inefficient. I love the old-fashioned, four-sided box graters, but the new Microplanes are terrific. I have three sizes (they work well on truffles too!). Be sure not to grate cheese too far in advance; grated cheese dries out quickly and loses its fluffiness. The Parmesan box graters from Alessi are beautiful, but expensive.

CLEAVERS

Another essential tool. Great for breaking up bones for stock, pounding out fish or meat, hacking through lamb chops. I like Chinese cleavers; American ones are fine; just don't get ones with plastic handles. German cleavers are spectacular, heavy and formidable. Cleavers are dangerous for kids, so please put them safely away.

COPPER PANS

My introduction to copper was my mother's Revere Ware skillet, pot and stock pot. The copper was entirely decorative, and the pans were terrible. When I went to Dehillerin and Simon, the famed stores in Paris and saw their copper equipment, I almost fell over. I wanted every pan, pot and bowl. Copper pans are very expensive, but they last forever. Please don't buy copper pans that are tin lined; the "tin" is all lead, which is bad. Buy brands such as Mauviel, Paderno or American All-Clad. The Italian company Paderno makes excellent pans, but they are hard to find. Williams-Sonoma carries a wide variety of beautiful copper. I like the following: an 8-inch sauté pan, an 8-inch saucepan (sloping sides), an oval fish pan (10 inches or so), a copper bowl for pastry, a copper sugar pot (quite beautiful!), a copper roasting pan, a *rondeau*, a tiny saucepan (about 1 quart), a set of copper measuring cups and finally a 16-inch *sauteuse*. That's about $2,000 retail. But considering what we pay for fancy ranges and dishwashers, it's a wise investment. To make copper pots gleam, here is an effective and all natural cleaner: Mix 1 cup white vinegar, 1 cup rock salt, and 1 cup flour to a smooth paste. Wash the copper with soap and hot water, rub the paste on the copper and let sit for an hour. Wash it off, and you will be amazed. Good for the environment and the look of your kitchen.

CUTTING BOARDS

I hate plastic. I hate rubber. New York City's restaurant health inspectors have decided that we can only use colored plastic ones: red for meat, white for poultry, green for vegetables, etc. That makes sense if you use only plastic. But wood is a natural antibacterial agent; it cleans perfectly, does not retain odor, looks beautiful and lasts as long as your kitchen. At Chez Panisse, we washed the boards down collectively (we were in Berkeley after all) with hot water and soap, then scraped them well with a pastry tool. This removed all the soapy scum and the boards would dry to look like new. If your wood boards are at all smelly, add a tablespoon of hydrogen peroxide to a cup of hot water and scrub the wood with the mixture. Then with a heavy spatula or pastry scraper, scrape hard against the grain to remove all the scum. After they dry, I like to season my wood boards with some almond or olive oil (a teaspoon is all you need). John Boos makes stellar butcher's block. Their prices are quite reasonable. Please don't buy "coated" butcher block—it's all plastic.

DISHWASHERS

The most important equipment in any cook's life! I would choose one that is stainless steel inside, quiet as a mouse, quick as can be, and has a short wash cycle and uses extremely hot water. Using an organic soap with hot water is better for the environment and will clean perfectly. Also, you can wash wine glasses with water only.

ESPRESSO MACHINES

I love my Aussie Breville.

FISH SPATULAS

This French tool is a work of art. I love the shape and its gentle flexibility. With it, you can stir a sauce, flip a burger, nudge a filet of fish, and coddle a French fry. Buy the best one you can and make sure the handle is fireproof. The all-metal ones are not good—they conduct heat and are slippery.

FOOD PROCESSORS

For a while, at the height of my arrogance, I refused to allow my cooks to use any of the available modern conveniences. They were not allowed to have a deep fryer, nor a Bermixer and most certainly not a Cuisinart. It's true that the best cooks can cook a wonderful meal under any circumstances. I wanted my staff to be prepared for any contingency and to rely on just three tools: a spoon, a knife and a fork. But as I have mellowed somewhat and relented, the Cuisinart has entered my kitchens. At home we use a standard heavy-duty machine. They do take some time to use properly, they are a pain in the ass to clean, and the attachments are weird, but the sum of the parts equals a marvelous tool. They make perfect chips, great pastry, and wonderful shoestrings, perfect purée and delicious pizza dough. Smaller machines (less than 2-quart capacity) are a bit silly I think.

HAND BLENDERS

We call them Bermixers, named after one of the companies that introduced these marvelous machines in the 1970s. The early ones resembled small outboard motors and they were heavy and expensive, but they revolutionized sauce and soup making. They have shrunk both in size and expense, and the newest ones are a kitchen marvel. I love mine; it makes fantastic sauces, puréed vegetables, tomato purée for pizza, etc. They are a perfect tool and cost about $30.

JUICERS

I use my hand juicer from Braun every morning for fresh grapefruit or orange juice. Easy to clean, bulletproof and elegant; you can't go wrong.

KIDS' TOOLS

I have a multitude of kids' cooking items. All of them will help your children learn to enjoy cooking and be safe: A small rolling pin, baby whisk, plastic knives (they can cut but are very safe!), small tongs, wooden spoons, a baby spatula. Basically a kitchen in miniature. Also helpful for kids: aprons, mitts, a step stool, goggles, etc.

KITCHEN FORKS

Here is an almost forgotten tool: the kitchen fork. It is 10 inches long, beautiful, sharp (for testing the doneness of meat), strong (for picking up a whole roast) and delicate (for gently flipping a filet of fish). It is essential for carving.

KITCHEN TOWELS

Sounds easy, huh? Not really. A good towel is sturdy, all cotton, colorful, hardy, absorbent and easy on the hands. I don't like kitchen mitts; they are dangerous if torn and when wet they are a nightmare. Use towels. Cotton is an excellent heat shield for your hands. Look for them in flea markets; someone's hand-me-downs will serve you well. At Chez Panisse we were allowed two towels a day. Use paper towels to clean cutting boards and save your towels for the oven or to hold a sauté pan.

KNIVES

I love German knives and own many Japanese ones as well. You need to take special care of Japanese knives. The metal blade tends to be very brittle, and the knives should never be dropped into the sink. I would never put them in a dishwasher or let the kids use them. German knives (I favor Dick) are sturdier, use a stronger steel alloy, but they dull faster than the Japanese ones. I like the ones made from phenolic composite material.

I recommend two 4-inch paring knives (I have a Damascus-steel Japanese knife that has a beautiful shape and a gorgeous handle), a boning knife (German), a fish knife (French), an 8-inch chef's knife (German or Japanese), a bread knife (Japanese), a sharpening steel and a sexy Japanese knife to use for all fish and vegetable preparation. You can augment your collection with a sushi knife, a fluted one, a flexible one for slicing smoked salmon and roast beef and finally a ceramic one for vegetables.

LADLES

I like the Swiss-made variety. These are unibodied, with no welds, and heavy duty. I have four sizes: 1 ounce, 2 ounce, 4 ounce and 8 ounce.

MANDOLINES

I have four: a heavy-duty one from Paris, a delicate plastic one from Japan, a Swiss one, and a dull but useful one for the kids.

MEASURING CUPS AND SPOONS

I use glass Pyrex quart-size ones, copper cups in all the denominations, measuring spoons, Pyrex glass vessels and a beaker set from a chemistry lab.

METAL STRAINERS

I adore the fine stainless-steel mesh strainers from Switzerland. I like them conical, rounded and flat. You can strain soup, sauces, stocks and even make delicate bread crumbs. The *tamis* from France are great for sifting and making purées. I have a copper pasta colander from Italy that's wonderful for draining pastas. I have a four-tier set that works for soups, mashed potatoes, fish stock, etc. Buy the most expensive; the cheap ones are flimsy. Plastic ones are silly—they melt! The Chinese spiders are inexpensive and come in many sizes. I adore them.

MEZZALUNAS

The curved, two-handled blade called the mezzaluna is a remarkable piece of equipment—like having a team of butchers. I love it, but it's hard to find. Buy one that can go in the dishwasher, but be careful using it around your kids.

MIXERS

Buy the best. There is a good selection of stand mixers now: De'Longhi, KitchenAid, and Electrolux all make fantastic machines. Collect at least four attachments: a whisk, paddle, dough hook, and the grater attachment. Also, it's worth it to buy two stainless-steel bowls. I think the old-fashioned man-powered eggbeaters are great. The more modern (1940s–1960s) versions are in so many kitchens. I like them—they clean easily and are light, productive and cute!

MORTARS AND PESTLES

I own a gorgeous burl olive wood set I purchased many years ago in Nice at the wonderful olive oil store Alziari. It is just about perfect, voluptuous, even better as a salad or sauce bowl. It is not cold like marble or impersonal like porcelain. The wood helps grind the herbs or shallots or meat.

NONSTICK PANS

I must admit that the early-generation nonstick surfaces are scary as cooking media. They are probably great for stealth bombers and camouflaging battleships from radar, but for cooking? Luckily engineers have developed healthier alternatives. Search out GreenPan Cookware and Thermolon Technology.

PARCHMENT PAPER

Parchment paper has many uses, from baking fish *al cartoccio* to baking breads and tarts. I find laying parchment paper on a cookie or baking sheet aids the baking process and makes cleaning up far easier.

PASTA COOKERS

A heavy pot with at least a 12-quart capacity is correct for boiling pasta. A pasta cooker (a steel cylinder with a metal handle to hold the pasta) is also very useful. I would say the rule of thumb is a minimum of 10 quarts of water for every dry pound of pasta. I have tried smaller pots; believe me, they don't work!

PASTA MACHINES

I love my little Atlas. It has served me perfectly well and been a friend for years. Cheap, strong, tiny, it makes great noodles. Do clean your machine well after every use. I use a vacuum cleaner to suction up the flour (don't tell my wife) and a dry rag, never wet, which is bad for it.

PEPPER MILLS

It seems obvious, but not all mills are equal. I love the Indian copper ones; and the American Vic Firth brand is my favorite of the conventional types. Peugeots are still fantastic, especially the small hand-size ones. I use a coffee grinder for spices. Buy a cheap one, and remember to clean it well—no water, just wipe with a stiff paint brush or pastry brush.

PIZZA STUFF

I do think a stone for the oven floor is a nice addition. But the old-fashioned perforated round and rectangular aluminum pans are quite effective. An inexpensive alternative to a stone is to stick an untreated and unglazed 12 x 12-inch terra-cotta tile (Mexican Saltillo) on a sheet pan and place the sheet pan in the oven for an hour to preheat. Baking your *ciabatta* on it will give fantastic results. I use a baking sheet as well, especially the double one. (Preheat it in the oven and use a peel—a big spatula-like tool for pizza—to slide the dough onto the surface.) Peels are steel or wood. Wood peels are great for many things. The metal ones are nice, but a big metal spatula does practically the same thing.

PLIERS AND TWEEZERS

Tweezers are good to retrieve lost pieces of toast from the toaster, remove fish bones, and turn a delicate something in a sauté pan. Pliers are good for fish, poultry, meat, etc. Try and buy stainless-steel ones. The hardware variety just gets rusty and gross.

RICERS

This old-fashioned tool is marvelous. It does the best job for mashed potatoes, smoothing sauces and stocks and polenta. And it lasts forever.

ROLLING PINS

I admit to a certain fetish regarding rolling pins. To keep her pastry cold, my mother had a plastic one that she filled with water and froze. Good idea, bad execution. That pin was impossible to hold. I advise having three: a tiny one for the kids, a tapered one for pies and pasta and a heavier one for puff pastry and bread.

SALAD SPINNERS

I love the Swiss cord type; they work!

SALT AND GRINDERS

I use four basic salts: white sea salt (Maldon is the paradigm); gray or pink raw sea salt; kosher salt, which has a nice texture and works great in all cooking, even pastry, and finally table salt or fine salt. Experiment. Salts do vary: some, like Maldon, can clump, kosher can lose potency and others dry out or get moist. The grinder I use has a special knob denoting its use for salt only. I use Maldon or gray coarse sea salt in the grinder.

SAWS

I have a bone saw. It is wonderful. It looks like a standard hacksaw. The shape is perfect to saw around big bones and carcasses. I am not telling you that you should buy one, but when that leg of lamb needs a trim, they do come in handy.

SCALES

I have three: an old-fashioned balanced type, an electronic gizmo and a standard one that does both metric and American measurements.

SCISSORS

The Fiskars brand of scissors that debuted in the 1980s revolutionized the industry. Razor sharp, they can cut almost anything. They clean nicely and come in a myriad of sizes. They are, however, not perfect for all tasks. I like heavy poultry shears, which cut through the most difficult of bones and break apart for cleaning. I do like the tiny ones for tight corners and a surgically sharp pair for cutting through the smaller bones. Quail bones especially need a tiny pair.

SHARPENING TOOLS

For Japanese knives a wet stone is mandatory. Do not let that guy in the funny truck sharpen any of your knives. He uses a grinding wheel that is good for horseshoes only. I love big steel sharpeners (the smaller ones are dangerous). Always sharpen away from you. Any lack of concentration and you risk injury. I love the new surgeon's-style knife-sharpening tool, which has two diamond sticks embedded inside. It sharpens at a precise angle. My Forschner sharpener cost $30 and is worth every penny. It's safe, easy and foolproof. Your knives will be very happy. I am not a huge fan of the electric ones; they seem to do nothing but grind the blades unevenly.

SILPATS

These nonstick inserts for baking sheets are wonderfully modern tools. A Silpat makes cookies cook like a dream. They also make muffin Silpat molds, so no butter is required.

STEAMERS

The Japanese and Chinese ones are good looking, come in many sizes and are easy to use. They are a bit hard to clean, but they are cheap and therefore easy to replace. The stainless-steel variety will last forever and is very sturdy. But in a pinch, a wok and a bowl placed inside over an inch or so of water works as well as anything. To steam a duck or goose, place the roasting grids in a pan, then add an aromatic liquid (water with star anise and mint, or red wine with water and cinnamon) and *voilà*—you have a great steamer.

STOVES

The mark of any good cook is her choice of stoves. I think the technology will change radically in the next few years. As we better understand insulation, energy use and its effect on the environment, gas and electric stoves will evolve; induction and other fuel-efficient technologies will prevail. Even the dreaded microwave will make amazing changes. I find that sometimes a cheaper stove like a standard GE works as well as the fancier brands. My Viking, now eight years old, has been perfect, other than some routine mechanical issues (we use it a lot). I love the look of the Miele and Gaggenau as well as stoves from Italian companies like Molteni (really French) and Zanussi. If I were to design the perfect kitchen, I would have a fireplace thirty-six inches above the floor that would double as a pizza oven and grill, a Wolf range top that included induction and an electric wall oven that was either a regular GE or similar model or the more expensive Viking or Miele.

TART PANS

Buy an assortment. For parties, I have eight little fluted ones (the kind in two parts) and eight rings. I love my copper tarte tatin pan and its lid; it is wonderful for all upside-down desserts or for any *torta*. Pyrex pans are fine as well. If you buy three sizes—an 8-inch square, 8 x 11-inch and 14 x 5-inch rectangle—you'll use them all.

TERRA COTTA

The Italians have used terra-cotta cooking vessels for thousands of years. Pottery shards from Etruscan digs have proven that terra cotta was the cooking vessel of choice before iron. They are works of art. The rules for use in our times are simple: Season them before they are used and cure them by heating gently with salt and a layer of olive oil. They will not last forever, but with careful use, they will give you many years.

THERMOMETERS

I cannot do without them. I have one in the fridge and the freezer and one or two in every oven. I want all my cooks to carry the electronic probe type. They are essential for preparing all types of foods—cold, hot, cooked, raw, etc. I have a probe that has a long cable so it can be used in the oven for roasts and in the fridge to test the temperature there.

TOASTER OVENS

I used to hate them. They took up space and they were plastic, ugly and were not really serious tools. Lately there has been a toaster oven renaissance; they are beautiful and strong. We have a De'Longhi (though Breville and others are wonderful). It heats in an instant and is good for baked pasta, pizza, breads, baked potatoes and reheating leftovers.

TONGS

Ah, the ubiquitous tongs. Many pro chefs use tongs like an extension of their arms, for stirring, sautéing, flipping. I have a friend who refuses to use them; in his opinion they are crass, dirty and ruin food. He feels that one is better served using a spatula and kitchen fork. I am in between: A good pair of tongs is essential on a grill, for large pieces of meat, for whole fish, etc. Buy the pro models; the cheaper ones are flimsy.

VEGETABLE PEELERS

I have about ten. I have one with grooves, one that is ergonomically superior, one that is as sharp as a surgeon's knife, one that is good for lefties (my wife) and one that also has a stripper for string beans (a great tool). I really enjoy the ones from Oxo.

WELDERS' GLOVES

These are a dream. My dear friend Craig uses them to extract embers from the charcoal grill and clean a fireplace. I use them for baking and for the grill. They last forever, prevent burns and look great!

WHISKS

I have about six; you need at least three—one for egg whites, a stiff, straight one for sauces and finally a balloon whip for whipping cream. Again, buy Swiss.

WINE KEYS

Buy a sturdy one. The fancier, the sillier. I have one that is quite heavy duty and cheap; it also cuts the foil nicely.

WOODEN SPOONS

It may seem patently obvious, but wooden spoons are essential. I have used them to fix a broken oven door, shoo away a fish-crazed kitten, roll out pastry and more. I suggest you buy an assortment: I adore the tiny ones; they are good for measuring, stirring small pots, great for kids. Large wooden spoons are the most versatile tools in the kitchen. They are perfect for any one of a dozen different tasks: serving salad, whipping eggs for a frittata, stirring a soup or testing the doneness of a Guinea fowl. A wooden spatula is amazing; it can save an errant pancake or Brussels sprouts from near death, and coat the bottom of a pan.

INGREDIENTS AND COOKING METHODS

ai ferri from the grill

al forno from the oven

arugula *Eruca sativa,* also known as arugula or rocket, is a species of *Eruca* native to the Mediterranean region and cultivated throughout it.

Asiago Pressato Asiago cheese is an Italian cow's milk cheese, which, depending on the various aging processes it undergoes, can assume different textures, from smooth, like fresh Asiago cheese (*Asiago pressato*), to crumbly, like aged Asiago cheese (*Asiago d'Allevo*), whose flavor is reminiscent of sharp Cheddar and Parmesan. The only "official" Asiago cheese is produced in the alpine town of Asiago, in the Veneto region, but is now also made in the province of Trento.

black pepper Native to south India, black pepper is produced from the green, unripe berries of the pepper plant. The berries are cooked briefly in hot water to clean and prepare them for drying. Once dried, the fruit becomes black peppercorns. White pepper is black pepper with the husks removed. Green pepper is made from unripened peppercorns and needs to be brined or dried.

blood orange This is a variety of orange (*Citrus sinensis*) with crimson, blood-colored flesh. The distinctive dark flesh color is caused by the presence of anthocyanin, a pigment common to many flowers and fruits, but uncommon in citrus fruits.

Bolognese A meat-based sauce for pasta originating in Bologna, Italy, this sauce is sometimes taken to be a tomato sauce, but authentic recipes have only a small amount of tomato. The people of Bologna traditionally serve their famous *ragù* with freshly made tagliatelle (*tagliatelle alla bolognese*) and their traditionally green lasagne. The recipe, issued in 1982 by the Bolognese delegation of Accademia Italiana della Cucina, limits the ingredients to beef, pancetta, onions, carrots, celery, tomato paste, meat broth, white wine, and (optionally) milk or cream. *Soffrito* (the carrot, celery and onion dice) is always the base. Prosciutto, mortadella or porcini are added to the *ragù* to further enrich the sauce. Traditionally white wine is used, not red. The sauce is supposed to retain some acidity and remain more meat-colored than tomatoey. I add a little (½ cup) cream at the end; it isn't orthodox, but it works.

brasato To braise. I love this style of cooking. In Italy this usually means slow-cooked over an open fire in a copper vessel.

bruschetta In Tuscany, it is called *fettunta,* meaning "oiled slice." In Abruzzo, local olive producers have a simple dish that is the essence of bruschetta. They thickly slice some peasant bread, grill it and liberally douse it with first-run olive oil, chili peppers and maybe a slice of cheese. This appeals to my sensibilities.

Brussels sprouts A member of the *Brassicaceae* family, which is a cultivar of a wild cabbage grown to resemble miniature cabbages. The same family includes cabbage, collard greens, broccoli, kale and kohlrabi. The first plantings in California's Central Coast began in the 1920s. Currently several thousand acres are planted in coastal areas of California, which offer an ideal combination of fog and cool temperatures year-round. The harvest season lasts from June through January.

bucatini A thick, hollow spaghetti. The name comes from *buco,* meaning "hole," and *bucato,* which means "pierced." Although primarily associated with Roman cooking, the original regions for *bucatini* are Lazio, Campania and Liguria.

calamari Frozen ones are no good; they are rubbery and tasteless. Freshness is the key. Don't buy them if they seem white rather than opaque. In 2007, a colossal squid weighing a thousand pounds and measuring thirty-three feet in length was caught off the coast of New Zealand. That would have fed my customers at Barbuto for a few months.

cannellini White kidney-shaped beans. Cannellini in English means "little rods." The common bean, *Phaseolus vulgaris,* is an herbaceous annual plant from South America and is now grown worldwide for its edible bean, popular both dry and as a green bean.

caper This is the edible bud and fruit of the caperberry plant. Capers are a distinctive ingredient in Sicilian and southern Italian cooking, used in salads, pasta salads, pizzas, meat dishes and pasta sauces. The bush is native to the Mediterranean, where it grows wild on walls or in rocky coastal areas.

Carnaroli The luxurious Arborio-like rice of the Po River valley, with sturdy, chubby grains, makes the finest risotto.

chickpeas This edible legume of the family *Faboideae,* was one of the earliest cultivated vegetables. The name can be traced back through the French *chiche* to Latin *cicer* (from which the Roman cognomen Cicero was taken).

chili pepper Also known as a chili or chile, this is the fruit of the plant from the genus *Capsicum,* a member of the nightshade family, *Solanaceae.* Christopher Columbus was one of the first Europeans to encounter them (in the Caribbean) and called them "peppers" because of their similarity in taste (though not in appearance) with the old-world peppers of the *Piper* genus.

The "heat" of chili peppers is measured in Scoville units (SHU). Bell peppers have a SHU of 0; New Mexico green chilies, about 1,500; jalapeños, 3,000 to 6,000; and habaneros, 300,000. They are rich in vitamin C and I love them.

ciabatta "Slipper" in English, this wonderful white bread is made with wheat flour, a touch of milk and yeast. The loaf is somewhat elongated, broad and flattish and, like a slipper, should be somewhat collapsed in the middle. *Ciabatta* was first produced in Liguria, although nowadays at least one type of *ciabatta* can be found in nearly every region of Italy. The *ciabatta* found in Tuscany, Umbria and Marche vary; the bread can have a firm crust and dense crumb or a crisper crust and more open texture. Like all my dough, *ciabatta* dough needs to be very wet, so when it hits that hot stone hearth, it puffs magically. The water between the crusts is vaporized and makes beautiful holes in the *ciabatta.*

cod Young Atlantic cod or haddock is called scrod. The Atlantic cod, which can change color at certain water depths, has two distinct color phases: gray-green and reddish brown. Cod feed on mollusks, crabs, starfish, worms, squid and small fish. Some migrate south in winter to spawn.

cozze Mussels are bivalves of the marine family *Mytilidae,* which attach to pylons by means of their beards. The mussel's shell is composed of two halves, which are joined together on the outside by a ligament and are closed when necessary by strong internal muscles. Most mussels are cultivated by the "bouchot" technique: the sprat (baby mussels) are planted at sea and attach themselves to ropes. They need fresh water that is loaded with micro-organisms. They do a great job of filtering water.

cremini mushrooms Button mushrooms (or Paris mushrooms), naturally occurring in grasslands, fields and meadows across North America, are one of the most widely cultivated mushrooms in the world. The cremini mushroom is an immature portobello, a large brown mature mushroom.

endive *Cichorium endivia* is a leafy vegetable belonging to the daisy family. Also known as chicory, the family includes radicchio, puntarelle and Belgian endive. Endive is rich in many vitamins and minerals, especially in folate and vitamins A and K, and is high in fiber.

fennel A member of the anise family, this bulb vegetable is used raw, cooked in broth, grilled or sautéed.

focaccia This flatbread topped with olive oil, salt and other ingredients is thought to be an early prototype of pizza. The basic recipe probably came from the Etruscans or ancient Greeks. My pal Joey Campanaro argues that the Etruscans invented everything Italian and were wiped out by the jealous Romans. Focaccia is usually synonymous with the region of Liguria and most specifically Genoa and Cinque Terre, the magical seaside duchy near Genoa.

garlic *Allium sativum* L., commonly known as garlic, is a species in the onion family *Alliaceae*. Its close relatives include the onion, shallot, leek and chive. Garlic has been used throughout recorded history for both culinary and medicinal purposes. The leaves, stems (scape), and flowers (bulbils) are also edible and are most often consumed while immature.

In 1858, Louis Pasteur observed garlic's antibacterial activity, and it was used as an antiseptic to prevent gangrene during the world wars.

gnocchi This is the Italian name (singular *gnocco*) for a variety of dumplings. The word *gnocco* means "lump" and comes from *nocchio,* a knot in the wood. The Roman legions introduced it during the empire's enormous expansion into the European continent. The use of potato in this dumpling is a relatively recent innovation, occurring after the introduction of the potato to Europe in the sixteenth century.

gremolata (or gremolada) A chopped herb condiment typically made of garlic, parsley and lemon peel, it is a traditional accompaniment to the Italian braised veal shank dish *osso buco alla milanese.* Although it is a common accompaniment to veal, the citrus in gremolata makes it an appropriate addition to seafood dishes.

grissini As a child, Vittorio Amedeo II, Duke of Savoy, was very frail and sickly. His mother called a famous physician of the time, Don Baldo Pecchio from Lanzo Torinese. The doctor diagnosed food poisoning and, remembering certain small *grissias* his mother baked for him when he suffered from a similar intestinal malady as a child, ordered the court's master baker to prepare a bread that was baked twice to destroy any micro-organism present in the dough. The end result was the *grissino,* hygienically perfect. Vittorio Amedeo II, miraculously healed by the *grissino,* grew to become the first Savoy king. At Barbuto we use a pasta machine to roll out sheets of pizza dough that are hand-cut and -stretched and then baked quickly and dried to crunchy perfection in a low oven.

honey In the Roman Empire, honey was used instead of gold to pay taxes. Pliny the Elder devotes considerable space in his book *Naturalis Historia* to the bee and honey and its many uses. Because of the natural presence of *Botulinum* endospores in honey, children under a year of age should not eat it. I especially like Italian chestnut honey, which has a warm, voluptuous taste.

Meyer lemon A hybrid lemon, from China, found by botanist Fred Meyer in 1903, it's juicier than regular lemon and less acidic. Some liken its flavor to a cross between a tangerine and a lemon.

nettles These grow wild just about everywhere and are easy to grow in your garden. Both the stinging variety and the nonstinging ones can be eaten, and both are rich in vitamins and minerals. Miner's lettuce or dark green spinach can be used as a substitute, but nettles are delicious and unique.

olive oil This is a huge subject. From a cook's perspective, here are the important points:

1. Extra-virgin is the best but should not be used for sautéing at high temperature because its smoking point is too low (about 400°).
2. Pomace is cheap and can vary widely in quality. It is good for dressings, frying, sautéing, mayo, etc.
3. Real Tuscan oil will always be expensive; if it isn't, it ain't Tuscan.
4. Spain prides itself on softer oils than Italy; some call the flavor buttery. French oil, especially from Provence, is similar to Spanish but is mellow and can be tastier. Tuscan oil is peppery, suitable for any raw dish from fish to vegetables. I also like Moroccan, Algerian, Israeli and Tunisian oils, but their quality can vary widely.
5. Large containers are only good for restaurants or for huge consumption; you are better off buying 375-milliliter or 1-liter bottles.
6. Olives are harvested in autumn and winter, so look for early-harvest release oils from Italy and Spain. They are fantastic.
7. Oil goes bad! Take care and always be objective.
8. Don't overuse it; a little goes along way.
9. For a good everyday oil, blend your own; it's fun!
10. Olive oil is better for us than other fats, but it is a fat and you can overuse it.

More than 750 million olive trees are cultivated worldwide, 95 percent of which are in the Mediterranean. Among the many different olive varieties in Italy are Frantoio, Leccino Pendolino and Moraiolo; in Spain the most important varieties are the Picual, Arbequina, Hojiblanca and Manzanillo de Jaén; in Greece, Koroneiki; in France, Picholine; in California, Mission; in Portugal, Galega; in Croatia, Oblica and Leccino.

All production begins by transforming the olive fruit into olive paste. This paste is then malaxed (crushed) to allow the microscopic oil droplets to concentrate. The oil is extracted by means of pressure (traditional method) or centrifugation (modern method). After extraction the remnant solid substance, called pomace, still contains a small quantity of oil. Pomace olive oil means oil extracted from the pomace using chemical solvents—mostly hexane—and by heat.

pancetta Often called Italian bacon, a true enough description, but unlike American bacon, which is usually smoked, pancetta is unsmoked pork belly that is cured in salt and spices for a few weeks. Outside of Italy, pancetta most often comes rolled (*rotolata*) so that the fat and muscle spiral around each other. Pancetta can also be made as a slab (*stesa*) so that the fat is mostly on one side. Rolled pancetta is normally cut into circular paper-thin slices before being fried, while slab pancetta is usually chopped or diced before being added to a dish. We make our own at Barbuto, and it takes about three weeks to cure it properly.

pappardelle The name of these large fettuccine noodles derives from the verb *pappare*, "to gobble up." Fresh pappardelle are ¾ to 1 inch wide and may have fluted edges. Dried egg pappardelle have straight sides. This noodle, a cousin to the smaller tagliatelle, was traditionally paired with rich wild boar and hare sauces.

Parmigiano-Reggiano A hard, fat, granular Italian cheese made from raw cow's milk that is named after the producing areas of Parma, Reggio Emilia, Modena and Bologna in Emilia-Romagna, and Mantova in Lombardy. The whole milk of the morning milking is mixed with the naturally skimmed milk of the previous evening's milking (it is left in large shallow tanks to allow the cream to separate), resulting in a part-skim mixture. The milk is pumped into copper-lined vats. Starter whey is added, and the temperature is raised to 33 to 35°C. Calf rennet is added, and the mixture is left to curdle for ten to twelve minutes. The curd is then broken up mechanically into small pieces. The temperature is then raised to 55°C. The curd is left to settle for forty-five to sixty minutes. The compacted curd is collected in a piece of muslin before being divided and placed in molds.

Traditionally the remaining whey in the vat was used to feed the pigs from which prosciutto di Parma (cured Parma ham) was produced. The barns for these animals were usually just a few yards away from the cheese-production rooms.

The cheese is put into a stainless-steel round form that is pulled tight with a spring-powered buckle so the cheese retains its wheel shape. After a day or two, the buckle is released and a plastic belt imprinted numerous times with the Parmigiano-Reggiano name, the plant's number and the month and year of production is put around the cheese and the metal form is buckled tight again. The wheel is then put into a brine bath to absorb salt for twenty to twenty-five days. After brining, the wheels are transferred to the aging rooms for twelve months.

At twelve months, the Consorzio Parmigiano-Reggiano inspects each cheese. A master grader whose only instruments are a hammer and his ear tests the cheese. By tapping the wheel at various points, he can identify undesirable cracks and voids within the wheel. Those cheeses that pass the test are then heat-branded on the rind with the Consorzio's logo.

The only additive allowed is salt, which the cheese absorbs while being submerged for twenty days in brine tanks saturated to near total salinity with Mediterranean sea salt. The product is aged an average of two years. The typical Parmigiano-Reggiano wheel is about 7 to 9 inches high, 16 to 18 inches in diameter, and weighs an average of 80 pounds.

pecorino pepato Sheep's milk cheese native to the town of Ragusa in southern Italy.

polenta Made with ground yellow or white cornmeal (ground maize), it can be ground coarsely or finely depending on the region and the texture desired. As it is known today, polenta derives from earlier forms of grain mush (known as *puls* or *pulmentum* in Latin or more commonly as gruel or porridge) commonly eaten in Roman times and after. Early forms of polenta were made with such starches as the grain farro and chestnut flour, both of which are still used in small quantity today. Polenta is often cooked in a huge copper pot known in Italian as a *paiolo*. In northern Italy there are many different ways to cook polenta.

Polenta is traditionally a slowly cooked dish. It sometimes takes an hour or longer, and constant stirring is necessary. The time and labor intensity of traditional preparation methods has led to a profusion of shortcuts.

pomegranate A native to Persia, it was cultivated and naturalized over the whole Mediterranean. It is widely cultivated throughout India and the drier parts of southeast Asia, Malaysia, the East Indies and tropical Africa. Spanish settlers introduced the tree into California in 1769. There is a great myth that a pomegranate was the fruit that tempted Eve. I believe it: it is terribly sensuous, delicious and good for you. I can see the juice dripping down Eve's elbow.

portobello mushrooms These are distinguished by their large size, thick cap and stem and a distinctive musky smell. Because of the size and thickness of their fleshy caps, they can be cooked in a range of different ways, including grilling and frying.

punterelle Ah, the greatest guest of winter in Rome. This wild form of chicory is bizarre and gorgeous, kind of an exploded version of frisée. It is nutritious, good raw or cooked and perfect with anchovy or tapenade. I like them dipped in a romesco or any good salsa. They are hard to find, but if very fresh, they can last quite a while in the fridge. I can't think of a substitute, but baby fennel comes close.

radicchio A leaf chicory sometimes known as Italian chicory, it grows in tight, leafy heads of white-veined red leaves. With its bitter and spicy taste, it adds color and zest to salads. When it is grilled or roasted, the flavor mellows. Radicchio has been cultivated since ancient times. Modern cultivation of the plant began in the fifteenth century, in the Veneto region.

rigatoni This tube-shaped pasta is larger than penne and ziti, is usually ridged (rigati means "ridged") and its end does not terminate in an angle, like penne. Rigatoni can be coupled with many different sauces from creamy to chunky. Consequently, it is a popular choice for restaurants that stock only one tube-shaped pasta. The tube may also be stuffed with cheese or other soft foods. In surveys rigatoni is the most popular pasta in Italy.

romesco A sauce originating in Tarragona, Catalonia, Spain, that is typically made from almonds and/or hazelnuts, roasted garlic, olive oil and *nyores* (small, dried red peppers). Other common ingredients include roasted tomatoes, red wine vinegar and onion. Leaves of fennel or mint may be added, particularly if served with fish or escargot. It is perhaps most often served with seafood but can also be served with a wide variety of other foods including poultry and vegetables, particularly *calçots* (a milder and bulbous variety of green onion).

salsa verde The basic recipe is probably from the Near East and, as such, is probably at least two thousand years old. Roman legionaries brought it to Italy, from where it was exported to France and Germany. The Italian *salsa verde* is a cold rustic sauce and includes parsley, vinegar, capers, garlic, onion, anchovies, olive oil and possibly mustard. Traditionally, ingredients were coarsely chopped by hand, but now it is frequently blended into a coarse sauce using a food processor.

San Daniele prosciutto The origins of prosciutto di San Daniele go back far into Italian antiquity. The curing process is at least as old as the Romans, maybe older. Prosciutto di San Daniele is by definition a sea-salt-cured thigh of a special variety of pig. The shape of the thigh is distinctive. The meat is purple-red. When sliced thinly (as it should be), the flavor and texture are ethereal. Domestic prosciutto is a poor cousin. Buy well, and don't wince at the price. Prosciutto di Parma can be as good, and I do love the hams from Spain, especially jamón ibérico from northern Spain. But nothing beats a San Daniele.

sopressata An Italian dry-cured salami, typical of Apulia and Basilicata. The name is said to come from the fact that it is often pressed with a weight while drying, giving the whole sopressata a characteristic flattened shape. The meat is typically coarsely chopped, rather than ground as with salami. This gives it an uneven "rustic" appearance when sliced. Sopressata is a specialty of southern Italy and often includes hot pepper (though, as with all salami, seasonings vary). The sausage is hung to dry for anywhere between three and twelve weeks.

speck A distinctively juniper-flavored ham originally from Tyrol and cured like prosciutto and other hams, *speck* is made from the hind leg of a pig, but, unlike other prosciutto, it is boned before curing. After it is cured in salt and various spices, the smoking process begins. *Speck* is cold-smoked slowly and intermittently for two to three hours a day for a week. It is then aged for five months.

walnuts I lived for a time on Walnut Lane, near the original Ka Tal vineyard in Napa, where the walnut trees are magnificent. They are more than 150 years old and still producing and are gorgeous when they blossom in spring. The nut is ripe in October, but green (young) walnuts are a great Italian specialty, especially cooked in honey and spices.

zucca Butternut squash.

SOURCES

All-Purpose Italian Food Stores

Agata & Valentina

The most elegant Italian store in New York. With prepared foods and a vast selection of Italy's best food products, they prove that New Yorkers love Italy.

www.agatavalentina.com

Annie's Homegrown

I love Annie's!

www.annies.com

Antico Mercante

Interesting varieties. A good shop.

www.anticomercante.com

Balducci's

They should be enshrined. I miss them terribly from Sixth Avenue, but time marches on!

www.balduccis.com

BuonItalia

OK, I use them every day; they offer everything I need. They can be very Italian (stubborn?)—"A second delivery? Are you crazy?" But I could not do without them for cheese, oils, truffles and more. It's one-stop shopping of quality.

www.buonitalia.com

Citarella

I have been buying fish from my buddy Joe Gurerra for more than thirty years! He now has his answer to Balducci's and other prepared food markets, but his niche is still fish.

www.citarella.com

Di Bruno Bros.

Emilio Mignucci is the duke of Philadelphia. In taking over this long-held family business, he has turned his professional chef skills into a thriving, bustling set of old-fashioned Italian shops, coupled with modern technique. Wonderful.

www.dibruno.com

Eden Organic

The first "organic" pasta for the masses. A good choice, and well made. I use it at home.

www.edenpasta.com

Eli Zabar

A New York food genius. I don't how he does it. From growing his tomatoes on his roof, to bread, to olive oils and vinegar, he is a food god.

www.elizabar.com

Fairway

Another New York landmark. They annoy me, I love them, I hate them, but they offer more produce, meat and cheese than any other place in New York. A truly wild shopping ride, worth the trip!

www.fairwaymarket.com

Manicaretti

They are trendsetters who dared push the price of true artisanal goods where they should be, and make the best pastas I know of. But they offer so much more.

www.manicaretti.com

Zabar's

Close to me, but a pain to shop in. That's its charm. If you go just before Thanksgiving, oh my god! They offer a tantalizing array of all cookware and are New York in a nutshell.

www.zabars.com

Zingerman's

A Midwest institution. A great, all-purpose store.

www.zingermans.com

Salumi

Boccalone

Try them. I think you will be happy. www.boccalone.com

Creminelli

www.creminelli.com

Fatted Calf

www.fattedcalf.com

Fra' Mani

My pal Paul Bertolli. He is the man.
www.framani.com

Volpi

www.volpifoods.com

Cheese and Dairy

Animal Farm

Thomas Keller's restaurant The French Laundry uses them. Nothing wrong with that!
www.animalfarmvt.com

Bedford Cheese Shop

www.bedfordcheeseshop.com

Cowgirl Creamery

Peggy Smith, my friend, is a goddess of all things cheese.
www.cowgirlcreamery.com

Formaggio Kitchen

www.formaggiokitchen.com

Murray's

We buy from Murray's, which says it all. They have much more than cheese, but cheese is their thing.

www.murrayscheese.com

Vermont Creamery

I love their butter!

www.vermontcreamery.com

Fish

Browne Trading Company

Impeccable fish and crabs.

www.brownetrading.com

Harbor Fish Market

www.harborfish.com

Louisiana Fresh Seafood

www.louisianaseafood.com

Pike Place Fish

For scallops, spot prawns, salmon, Dungeness crab and more.

www.pikeplacefish.com

Wild Edibles

All things that swim.

www.wildedibles.com

Meat and Poultry

Coleman Natural

A decent source of beef, pork and lamb.

www.colemannatural.com

D'Artagnan

Arianne Dagan is a marvelous woman. Funny, witty, full of life. She has a vast array of all the things we like to cook. Almost one-stop shopping.

www.dartagnan.com

Flying Pigs Farm

I hear good things.

www.flyingpigsfarm.com

Lobel's

Another New York institution. Unbelievably beautiful meat. I wish we could clone them!

www.lobels.com

Niman Ranch

Bill Niman is gone, but they have good stuff.

www.nimanranch.com

Schaul's

www.schauls.com

Summit Creek Natural Lamb

www.summitcreeklamb.com

Olive Oil

Stephen Singer, Olio

Stephen has the best olive oils and special *balsamicos*. The older ones are the crown jewels.

www.stephensingerolio.com

See the all-purpose stores as well.

Tartufi

Gustiamo

www.gustiamo.com

Sabatino Tartufi

Fresh white truffles.

www.sabatinotartufi.com

Urbani Truffles

Imported and domestic caviar, white and black truffles, and other gourmet products.

www.urbanitruffles.com

Flour

King Arthur

My only choice for flour at home.

www.kingarthurflour.com

Tableware

Bormioli Rocco

This company provides the best of Italy. Useful, well made, artistically exuberant and reasonably priced. It doesn't get better than that.

www.bormioliroccousa.com

Richard Ginori 1735

I have been using this venerable firm's plates and tableware since Jams. They are, without parallel, the finest china in the world. Our everyday plates at home have survived daily abuse and are as charming as the day we got them. Outstanding.

www.richardginori1735usa.com

Sambonet

Simple, elegant, perfect, these table pieces have survived the abuse of my staff, customers and myself. They look better with use than they did new. The stainless-steel version is quite well priced. I use the Hanna version, of course—my daughter's name!

www.sambonet-flatware.com

Italian Cookware

Alessi

A terrific design house, these guys show the rest of the world the path. They have a silver sauté pan that costs around 2000 Euros. I have always lusted after one!

www.alessi.com

Bridge Kitchenware

A New York institution. I used to be scared of the old man, but times have changed and sadly they have moved from New York to New Jersey. But the choices are as good if not better. The Dehillerin of the United States.

www.bridgekitchenware.com

Italian Kitchen Tools

Chef knives, espresso machines and pasta machines.

www.italiankitchentools.com

Korin

They're not Italian, but they are essential.

www.korin.com

Majolica

Gorgeous terra-cotta Italian cookware, and they have those beautiful hand-painted plates from Italy, especially the ones from the Amalfi coast.

www.italianmajolica.com

Mario Batali: The Italian Kitchen

Mario Batali, say no more!

www.italiankitchen.com

Paderno

www.paderno.com/us

Ruffoni

Their Italian copper cookware is pricey but really good. As with all Italian design, it's just more interesting than the rest.

www.ruffonicookware.com

Terra Allegra

Terra-cotta and enamel Italian cookware, reasonable prices.

www.terraallegraimports.com

All-Purpose Cookware Stores

Broadway Panhandler

A New York standard for years, they have great depth and many unusual items, well priced.

www.broadwaypanhandler.com

Chefs Catalog

A superb place for all kitchen wares, small to large—and reasonably priced.

www.chefscatalog.com

Crate & Barrel

A surprising shop, priced well, and they seem to have all those gadgets that you really want.

www.crateandbarrel.com

Fante's Kitchen Wares

A superb cookware store.

www.fantes.com

Kitchen Kaboodle

www.kitchenkaboodle.com

Kitchen Kapers

A good source, reasonably priced.

www.kitchenkapers.com

Sur La Table

I adore these shops. They are designed along the same lines as Williams-Sonoma but have their own flair.

www.surlatable.com

Williams-Sonoma

The prince of the kitchen, Chuck Williams, created magnificent stores that are a cooks' night in a candy shop. The store in New York's Time Warner Center is colossal; it has a vast knife collection, the best pots and pans, books and more. I willfully get lost there.

www.williams-sonoma.com

Large Appliances

American Range

Impressive American-made home stoves, almost commercial quality.

www.americanrange.com/residential

Bertazzoni

These cooking products originated in Emilia-Romagna, and that's not a bad thing. They are quite handsome.

www.bertazzoni-italia.com

Electrolux Icon

The company that owns Molteni, this is their more practical but still stellar range.

www.electroluxicon.com

Fratelli Onofri

Italian made, with a different design than American products. They seem well made.

www.fratelliappliances.com

Molteni

Fantastic and outrageously priced, but who cares? If you want a Ferrari in your kitchen, buy one!

www.molteni.com

Viking

I own a blue Viking. That says a lot.
www.vikingrange.com

Wolf

I love these stoves, now owned by Sub-Zero. They are impeccable.
www.wolfappliance.com

Books

Kitchen Arts & Letters

Noah Waxman's store, where else?
www.kitchenartsandletters.com

ACKNOWLEDGMENTS

Of course, to my parents who understood and appreciated good food. They tirelessly exposed us to the best Italian, Chinese, Japanese and other places in San Francisco. Original Joe's on Clement Street was a real inspiration. As I grew older, I ate at Giovanni's in Berkeley many times, as well as Tommaso's in San Francisco. Vanessi's was always the special night out, the wellspring for my open kitchens.

To Fabrizio and Alessandra Ferri, my elegant partners, for believing in my ability to cook Italian food. To my gracious and understanding partners Philip Scotti and Arnold Penner, who nudged me into viability. To Joey Grill, for your everlasting support.

I must applaud all the many chefs who helped to make Barbuto a joyful and nurturing environment. I have never truly thanked Lynn McNeely, my opening chef at Washington Park and Barbuto, in a germane way. He showed me how to make great gremolata, pesto, wonderful *torta al limone* and other soulful dishes. He was the heart of Barbuto in the opening days. To Justin Smillie for his enthusiasm, creativity and very hard work. To Roel Alcudia, who took over the reins and is having a great time.

And, of course, to my dear pastry chef Heather Miller. She lived through the hell of editing this book. She politely pointed out my deficiencies and elegantly suggested alternatives. And her skills as pastry chef are unparalleled.

To all my employees who helped make Barbuto a great success, through the cold of economic winter to the thaw that exists today, my deepest gratitude.

To my agent Jane Dystel, who has always had my back. To Sydny Miner for believing enough in my Italian cookery to bring this book to Simon & Schuster. To the lovely Ruth Fecych, who calmly edited out the bad grammar and repetitive verbiage. And finally to Michael Szczerban, who came in at the end and put it all together.

I need to thank all my great customers, some of you who dine at Barbuto three or more times per week!

As usual to my family for letting me work crazy hours and for visiting me when I needed them the most.

To Colman Andrews for pushing open doors to a world I had no idea of. To Piero

Selvaggio for tirelessly explaining his passion for all things Italian. To the late Mauro Vincente who showed me how to "act" Italian and taste like one. To Rose Gray and Ruthie Rogers at the River Café in London, who showed the world that great Italian food doesn't happen only in villages in Italy.

To Alice Waters for giving me a reference point and a standard to work from.

To my dear friends Christopher Hirsheimer and Melissa Hamilton, who make magical pictures with seemingly no effort whatsoever!

And finally to Arny, I have no idea how you stay so calm—your son.

INDEX

A

aioli:
    baccalà on grilled toast with, 52
    basic, 219
    chili, calamari with wilted frisée and, 61
    fried whitebait with, 40
    in *moleche fritto*, 53
Alexander's overflow pie, 88
almond(s):
    in *biscotti al cioccolato*, 213
    frangipane, for lemon raspberry *crostata*, 205–6
    in lemon raspberry *crostata*, 205–6
    paste, in *torta al limone*, 195–96
    in Romesco sauce, 221
    in *torta al cioccolato con pignoli*, 215
    in *zuppa inglese*, 197
anchovy(ies):
    in *salsa verde*, 235
    sauce, poached artichoke hearts with fried egg and, 7–8
    white, Long Island chicory and garlic toast, 16
Andrews, Colman, xvi, 45, 139
angel hair pasta with crabmeat, jalapeño and mint, 116
antipasti, 22–61
    asparagus wrapped with prosciutto, 37
    baccalà on grilled toast with aioli, 52
    balsamic-marinated quail with hazelnuts and field greens, 48
    bruschetta of wild mushrooms and goat curd, 34
    calamari with wilted frisée and chili aioli, 61
    ciabatta, chunked Parmesan and twelve-year-old *balsamico*, 38–39
    crostini with smoked trout and mascarpone, 31
    fried whitebait with aioli, 40
    fritto misto di mare, 47
    gnocco fritto with griddled sausage, 60
    griddled razor clams with spicy dressing, 42–43
    grilled or roasted prosciutto-wrapped figs with Gorgonzola, 57
    grilled porcini, 41
    ippoglosso tartare, 29
    lardo on toast, 28
    moleche fritto, 53
    oven-roasted mussels with cilantro and red chilies, 44
    pesce crudo, 25
    prosciutto *con burrata*, 26–27
    risotto pancakes with fontina, 56
    sautéed mushrooms on creamy polenta, 49
    sea scallop and cherry tomato skewers with spicy chilies, 54
    swordfish carpaccio, 32
    terrine of artichoke and ham, 33
    three crostini, 35–36
    vegetable *fritto misto*, 45–46
Antonucci, Francesco, xvi
Arborio rice, poached, 236
artichoke(s):
    bucatini with *cipolline*, fava beans and, 112
    and ham, terrine of, 33
    poached, hearts with fried egg and anchovy sauce, 7–8
    in vegetable *fritto misto*, 45–46
arugula, 2, 247
    in balsamic-marinated quail with hazelnuts and field greens, 48
    in lobster *alla piastra*, 142
    in pork chop *alla milanese*, 164–65
    in *salsa verde*, 235
    wild, salad with shaved Parmesan and extra-virgin olive oil, 10–11
Asiago cheese, 247

269

asparagus:

    and poached eggs, 6

    raw shaved, with lemon dressing, 4

    soup, 69

    in vegetable *fritto misto,* 45–46

    wrapped with prosciutto, 37

B

baccalà on grilled toast with aioli, 52

bacon:

    in *gnocco fritto* with griddled sausage, 60

    in handkerchief pasta with pork meatballs,
        113–14

    pizza with potato, green garlic, *robiola* cheese
        and, 83

baguette:

    in crostini with smoked trout and
        mascarpone, 31

    in *ippoglosso* tartare, 29

    in Long Island chicory, white anchovy and
        garlic toast, 16

balsamic vinegar (*balsamico*):

    ciabatta, chunked Parmesan and, 38–39

    -marinated quail with hazelnuts and field
        greens, 48

    skate with brown butter and, 146–47

    in squab with soft polenta and game sauce,
        179–80

Barbera, in Guinea fowl with chestnuts, 184

Barbuto restaurant, x, xi–xiii, 22, 26, 49, 97, 109,
    116, 120, 157, 174, 207

basics, 216–36

    aioli, 219

    blood orange dressing, 227

    Bolognese sauce, 220

    chicken stock, 218

    gremolata, 222

    JW roasted tomato sauce, 232

    lamb jus, 230

    lobster dressing, 229

    mascarpone, 233

    my salad dressing, 223

    pesto, 224

    poached Arborio rice, 236

    pork braising sauce, 231

    preserved lemons, 234

    roasted chili salsa, 226

    roasted garlic sauce, 228

    romesco sauce, 221

    salsa verde, 235

    walnut and winter pestos, 225

basil:

    in *bucatini* with artichokes, *cipolline* and fava
        beans, 112

    cherry tomatoes with, 131

    gnocchi with spring vegetables and, 93–94

    in Margherita pizza, 84

    in pesto, 224

    in pizza with chanterelle mushrooms, fontina,
        sweet onion and nettle purée, 81

    in pizza with potato, green garlic, bacon and
        robiola cheese, 83

    purée, in Justin's stromboli, 89

    in *salsa verde,* 235

    in swordfish carpaccio, 32

    in tomato with fresh herbs with crostini, 35–36

    in wild salmon baked in rock salt with
        tarragon and lemon, 152–53

bass, in *fritto misto di mare,* 47–48

Bastianich, Lydia, xvi

Batali, Mario, xvi, 116, 128, 151

bay leaves, in striped bass with new potatoes and
    picholine olives, 139

Bazzi, Aldo, 211

beans:

    borlotti bean minestrone, 64

    cannellini beans, guinea fowl braised with
        Savoy cabbage and, 181–82

    fava bean purée, crostini with, 35

    fava beans, *bucatini* with artichokes, *cipolline*
        and, 112

    lima bean, corn and tomato soup with pesto,
        71

beef:

    in handkerchief pasta with pork meatballs,
        113–14

    hanger steak with *salsa piccante,* 160

    in pappardelle with meat *ragù* and poached
        egg and, 111

    shoulder, in Bolognese sauce, 220

    T-bone steak *ai ferri,* 166–67

butter *(cont.)*
    in *torta al limone*, 195–96
    in trout with hazelnuts, 149
butternut squash, in goose for Christmas,
    190–91

C

cabbage, red, in chicken Piedmont-style, 185
cabbage, Savoy:
    guinea fowl braised with cannellini beans and,
        181–82
    in Lombardia-style pork ribs, 170
cakes:
    torta al cioccolato con pignoli, 215
    torta al limone, 195–96
calamari:
    in pizza *ai frutti di mare*, 86
    with wilted frisée and chili aioli, 61
calf's liver, *fegato di vitello con arancia*, 168–69
cannellini beans, guinea fowl braised with Savoy
        cabbage and, 181–82
caramel panna cotta, 207
carpaccio, swordfish, 32
Carpaccio, Vittore, 32
carrots:
    baby, in terrine of artichoke and ham, 33
    in Bolognese sauce, 220
    in char poached with aromatic vegetables and
        lemon dressing, 150
    in chicken stock, 218
    in *coniglio al vino bianco*, 186
    in Guinea broth with fresh noodles, 66
    in Guinea fowl braised with cannellini beans
        and Savoy cabbage, 181–82
    in Guinea fowl with chestnuts, 184
    in Lombardia-style pork ribs, 170
    in rigatoni and spicy duck *ragù*, 110
    with saffron and orange, 123
    thumbelina, in gnocchi with spring vegetables
        and basil, 93–94
    turnip and radish, shaved, with garlic dressing
        and green olives, 19
    in vegetable *fritto misto*, 45–46
Casella, Cesare, xvi, 28

cauliflower roasted with pine nuts and cream,
    128–29
celery:
    in Bolognese sauce, 220
    in Guinea fowl braised with cannellini beans
        and Savoy cabbage, 181–82
    in Guinea fowl with chestnuts, 184
    in rigatoni and spicy duck *ragù*, 110
celery root, in Guinea broth with fresh noodles,
    66
Cerruti, Antonio, xiii
chanterelle mushroom(s):
    in bruschetta of wild mushrooms and goat
        curd, 34
    pizza with fontina, sweet onion, nettle purée
        and, 81
char poached with aromatic vegetables and
    lemon dressing, 150
cheeses, *see specific cheeses*
chestnuts, guinea fowl with, 184
Chiarello, Michael, 57
chicken:
    al forno with *salsa verde*, JW, 174–75
    Piedmont-style, 185
    stewed, with Meyer lemon, garlic and white
        wine, 189
chicken stock, 218
    in lamb jus, 230
    in Lombardia-style pork ribs, 170
    in pizza with grilled *trevigiano* and fontina,
        85
    in pork braising sauce, 231
    in quail with Concord grapes, 178
    in roast duckling with dates, black olives,
        small onions and kumquats, 187–88
    in roasted garlic sauce, 228
chicory, Long Island, with white anchovy and
    garlic toast, 16
chilies, 249
    Fresno, in Romesco sauce, 221
    in hanger steak with *salsa piccante*, 160
    in pork chops with *salsa rossa*, 162
    red, broccoli rabe with, 127
    red, oven-roasted mussels with cilantro and,
        44
    in rigatoni and spicy duck *ragù*, 110
    roasted, salsa, 226

garlic *(cont.)*

toast, Long Island chicory, white anchovy and, 16

in walnut and winter pestos, 225

-walnut pesto, whole-wheat pasta with, 100

in wilted kale and *pepperoncini,* 130

in *zuppa di mare,* 70

gelato *gianduja,* 200

Ghirardelli, Domenico, xiii

gnocchi with spring vegetables and basil, 93–94

gnocco fritto with griddled sausage, 60

goat cheese:

crostini with prosciutto and, 35–36

pizza with Swiss chard, picholine olives and, 82

goat curd, bruschetta of wild mushrooms and, 34

goose for Christmas, 190–91

Gorgonzola, grilled or roasted prosciutto-wrapped figs with, 57

Gray, Rose, xvi

gremolata, 222, 250

Gruyère cheese, in *trofie* with peas, pancetta and spring onions, 115

Guérard, Michel, xv

guinea fowl:

braised with cannellini beans and Savoy cabbage, 181–82

broth with fresh noodles, 66

with chestnuts, 184

H

halibut:

alla milanese, 151

in *fritto misto di mare,* 47–48

ippoglosso tartare, 29

Hallowell, Charlie, 73, 81

ham and artichoke, terrine of, 33

handkerchief pasta with pork meatballs, 113–14

hanger steak with *salsa piccante,* 160

hazelnuts:

balsamic-marinated quail with field greens and, 48

in *biscotti al cioccolato,* 213

in *brutti malfatti,* 201

in caramel panna cotta, 207

gelato *gianduja,* 200

in raw shaved asparagus with lemon dressing, 4

in Romesco sauce, 221

trout with, 149

honey, in JW pizza dough, 75

I

ingredients and cooking methods, 247–55

ippoglosso tartare, 29

Italian restaurants, xiii–xiv, xvi

J

jalapeño(s):

angel hair pasta with crabmeat, mint and, 116

in *ippoglosso* tartare, 29

in sea scallop and cherry tomato skewers with spicy chilies, 54

in *zuppa di mare,* 70

Justin's stromboli, 89

K

Kahlúa, in tiramisù, 211–12

kale, wilted, and pepperoncini, 130

Kayser, Paul, 174

kid's pasta with cream, Parmesan and butter, 109

kitchen tools, 237–46

kumquats, roast duckling with dates, black olives, small onions and, 187–88

L

ladyfingers, in tiramisù, 211–12

La Frieda, Pat, 154

in pork chops with *salsa rossa,* 162

red, in Guinea broth with fresh noodles, 66

in rigatoni and spicy duck *ragù,* 110

in risotto with sweet peas, pea shoots and Parmesan, 95–96

in Romesco sauce, 221

small, roast duckling with dates, black olives, kumquats and, 187–88

spring, in char poached with aromatic vegetables and lemon dressing, 150

spring, *trofie* with peas, pancetta and, 115

in squab with soft polenta and game sauce, 179–80

strozzapreti with octopus, red wine and, 119

in T-bone steak *ai ferri,* 166–67

in vegetable *fritto misto,* 45–46

in wilted kale and *pepperoncini,* 130

in *zuppa di mare,* 70

onions, sweet:

in cold tomato and tarragon soup, 68

in *fegato di vitello con arancia,* 168–69

in hanger steak with *salsa piccante,* 160

in Lombardia-style pork ribs, 170

pizza with chanterelle mushroom, fontina, nettle purée and, 81

in roasted chili salsa, 226

in roasted garlic sauce, 228

in scallops with preserved lemon and wilted spinach, 141

in stewed chicken with Meyer lemon, garlic and white wine, 189

orange(s), 247

blood, and shaved raw fennel with black olives, 18

blood, dressing, 227

carrots with saffron and, 123

fegato di vitello con arancia, 168–69

in wild salmon baked in rock salt with tarragon and lemon, 152–53

orange juice, in sea scallop and cherry tomato skewers with spicy chilies, 54

orange zest, in gremolata, 222

oregano, eggplant and, 125

P

pancakes, risotto, with fontina, 56

pancetta, 252

cherry tomato, *burrata* and scallion pizza, 77

in Guinea fowl braised with cannellini beans and Savoy cabbage, 181–82

in pappardelle with meat *ragù* and poached egg, 111

peas with mint and, 124

pizza with an egg, tomatoes and, 87

in *porchetta,* 163

trofie with peas, spring onions and, 115

in warm dandelion greens with scrambled eggs and chives, 20

panna cotta, caramel, 207

Paoletti, Johnny, xv

pappardelle with meat *ragù* and poached egg, 111

Parmesan cheese, 252–53

in Alexander's overflow pie, 88

in asparagus and poached eggs, 6

in *bucatini* with artichokes, *cipolline* and fava beans, 112

in cauliflower roasted with pine nuts and cream, 128–29

ciabatta, twelve-year-old *balsamico* and chunked, 38–39

eggplant, pepper and roasted tomato pizza, 78

in goose for Christmas, 190–91

in grilled polenta with mascarpone, 133–34

in handkerchief pasta with pork meatballs, 113–14

kids' pasta with cream, butter and, 109

in linguine with wild mushrooms, 106–7

in Margherita pizza, 84

in pancetta, cherry tomato, *burrata* and scallion pizza, 77

in pappardelle with meat *ragù* and poached egg, 111

in pesto, 224

in pork chop *alla milanese,* 164–65

risotto with sweet peas, pea shoots and, 95–96

in sautéed mushrooms on creamy polenta, 49

in spaghetti *alla carbonara,* 104

radish(es) *(cont.)*
> in char poached with aromatic vegetables and lemon dressing, 150

raspberry(ies):
> lemon *crostata*, 205–6
> in *zuppa inglese*, 197

Ratto, Alan, 133

ravioli, fresh, with pumpkin and sage butter, 97–98

red cabbage, in chicken Piedmont-style, 185

red pepper flakes:
> in *salsa verde*, 235

red snapper:
> in *pesce crudo*, 25
> stuffed with olives and lemon, 145

red wine:
> in goose for Christmas, 190–91
> in grilled T-bone lamb chops with rosemary and garlic, 158–59
> in leg of lamb braised for seven hours, 157
> in pappardelle with meat *ragù* and poached egg, 111
> in rigatoni and spicy duck *ragù*, 110
> in roast duckling with dates, black olives, small onions and kumquats, 187–88
> in squab with soft polenta and game sauce, 179–80
> *strozzapreti* with octopus, onions and, 119

red wine vinegar, in my salad dressing, 223

rice, 248
> poached Arborio, 236
> risotto pancakes with fontina, 56
> risotto with sweet peas, pea shoots and Parmesan, 95–96

rigatoni and spicy duck *ragù*, 110

risotto, *see* rice

robiola cheese, pizza with potato, green garlic, bacon and, 83

rock salt, wild salmon baked in, with tarragon and lemon, 152–53

Rogers, Richard, 45

Rogers, Ruthie, xvi, 45

romesco sauce, 221, 254

rosemary:
> in *bigoli al pomodoro*, 101
> blossoms in balsamic-marinated quail with hazelnuts and field greens, 48

fried polenta with, 135

grilled T-bone lamb chops with garlic and, 158–59

in JW roasted tomato sauce, 232

in lamb jus, 230

in leg of lamb braised for seven hours, 157

spaetzle with, 132

rosé wine, in *tagliorini* with shrimp and saffron, 117

rum, in *semifreddo*, 209

S

saffron:
> carrots with orange and, 123
> *tagliorini* with shrimp and, 117

sage:
> butter, fresh ravioli with pumpkin and, 97–98
> leaves, in *coniglio al vino bianco*, 186
> in *salsa verde*, 235

salads, 2–20
> artichoke hearts, poached, with fried egg and anchovy sauce, 7–8
> asparagus, raw shaved, with lemon dressing, 4
> asparagus and poached eggs, 6
> baby beets, farmer's cheese, beet top greens and walnut oil, 15
> baby spinach, Maine sardines and pine nuts, 9
> blood orange and shaved raw fennel with black olives, 18
> Brussels sprouts, raw shaved, with pecorino and toasted walnuts, 14
> dandelion greens, warm, with scrambled eggs and chives, 20
> Long Island chicory, white anchovy and garlic toast, 16
> shaved carrot, turnip and radish, with garlic dressing and green olives, 19
> tomato, *burrata* and lavender blossom, 13
> wild arugula, with shaved Parmesan and extra-virgin olive oil, 10–11

salmon:
> steak, seared fennel and tarragon, 148
> wild, baked in rock salt with tarragon and lemon, 152–53

T

W

walnut(s), 255

-garlic pesto, whole-wheat pasta with, 100

toasted, raw shaved Brussels sprouts with pecorino and, 14

and winter pestos, 225

walnut oil, baby beets, farmer's cheese, beet top greens and, 15

Waters, Alice, ix, 4, 53

Waxman, Alexander, 22, 73, 88

Waxman, Foster, 73

Waxman, Hannah, 73, 91, 146

Waxman, Jonathan, ix–x

Waxman, Sally, 158

whitebait, fried, with aioli, 40

white fish fillet, in *fritto misto di mare,* 47–48

white wine:

in Bolognese sauce, 220

in char poached with aromatic vegetables and lemon dressing, 150

coniglio al vino bianco, 186

in lamb jus, 230

in linguine with Manila clams, mussels and fennel, 118

in lobster dressing, 229

in risotto with sweet peas, pea shoots and Parmesan, 95–96

in roasted garlic sauce, 228

stewed chicken with Meyer lemon, garlic and, 189

in vegetable *fritto misto,* 45–46

in *zuppa di mare,* 70

whole-wheat pasta with walnut-garlic pesto, 100

Willinger, Faith, 100

Z

zuppa di mare, 70

zuppa inglese, 197

in gelato *gianduja,* 200